CANADA UNSCRIPTED

Books by Vic Sarin

Eyepiece: Adventures in Canadian Film and Television. Paperback, 2017.

Gung Ho Filmmaking,

Audiobook, 2019.

CANADA UNSCRIPTED

VIC SARIN

IN CONVERSATION WITH

WILLIAM SHATNER · TANTOO CARDINAL · DAVID SUZUKI
ADRIENNE CLARKSON · PETER MANSBRIDGE · LOUISE LORE · DENYS ARCAND
ALANIS OBOMSAWIN · GARY EVANS · GEORGE STROUMBOULOPOULOS
BRIAN STEWART · TRINA MCQUEEN · MARK STAROWICZ · BOB MCDONALD
KRISTIN KREUK · MARTIN DUCKWORTH · JOHN KENNEDY · TREVOR EVANS
ROSEMARY RADCLIFFE · CHRISTOPHER HINTON · IAN WEIR

DURVILE & UpRoute

DURVILE.COM

Calgary, Alberta, Canada

DURVILE & UpRoute
CERTIFIED CANADIAN PUBLISHER

Durvile Imprint of Durvile Publications Ltd.
Calgary, Alberta, Canada
www.durvile.com

DURVILE.COM

Library and Archives Cataloging in Publication Data

CANADA UNSCRIPTED
CONVERSATIONS WITH CANADIAN MEDIA ICONS

Editor and Interviewer: Sarin, Vic

Authors: Shatner, William; Cardinal, Tantoo; Suzuki, David; Clarkson, Adrienne; Mansbridge, Peter; Lore, Louise; Arcand, Denys; Obomsawin, Alanis; Evans, Gary; Stroumboulopoulos George; Stewart, Brian; McDonald, Bob; Duckworth, Martin; McQueen, Trina; Starowicz, Mark; Kennedy, John; Kreuk, Kristin; Evans, Trevor; Radcliffe, Rosemary; Hinton, Christopher; Weir, Ian

1. History | 2. Biography | 3. Canadian Media | 4. CBC | 5. National Film Board

The Durvile "Reflections" Series
Issued in print and electronic formats
ISBN: 978-1-990-73595-0 (pbk) | 978-1-990-73597-4 (e-pub)

Front cover design Austin Andrews. | Book design by Lorene Shyba.

Durvile Publications acknowledges financial support for book development and production from the Government of Canada through Canadian Heritage, Canada Book Fund and the Government of Alberta, Alberta Media Fund.

Canada Alberta Government

We acknowledge the Traditional Land of the Treaty 7 Peoples of Southern Alberta, including the Siksika, Piikani, and Kainai of the Blackfoot Confederacy; the Dene Tsuut'ina; and the Goodstoney, Chiniki, and Bearspaw Stoney Nakoda First Nations. We also honour the Homeland of the Otipemisiwak Métis Nation of Alberta.

While every effort has been made to verify the accuracy of names, titles, and other references, whether quoted verbatim or paraphrased, this work is based audio transcriptions. Some names of individuals or productions may be inadvertently misspelled or misidentified. The publisher regrets any errors and welcomes verified corrections for future editions.

Durvile & UpRoute is committed to protecting our natural environment. This book is made of material from well-managed FSC-certified forests and other controlled sources.

Printed and bound in Canada. First Printing, 2025.

Product of Canada
Authors, Publisher, Printers

I hope this project helps
Canadians and newcomers alike
understand how the CBC and NFB
gave us a way to see ourselves,
to hear our own voices,
and to share them
with the world.

CANADA UNSCRIPTED
CONVERSATIONS WITH CANADIAN MEDIA ICONS
VIC SARIN, EDITOR AND INTERVIEWER

CONTENTS

CONTENTS

SONY

Introduction

VIC SARIN

As I look back on my life, I feel deeply thankful. My journey as a filmmaker has lasted 65 years, and 25 of those years were spent at CBC. It was during my time there that my career truly began to take shape. The CBC opened the door for me, offering not only a job, but an opportunity to learn, to grow, and to work alongside some of Canada's most talented people. Later, I founded Sepia Films in Vancouver, where I continue to focus on telling stories from many parts of the world and working with people from different cultures. But none of that would have happened without the CBC's support in those early years.

At CBC, I was given freedom. Freedom to tell stories. Freedom to experiment. Freedom to work with creative people who cared deeply about their craft. Whether in front of the camera or behind it, I was surrounded by people who helped shape Canadian television and film. The producers, writers, camera crews, editors, and sound people were just as important as the actors we saw on screen. I learned so much from them. Those years built the foundation for everything that followed in my life.

One memory from early in my career has always stayed with me. In 1968, I went on my first CBC assignment around the world. Our first stop was Somalia. As we set up the cameras and equipment, a group of local children gathered around us, curious about who we were. They kept asking, "Where are you from?" I answered, "Canada." Most of them didn't know where Canada was. Then suddenly, an older boy ran up and shouted, "Film Board! Film Board of Canada!" Even there, so far from home, people knew Canada through the National Film Board. That moment showed me how powerful stories can be. Long before many people had heard of Canada, they had seen its films.

Over the years, I came to know many filmmakers, actors, and artists who had started at the NFB. I admired the way the Film Board gave people room to be creative and try new things. Like CBC, the NFB trusted people to tell Canadian stories their own way. Both organizations believed in developing Canadian voices. They didn't try to copy Hollywood or anyone else. They simply let Canadians be Canadians.

That's why, after so many years, I felt it was time to celebrate these two special institutions. CBC and NFB have helped Canada find its voice. Our country is large, stretching across four and a half time zones, with many languages, cultures, and communities. Yet CBC and NFB helped bring us together. They allowed us to see ourselves reflected on the screen. They helped build our sense of identity.

When I started this project, my first idea was to speak with people I knew — friends and colleagues I had worked with over the years. Many of us worked side by side for decades. We often remember the stars, but behind every program there are countless people whose names you may not know — the writers, directors, camera people, and editors. Without them, none of the shows we love would exist.

But as I moved forward, I realized I needed to go beyond my own circle. The CBC and NFB touched so many lives. I wanted to hear from others, from different generations and different experiences. To my great joy, many people said yes. They were eager to share their stories, and slowly this project grew into something much larger than I first imagined. Together, these voices form a beautiful portrait of Canadian storytelling.

Originally, I had hoped to begin this work before the Covid pandemic. But like many things in life, plans changed. The pandemic delayed everything, and then I became busy with what would may be my final feature film, *The Lightkeeper*, filmed on location in Ireland. Time moved quickly. Sadly, some people I hoped to include in this project are no longer with us. Their absence is deeply felt. But I am grateful to those who were able to share their memories here.

Ever since I was young, I have loved the power of images. A single photograph or short film can say so much, even without words. No matter where we come from, we all share that same way of seeing. That's what makes film so powerful. I've always followed my heart more than my head. In the end, it's the emotion that matter, not the technology or special effect, but the feeling that stays with you long after the story is over.

When I think about the moments that last, they are never the big explosions or grand sets. It's always the simple, human scenes that stay in our hearts. I often think of the moment in *E.T.* when the boy touches the alien's finger and softly says, "E.T. go home." That small scene says everything about love and friendship. That is what storytelling is about, reaching the heart.

For me, falling in love with the camera changed my life. It became my guide and my companion. My father helped set me on this path when he gave me a gift for my 16th birthday: a 16mm Bolex camera with two rolls of Kodak film. That camera opened a door that would never close.

True success, for me, is not about money or fame. It is about the experiences: the people I meet, the stories I am able to tell, and the places my camera takes me. Canada gave me the chance to live this life, and for that I will always be grateful.

As I spoke to people for this project, I heard many wonderful stories. Some made me smile. Others touched me deeply. One story I'll never forget came from Adrienne Clarkson. She told me how she arrived in Ottawa as a child, after World War II. Her family lived on Sussex Drive. Every day she would ride the bus past 1 Sussex Drive — Rideau Hall — never imagining that one day she would live there herself as Canada's 26th Governor General. This is what Canada makes possible.

Another story that stayed with me came from Bob McDonald. He once took Buzz Aldrin, one of the first men to walk on the Moon, sailing on his boat. You might expect a meeting with such a famous man to feel larger than life. But Bob described how simple and ordinary their time was. It reminded me that no matter how great a person's achievements, they are still human. That's the beauty of these stories. They bring our heroes closer to us.

Most of all, I hope this project helps young Canadians and newcomers understand what CBC and NFB have given us. They allowed Canadians to tell their own stories, in their own voices. They helped us learn about our country — its land, its people, and its many cultures. They gave us the gift of seeing ourselves.

When I look back at those early years, I am amazed at what was accomplished with so little technology. There were no computers or digital tools. Yet even with simple equipment, people made programs that were bold, creative, and full of heart. They informed us, entertained us, and brought us together. And they did it without relying on crime, violence, or negativity. Instead, they offered hope, humour, and a strong sense of community.

There was something magical in those early days. People worked with passion. They loved their art, their music, and their storytelling. Even though the world has changed, I believe we still need that spirit today. Too often, modern shows focus on darkness and sadness. But what lasts are the stories that lift us up and remind us of what people can overcome.

This book and documentary film is my way of remembering that time. I hope others will remember too. Programs like *This Hour Has Seven Days*, *22 Minutes*, *Wayne & Shuster*, *For the Record*, *The Friendly Giant*, *Country Canada*, *Man Alive*, *Front Page Challenge*, *Juliette*, *The Fifth Estate*, and *The Nature of Things* — these shows helped shape Canadian broadcasting. They told us who we are.

It has been my great honour to witness these stories, to share in them, and now to help preserve them. My hope is that these stories will continue to inspire future generations of Canadian storytellers, just as they inspired me.

— *Vic Sarin,*
Vancouver, British Columbia,
2025.

billboard

billboard

billboard

Chapter 1

WILLIAM SHATNER

With a career spanning more than seven decades, William Shatner stands as one of Canada's most internationally recognized performers. In addition to his iconic role as Captain Kirk in Star Trek, *he has built a wide-ranging body of work as an actor, author, director, and producer. Beyond the screen, Shatner has received numerous awards, including Emmys, a Golden Globe, and the Order of Canada, while continuing to explore new creative projects well into his 90s.*

VIC SARIN: Just to give you some background—I came to Canada in 1963 from Kashmir, where I was born.

BILL SHATNER: Kashmir? No kidding. So you're either Pakistani or—

VIC: I'm Indian. Okay, tell me, Bill, do you remember Gordon Pinsent?

BILL: Do I remember him? Of course I do.

VIC: Gordon was like a messiah for me. He brought me to Canada.

BILL: Gordon Pinsent. Wow, I haven't thought of that name in years. There was this whole group of Canadian actors I knew... and didn't know. It's strange when I look back. I feel a mix of hurt and curiosity about why things were the way they were.

VIC: Let's start with your years in Montreal.

BILL: My father worked very hard. He sustained us well enough that we were comfortable—but there was never anything extravagant. Buying a bicycle, for example, was a big deal. We lived on Girard Street for three or four years, and then moved just a few blocks away to Marcil Avenue, still in the Notre-Dame-de-Grâce area. I stayed on Marcil for the rest of my time in Montreal. When I went to McGill, I'd take the number 15 trolley, get off near campus, and walk the rest of the way. At the time, McGill was down near the city centre, and we were out on the edge. But now, of course, it's all part of central Montreal. The city's grown around it.

As a kid, we had a little crew—the Marcil Gang. Half French-speaking, half English. One of my closest friends had a French name I've now forgotten. And across the street was Becky, this beautiful blonde girl. We'd play football right there on the road, and Becky was usually on the opposite team. The highlight of the game for me was tackling Becky. That was my introduction to boy-girl dynamics.

Not far from us—on the corner of Marcil and, I think, Markland—there was an old apple orchard. A few blocks further along was the Mundelene movie theatre. When I was a teenager, I'd go there almost every Saturday afternoon. Back then, admission was a dime—eventually a quarter, which felt outrageous. But I'd saved my allowance. My parents would come find me late at night, still glued to my seat, watching the same movies again and again. Beside the theatre was a drugstore with a soda fountain. I wish I could remember the owner's name. I'd use my spare change to get an ice cream or a treat, then head into the theatre. That little routine—drugstore, movie house—that's where my love of cinema was born.

VIC: Do you remember the first film that really left an impression on you?

BILL: Absolutely. It wasn't at the neighbourhood theatre, but downtown at a more upscale venue—plush seats, big screen. The film was *Snow White and the Seven Dwarfs*. It had just come out and it was the talk of the town. It was one of Disney's first animated features. I have a vivid memory of hanging onto a banister at the back of the theatre while my father tried to pull me away. I didn't want to leave. I wanted to stay for another showing. I was utterly captivated.

Back on Marcil Avenue, I spoke French, and had that tight-knit group of friends. And I've thought about this a lot over the years—those early roots, where it all started. On my mother's side, the Robins started a summer camp up in the Laurentians, near Sainte-Agathe. It was a working habitant farm—very traditional. They slaughtered pigs the old way, drained the blood, made sausages. All of that was going on while city kids like me were sent there for two weeks to cool off and maybe see a tree for the first time. There was a train track nearby. I still remember the sound of the steam engine's whistle—*whoo whooo* haunting, like a lone wolf's cry. It's a sound that stayed with me. I was always homesick at camp. The only things that helped were boxing—and something they called drama.

I'm six or seven years old and that was the time of World War II and the Nazis. Somebody in the camp had written a play that involved children in Nazi Germany being removed from their home and I was playing the part of a child who was leaving his dog. Lines were "I have to go. I don't know where I am going? And I want you to come with me." I must have done it so well that when the curtain came down and went up, the audience was crying and I thought, "Oh my God I made those people cry." Then after the play was over, my father picked me up and said, "That's my boy, Billy" That meant everything. His approbation was very hard to get. But that night, I had it.

VIC: So that's when the acting spark really caught for you?

BILL: Yes, from that moment, I never stopped. When I got home, I found a neighbourhood drama group run by a couple of ladies in their basement on Girard. I joined right away. Then we started putting on plays in a local park with an actual stage. By the time I was eight or nine, I was performing in front of live audiences. As a teenager, I moved into radio. CBC Radio in Montreal had a producer—Kaplan was his name—not Lionel Kaplan, who was a school friend, but another Kaplan. He was responsible for casting and took a chance on me. I joined a group of seasoned actors who were the Montreal branch of CBC's dramatic talent. Most of the drama came out of Toronto, some from Vancouver, but Montreal had its own tight circle. I learned microphone technique, how to use my voice. And because I spoke French, I was cast in French radio plays too. The French actors were so passionate! Sometimes they'd knock my script to the ground mid-performance and I'd have to scramble to pick it up. It was thrilling. That was my training ground. That's really where it all began.

VIC: You mentioned the French actors earlier—what was it like working with both the English and French performers at CBC?

BILL: Oh, it was great fun. The French actors were much livelier—more fun than the English ones. The English were reserved. Many of them were very English, and kept to themselves. But the French? They lived by *joie de vivre*. They'd shout, "We shoot upon sacred!" and slap my script right out of my hand during a scene. It was wild—and unforgettable. I was active on CBC Radio in Montreal as a teenager and did it for years, right up until I started at McGill. I'd graduated from high school in the west end of Montreal—West Hill, it was called. Doesn't exist anymore. We went to shoot something there once, and I said, "Let's go see the old high school." It had become a two-unit apartment building or something. Gone.

So, I'd played on CBC, and once I got to McGill, I threw myself into it all. Plays, musicals, radio. I wrote, directed, acted—I was in the McGill University musicals, and I did theatre on the side too.

There was this woman—Stanford, I think her name was. She ran amateur theatricals in Montreal, which I didn't even know at the time. By then, I was finishing a business degree from McGill. Not that I ever went to class. I graduated with maybe ten different courses in English and theatre—nothing to do with bookkeeping!

VIC: So you were building this whole theatrical life on the side of what was actually a business education?

BILL: Exactly. I barely scraped through. But Stanford offered me a job. She said, "I'm opening a summer theatre in Montreal, but the company's already full. I can take you on as an assistant manager." So, I took it.

Bruce Raymond was managing that theatre. He was well known in Canadian theatre circles and I worked under him. I was terrible at the job. But they heard me read. Ruth Springford—that was her name—had directed me in several plays. She saw something in me. Said I had a natural gift for style. I didn't know French style or English style, but I must've absorbed it by osmosis, or maybe I was copying someone. In any case, Ruth said, "You should be in the company." So just like that, I went from assistant manager to company actor.

The theatre was in a big park at the centre of Montreal, on the slopes of that old volcanic mountain the city's built around. At the end of the summer, Bruce said, "I'm going to Ottawa to produce the Canadian Repertory Theatre, the CRT." It was one of the only professional theatres in Canada at the time. And he invited me along. So, I went.

VIC: Was that the moment you committed to the life of a professional actor?

BILL: I think so. Though I failed again as assistant manager. But they hired me into the company. I spent three years there—doing a play a week out of a school theatre in Ottawa. I lived in the city on rope mattresses. If I wanted to see a movie or do my laundry, I had to skip a meal. It was complete penury. But also—exhilarating.

I still remember walking across the lawns on winter nights after the show. The Peace Tower bells would ring out—those clear, icy tones that sound like they've been frozen into icicles. It was beautiful. I'd walk to some chain restaurant and order a cheese sandwich, then head back to my rope mattress wishing for something more.

In the summertime, I went to Toronto. That was the Mecca. The New York of Canada. If you wanted to be an actor, you had to be there. The CBC was the fount of everything—TV, radio. Unless you were in theatre, which didn't pay. If you have to feed yourself, you had to do television or radio. That was the early '50s—1952, maybe. I was writing half-hour radio plays, hiring actresses. One of them I eventually married. We had three children together.

Toronto became my base. And around that time, I got invited to Stratford. So in winter, I'd work in Toronto. In summer, I performed at Stratford, for three years. That became my career.

Eventually, we took a play down to New York—*Tamburlaine* by Marlowe. I had a good part in it. It opened on Broadway for a limited run, and the reviews noticed me. I got good notices. That changed things. We later toured to Scotland, Edinburgh Festival. We performed *Oedipus* there. And then I returned to New York. An agent had taken an interest. That was the beginning of my New York career.

VIC: But even as your career took off internationally, you always returned to Canada. What kept bringing you back?

BILL: Well, I'll tell you. I love Canada. I still carry a Canadian passport. After all these years—I'm still Canadian. That never changed.

VIC: You've said you've always carried your Canadian identity proudly. What does Canada mean to you, really—on a deeper level?

BILL: I love the country. I love what it represents, all the usual things people say, sure, the clichés. But for me, there was always something more. As I struggled in New York and Los Angeles—trying to figure out how to support three children and keep working—in the back of my mind there was always this thought: If I fail, I can go back to Toronto. It wasn't that I ever doubted I'd be an actor. Never once did I consider leaving the profession. People would ask, "Did you ever think of giving it up?" Never. Not for a second. Maybe I should go be a banker or clean houses? No. That wasn't in me.

But there was comfort in the idea that Toronto was there. That I could return. Like a thumb-sucking safety blanket—I could always go back to where it started. Though, honestly, what made me think I'd even get work there again? Toronto had become home to incredible actors and a vibrant scene. Still, the thought kept me going.

VIC: Let's talk about that scene—those early CBC days in Toronto. Who were the people shaping it?

BILL: Well, remind me the name of the great radio producer—MacLeod? Mackay? The one who won all the awards in the '50s? Neither of us can seem to remember now, but he was legendary. Under his leadership, CBC radio drama won Peabody after Peabody. He ran the whole thing like a theatre company. It was a golden age. *(Ed' note: It was James Mavor Moore)* I was on the periphery of it. Guys like John Drainie—that name mean anything to you?—they were the core. He and others were brought up on Shakespeare, on radio drama, on proper diction. When the reviews came out of Stratford, critics always said the strength lay in the middle: the supporting actors. That was because these folks had been trained in voice, in elocution, in craft. They were theatre and radio actors. And in radio you had to enunciate, you had to create a world with just your voice. They could do that. They could do anything.

There were even brothers with their own theatre company. The older brother, the younger one, and a sister who married an English actor who ended up at Stratford. I'm sorry, I can't remember the names. But anyone with a sense of Canadian theatre history will know who I mean. *(Ed's. note. Likely he is speaking of Len, Robert and Charles Cariou, and Barbara Bryne.)* There was this passionate group of actors, singers, and producers in Canada at that time. And I was just outside it, looking in. Why? I don't know. Part of it was that I didn't drink. They'd finish a show and go out drinking, having parties, building camaraderie. I wasn't part of that. And it hurt.

VIC: Was it Guthrie who finally welcomed you into the fold?

BILL: Yes. Tyrone Guthrie, the man who founded Stratford. I arrived in the festival's second year. And he took me under his wing. I was pretty good, I think. I had a natural thing. I don't know where it came from, but it's always been there. I've never been anything but an actor. I've blundered through life, yes, but it was that blundering that led me to Guthrie. He gave me a part. He directed *Tamburlaine*, the play we took to New York. That play furthered my career. People noticed me. We later went to Edinburgh for the festival and did *Oedipus*. After that, I returned to New York, where an agent had taken an interest in me. That's really where the next chapter began. But why was I still on the outside? Why was I never fully part of the core? I don't know. But I felt it. Always. And it hurt.

VIC: It sounds like Stratford itself was shaped by that kind of elite, British-oriented sensibility. Was it difficult to break through that as a young Canadian actor?

BILL: Absolutely. In the '50s, Stratford was an elite world. Very English. Our own leader, Tom Patterson, had this vision. He goes to England, recruits Guthrie, and they start a theatre in his hometown: Stratford, Ontario, right there on the Avon River. It was meant to be.

Years later, when I had made some kind of name and was living in Los Angeles, I got a call. An actor—I don't remember his name—said he'd been with Stratford long after me. Now he was in California and wanted to start a Shakespeare company.

He said, "There's a Stratford, California. I want to open a Shakespeare festival there. Will you help me?" I said, "If it works out, I'll help you raise some money." Months later, he called again. Turns out Stratford, California is just two gas stations and a café—you can't start a theatre there! But he'd found another town, about fifty miles into the California foothills. Rich farming community. He was going to start the festival there. And I went up and helped. Helped raise money.

VIC: You helped start a Shakespeare festival in California. Was that connection to your Canadian roots part of what drew you to it?

BILL: Yes, absolutely. That call—those deep roots I feel from my beginnings in Canada—made me say yes. I agreed to help raise money in this town of maybe 200,000 or 300,000 people, right in the heart of the San Joaquin Valley. A rich farming community. That one "yes" led to a whole other life. I didn't move there, but I ended up with a second home up in the mountains. I met people I never would've known otherwise and had experiences I never would've had. And, in many ways, it led me to the horse passion I've had since middle age. Once I had enough money to buy a horse, it became a major feature in my life. And it all began because one itinerant actor called and said, "Would you help me raise money for a Shakespeare festival?"

The same thing happened back in Montreal. I was performing in summer theatre, and a woman—I can't remember her name—approached me and said, "We're starting a Stratford Theatre. Would you come as an actor?" That was the first year. And I said no. I was already committed to something in Montreal. Bruce Raymond had offered me a job in Ottawa. It felt more secure. I couldn't count on this new festival—it was just a dream at that point.

She came back the following year. By then, Stratford in Ontario was a raging success, so I said yes. And I joined. But it was very elite. They didn't hold open auditions. They approached you, almost like, "Would you like to go into business with me?" It was very curated. Very English.

VIC: Did you find it difficult to adjust to American friends in the arts, coming from that different Canadian culture?

BILL: I've lived most of my life alone. I got married when I was about 26 or 27. I relied on the woman I was married to, and on the three children we had together. I had a home. But even as I moved between cities—like when I left LA to do a series in New York—I was never quite surrounded by friends. I've known acquaintances, sure. But friends? That's different. My life has always been kind of enclosed. Maybe that's just me. Or maybe that's how it is for everyone. I mean, what is a friend? How do you retain one?

There's a real tension when there's a difference in success. If a friend says, "Can you lend me money?" and you do, something changes. The dynamic shifts. Being successful when your peers aren't—it creates barriers. I've written about this. I've thought about it deeply. Success changes relationships. Sometimes it isolates you.

VIC: You've accomplished so much, and yet you still describe yourself as an outsider. Do you still feel that way?

BILL: I am an outsider. No question. I know a few people. I do things that bring people together—like our *Monday Night Football* gatherings. My family, my extended family now—that's who I really connect with. But as for friends... again, what is a friend? That question still hangs in the air for me.

VIC: So with all of that behind you—what's important to you now?

BILL: Important now? You say I've done everything—but I haven't. There's so much more out there. Just before this conversation, I was in a meeting with people deciding whether to invest in a new medical device. Something out of science fiction. On *Star Trek*, we had that scanner—a tricorder. It could read your body and say, "You've got cancer," or "You've got an ingrown toenail."

Well, this group of scientists has actually invented something like it. They approached me a year ago to be involved. Today's meeting was with investors. I'm now the face of, or a spokesperson for, three or four companies working on truly futuristic projects. One company is working on extending human life by tapping into mitochondrial function. These companies are building the future—one that will go on long after I'm gone. And that's deeply satisfying. This morning, I had a moment of joy, not because I said, "Invest now," but because I saw something real. Something that felt like it leapt right out of *Star Trek* into reality. We're on the brink of such immense technical progress. We dreamed of this, and now we're using it. But it's a race. Technology could save us—or destroy us.

Take plastics, for example. There's a world meeting coming up, maybe in Paris, about plastic pollution. Plastics are everywhere now. In orbit. In the oceans. In our blood. We're choking on it. Something that was once seen as miraculous is now poisoning us. It's terrifying.

So I've made it part of my mission—my advocacy. I'm involved with companies and campaigns that bring attention to global warming, environmental collapse. The planet is burning. Just look around. Southern California is burning. Quebec has burned. I saw footage not long ago from Midway Point, out in the Pacific. The camera pans from a beautiful sunset to beneath the waterline, and it's just garbage. There's a swirling patch in the Pacific bigger than Texas—just garbage. That's where our food comes from. That's our protein. That's life.

VIC: And still, amid it all, you keep doing the work.

BILL:Yes. That's what I'm doing now. Advocating. Engaging. Asking questions. And—well—I've also got a hit show.

VIC: You're still creating at such a remarkable pace—albums, books, even hosting *The UnXplained*. Where does all that energy come from?

BILL: I don't know—it's just a ferment of creativity. Right now I've got *The UnXplained*, two albums up for awards—one spoken word, one musical. I've got a book out. I'm on fire creatively. I don't even know how or why.

But am I in some kind of "Federation Time"? Maybe. Except when I stop to think about it... finishing, I mean—I can't conceive of my death. Sure, I ache. My shoulder's sore. I've got all the usual ailments of being old. But the idea of death? I just can't see it.

And in the same way, I never really conceived of becoming an actor. It never occurred to me to say, "I want to be an actor." I just blundered on. That worked out. Or it didn't. And I wondered why. I never had a plan. I still don't. I don't even know if I've made a will. I do know that in my will, I want to be buried in the ground with a tree planted over me. Let the tree absorb my body's nutrients. There's even a song on my album called "I Want to Be a Tree." So even in old age, I'm still blundering forward. Instinct is all I've got.

VIC: It sounds like you've found peace—accepting life for what it is.

BILL: I talk a lot about the book of life. The book of our life—it's being written right now, even as you and I talk. This moment—this conversation—it's part of that. Right now I'm remembering things I haven't thought about in decades. Like Lani Pearson, a neighbour when I was five. We found a $5 bill in an empty lot on Shearwater Avenue. Being kids, we decided to divide it evenly. So we tore it in half. Here's yours, Lani. Here's mine. Why would I remember that? A child's act of love, of fairness. That's still with me. So here I am. I don't know what I'm doing. I don't know why I'm here, talking to you. But it feels right.

I remember the corridors of CBC, back when it was on Jarvis Street, not Church. That old building felt like a furtive hotel. You moved quietly, instinctively. No one knew what a camera was. You just did things.

There were people who seemed to know—like that producer, MacDonald? That's not his name, but someone like that. *(Ed's note: Mavor Moore.)* They always had a plan. I never did. I've met all kinds of successful people who seemed to know exactly what they were doing—projects, movies, theatre. They move with purpose. And yet, I'd speak to them like I knew what I was doing. But I didn't. I never have.

VIC: Looking back, did the National Film Board shape you as an artist?

BILL: Ah, the Film Board. When I was in Montreal, I knew nothing about film. I knew microphones. I knew how to make an entrance. Radio made sense. Television—you acted like it was the stage, just with cameras in the room. But then there was this new beast: film. The National Film Board of Canada—God, I hope it still exists—was one of the great filmmaking institutions in the world. Innovative, respected, vital. I can't remember exactly what the innovations were—but I remember the experience. Every so often, they'd hire me to do "a film."

"Stand here. Wait. Action. Speak, Bill." That was it. It was all new to me. The CBC cameras were massive, filled with vacuum tubes, fans blowing to keep them cool. Other actors would flinch when a camera rolled in for a close-up. Not me. It felt like a curious animal coming to say hello. I welcomed it. "Come on over, baby." I greeted it with affection. Film was the same. The Film Board taught me to be a film actor. Not to perform, but to be there. That was the magic. Be there. Be there. Be there.

VIC: What about the CBC? What productions stand out in your memory?

BILL: The big CBC productions came later, mostly in Toronto. In Montreal, during my school years, there wasn't much television. There was a small radio station that wasn't even part of CBC. They'd put on teenage dramas, and I was a big part of that. But proper CBC radio was the main stage in Montreal. Then, around the time I moved to Toronto, television was just arriving. In the U.S., it had a head start, but CBC adapted quickly. I remember working in a radio building where they'd clear space just to move the cameras around. And this just came flooding back—*Billy Budd*. I did a production of *Billy Budd* at CBC with... what was his name? That wonderful English actor who played Sherlock Holmes so often... it's on the tip of my tongue. Anyway, that was one of the standout moments.

It was Basil Rathbone. Yes, that's who it was. He played Sherlock Holmes in all those movies. Aquiline nose. Very English. Regal. He adopted me in a way during that production.

When we were introduced, he asked, "Are you nervous, Bill?"

I said, "No. Why?" And he said, "Because there are about thirty million people watching us."

Suddenly, I was hysterical.

What I remember most vividly is how nervous he was. After weeks of rehearsal, we went live, because everything was live back then. No taping. No do-overs. You hit your mark, said your lines, and hoped the cameras followed. It was like theatre, except you had five or six giant, heat-blasting cameras, cables underfoot, and stagehands darting around. Complete chaos.

So there we are, opening night. I'm Billy Budd. Rathbone, the captain, steps aboard the ship—and puts his foot straight into a bucket that someone had left there. He was so tense, so focused, he just kept going. Played the whole show with the bucket on his foot. And I'm supposed to be this young sailor facing persecution, trying to stay serious, while the captain's stomping around in a bucket.

VIC: Were those kinds of disasters common in those early CBC days?

BILL: Oh, constantly. Another time we had guns in a live show, blanks loaded with wax plugs. One of those plugs hit me right under the eye. A big blood blister swelled up. This was at the start of the show. We had an hour to go, and I had to perform with this balloon-sized welt on my cheek. It was wild. Another time, I was supposed to stab someone. But the prop knife went missing. There was a bar on set, so I grabbed a corkscrew and just... screwed him to death. Improvised the whole thing. I mean, that's what it was—improv, survival. You memorized your lines and hoped nothing exploded or hit you in the face.

There were people fumbling with cables, props going missing, actors forgetting lines. You had to maintain focus. It was like being in the eye of a storm. Pure theatre, but with cameras watching your every move.

VIC: Did you notice much difference between working in Canada and the United States back then?

BILL: Honestly? I don't know. Were Canadians behind the Americans? Or were the Americans just fumbling in fancier sets? A guy walking around with a bucket on his foot—that's universal comedy. A blood blister on your face while you're supposed to declare your love? That's tragedy and farce.

In Canada, the structure was looser. At CBC, there wasn't a hierarchy. Once the budget was approved, the producers disappeared. We were left to do the work. No one hovered. We'd gather around a table with the director, read the script, then go mount it for the stage or studio. In later years, yes, I dealt more with producers, but back then, it was just us.

As for freedom? I never thought about it. My job was to say the lines. Perform. That was the freedom.

This wasn't just in Toronto. It happened in Montreal too. Radio actors were passionate. John Drainie, he was the premier radio actor. Always there. Always strong. And because CBC and the National Film Board were publicly funded, there was space to take risks. They weren't answering to shareholders. They were answering to Canadians. That's what made it special. That's what made it possible.

VIC: Do you think we've lost that spirit now—what public broadcasting once offered?

BILL: It's fading, isn't it? CBC is still there, but it's not the same. Budgets are shrinking. The ratings are low. And they're piping in American dramas just to stay afloat.

Back in the '50s, television in Canada was an act of invention. It was funded by the government, yes, but built by artists. We had to improvise. We had to believe. And sometimes, we had to finish a live show with a corkscrew or a bucket on someone's foot. That's the kind of chaos that raised me.

VIC: Looking back at your incredible journey, do you give any credit to CBC and the National Film Board for helping you discover your path?

BILL: Well, I can't say it was any one person. But the organizations, yes—the CBC and the Film Board—that's where I worked. For over three years, I was part of it all. Television was just arriving in Canada. And Canadian radio? It was at the height of its powers. In fact, American radio looked north, to Toronto, to figure out how to do drama.

I keep trying to remember names. Norman Corwin! That's it. He wasn't Canadian, but he was a towering figure in radio. He wrote award-winning dramas for CBS. He even hired actors from the Mercury Theatre—Welles, Houseman... Corwin took me under his wing later on. I ended up doing a lot of his work. In some ways, I became one of the key voices in American radio dramas, and later on, in PBS productions. That passion for radio—it began in Canada, but it rippled outward.

VIC: Is there one production—one moment—that you still carry with you above the others?

BILL: *Billy Budd.* Without a doubt. That was the big one. We shot it in Toronto, but not in a regular studio. It was in a large theatre or stage setup. They built the whole ship. It wasn't the norm—it was grand, ambitious. And the radio actors from the CBC, the ones who carried those productions? They were the ones who went on to Stratford and made names for themselves.

They were the strength of the middle—the supporting roles that gave the productions real muscle. Their names are just out of reach right now, but I remember their presence, their voices.

VIC: Do you have any regrets? About anything?

BILL: Regret is a strange thing. You reach a fork in the road, and you go left. Something terrible happens and you think, I should've gone right. But the only reason you think that is because of what happened. You had no way of knowing. You didn't have the information at the time. You can't regret something you couldn't predict. So what do you do? You adapt. You tunnel through. You find a way forward. That's what life is. That's all you can do.

VIC: That's a perfect place to end—unless there's something more you'd like to share?

BILL: I'd love to talk about the 1920s... but no, no, I think I've said enough. It's been so kind of you to give me this time.

Chapter 2

TANTOO CARDINAL

Tantoo Cardinal is a trailblazing Métis/Cree actor whose work has opened doors for Indigenous voices in film and television. Raised in Anzac, Alberta, her memorable performances in Dances with Wolves, Legends of the Fall, Falls Around Her, North of 60, *and* Killers of the Flower Moon *have touched audiences around the world. Through each role, she honours the stories of resilience and belonging that have shaped her life and career.*

VIC SARIN: Tantoo, I want to say how grateful I am to you for giving me this time. I've followed your career for so long—

TANTOO CARDINAL: It's an honour for me too. Thank you.

VIC: When you get older, like me, it's often hard to bring back the memories. You remember the feeling, but not the details. Looking at you, everything's coming back. Our time working on *Loyalties*... it wasn't just about the film.

TANTOO: Yes, funny thing. *Loyalties* was shot right in my home territory. And now, my school is there too, just outside of Lac La Biche. About a half hour away, I've established my school—Taproot.

VIC: So you're still deeply connected with Alberta?

TANTOO: More so now than ever. I hadn't really been rooted anywhere for a long time. But I went back to where I was born—Fort McMurray. I'd grown up around there. When I turned 30, I returned, and everything was gone. Every place I'd lived had been erased, taken over by the oil sands and the industry. That was a kind of severance from my home territory. So, I began a practice of connecting with the earth, wherever I was. Wherever I lived, wherever I worked, I made that connection. Because the place I came from was gone.

You were talking about getting older... well, I think it depends on how you define it. When I got into my 50s, I started thinking about those old dreams again. The ones that never really go away, even after being told time and again, "That's hopeless. Just forget it." No matter how many times I threw those dreams into the pile of "forget about it," they kept coming back.

And that's how I ended up establishing the school. It was something that started inside me back in the '70s, and it's only recently come to fruition. We're starting our fifth year now. It took a long time. And it changed forms in my imagination many times. But when I finally launched it, I wanted it to be something really organic. I wanted it to move with the community, at the pace of the people. That's why I named the school "Taproot," because I wanted people to have the dialogue, the language, to remember our roots—to connect with the energy in those roots, the life, the juice that's still there.

I come from territory where they knew about the oil under the land back in the 1700s. That's how long they've known. And to get at that wealth, they had to put the people to sleep. There's so much in our world that pushes us to look outside of ourselves, to measure ourselves against something external. But that's what CBC did for Canada—it brought everything into one place. As a public broadcaster, the projects, the images, the stories, they included Indigenous voices. A lot.

I remember seeing those early NFB films, and the CBC stories too. Gordon Pinsent, for example—his work was so powerful. Because he insisted on being who he was, from where he came from. Just like Chief Dan George. And even watching the Olympics—when you see the Canadian coverage, you'll hear so many accents. People are still connected to who they are. Not diluted. Not flattened into some generic "Pan-American" thing. That's what CBC, and especially CBC Radio, gave me. It grounded me in our own thoughts, our own stories, our own perspectives.

VIC: Because art has its own international language, it creates a shared rhythm, a shared melody, instead of keeping people separate.

TANTOO: I do believe that. For me, the analogy is that the language of the whales, the water, and the wind is found in the arts. Art can express what words struggle to say. It can spark thoughts, images, feelings, and even decisions without uttering a word. It touches both the participant and the observer in ways that language often cannot.

VIC: What fascinated you when you were young?

TANTOO: When I was young, we didn't have television. We had radio. I remember the Alberta school broadcasts, though I'm not sure if that's what they were called. My uncle would run home from school to turn on the radio for the stories. That's how we got them. But my stories mostly came from the people who visited our house. When people gathered, they shared stories, in Cree, Dene, English, and sometimes this beautiful mixture with French. I grew up hearing all kinds of languages. I think that helped me become open to different sounds, different cultures. I'd imagine where people came from, who they were.

I was raised by my grandparents until I was about ten. Then it was just my grandmother. Listening to CBC Radio reminded me of those voices I was missing—those visitors from different places. You'd hear about where they came from, what people were doing down the railroad or across the land. There were stories full of character, politics, survival, and humour. It opened your mind beyond our small community. And I remember the National Film Board, too. I think they were the ones who did forestry films—forest fire prevention. They used to show them in schools and community halls. You'd get a short, a feature, and sometimes they'd bring films right into the classroom.

VIC: The Film Board helped filmmakers say what they wanted to say. I worked with many of them—Claude Jutra, Gilles Carle, John Brittain—all trained by the Film Board. It was a place to develop documentary talent.

TANTOO: Yes, I remember those short films. They'd bring them into the schools. One that stayed with me was about fiddlers: one from Quebec, one from Ontario. Real old-style fiddlers. The film followed them as they played tunes that had been forgotten in Ireland. The filmmakers took them to Ireland, where their playing helped Irish fiddlers rediscover those lost melodies. The contrast was amazing—the difference in style, how they finished a tune. And the Métis fiddlers from the North had such a ragged flourish, a raw, funky style. I felt this surge of pride watching it.

There's always been this loneliness in me, seeing what we had in the '50s—so deeply connected to the '40s, '30s, '20s—just disappear. That film was a kind of solace. It showed that someone had seen it. That it existed somewhere, even if we couldn't replicate it. These were people raised by the bush, on the land. In that kind of life, you depend on one another for everything—survival, food, company. Nobody's a stranger. Some early radio and film captured that feeling because it was still close to the roots of who we are.

VIC: Do you remember the first actual films you ever saw?

TANTOO: Yes. *Going Down the Road* and *Don't Let the Angels Fall*. I remember Gordon Pinsent most of all. And there was a series—I think it was *Wojeck*. It had an episode on heroin addiction that hit me hard. It told the truth. I've always been grateful for work like that. Because when we grew up, we knew those people. We spoke that language. So why hide it? Why dress it up or water it down? Truth is essential. It's how you move forward. Lies just muck up the path.

VIC: When did you first feel like you wanted to be part of this magic?

TANTOO: I remember hearing Cree in a movie—*The Sheriff of Fractured Jaw*—some old black-and-white Western. It was shocking. Then I saw another film with Cree code talkers. That inspired me.

But more often, I saw non-Indigenous actors playing Indigenous roles. I didn't know how the industry worked, but I knew who I was. Audrey Hepburn—so beautiful and talented, but she wasn't Indigenous, and no one seemed to care. Rita Moreno played Indigenous roles for years... badly. And when the industry finally shifted toward authenticity, suddenly there was no room for us. All the layered, complex roles dried up.

When I started out, my characters often didn't even have names. So, I filled them out myself—with my name, my story, my philosophy. There was no place for Indigenous women in film or in Canadian history. Our existence was hidden. But through it all, there were these little cracks in the wall—people who wanted to tell the truth. Some had grown up near Indigenous communities. Some were just seekers. Whatever their reasons, they wanted to start telling real stories—and including us.

VIC: I completely agree. Honesty is the most important thing in life. Do you feel the CBC or the Film Board helped move things toward more honest portrayals of Indigenous Peoples?

TANTOO: Over time, yes. Sometimes consciously, sometimes just through cause and circumstance. In Canada, I think our Indigenous voice has had a stronger platform than in other places.

In the U.S., the Black voice became powerful. In Canada, it's the Indigenous voice. That's one of our great differences—and responsibilities. Our people did a lot of educating, whether anyone was ready or not. There were leaders like Harold Cardinal and John Tootoosis. Parents who hid their kids so they wouldn't be taken to residential school. Those children preserved knowledge, and now they're feeding it back into the culture. Despite the attempted genocide, some of that wisdom has survived because of persistence, resistance, and allies.

I know I wouldn't have made it without allies like Anne and Sharon, who wrote the script for *Loyalties*. That was a long journey. But they knew they had to tell that story—and that there were actors who could carry it. They weren't looking to cast someone from Juilliard and put war paint on them. That was the go-to back then. I had to do some tough, painful scenes, because I didn't want them to have the excuse, "Well, there are no Native actors."

Whenever I had the chance, I took it. Even if I wasn't ready. I'd work with the team—wardrobe, hair, dialogue—because that was part of my responsibility. And most of the time, there was someone listening. Even if change came slowly... glacially... there was movement. And now we've hit a tipping point. There's so much more material, so many more voices.

VIC: Your recent success in *Killers of the Flower Moon*—do you feel like that film gave you the arc toward truth and honesty that you've always fought for?

TANTOO: It triggered a grief I had buried. That movie brought it all back. I thought we had come further than that. But there was so much ignorance in that film. And then, to be standing on the red carpet afterwards and hearing people say, "Oh, it was like a documentary"—it was horrifying. I've come through the journey of living in the brown world. That era in the film? It was a time of cultural genocide, of atrocity. And to see an Indigenous woman on screen lighting a smudge while this white man—this philanderer, woman-beater, drunk, murderer—just sat there still and serene.... That scene broke me. Because I know how long it took before someone could even light a smudge in their own home with a white man present. That was a real fight. So many people lived through that oppression.

And so there went the opportunity. The chance to tell the real story of what cultural genocide looks like. How it feels. What it does to people. Why so many women are beaten, murdered, and missing. It's not "la la la." It's not a costume drama. It's deep. It's devastating. That film was really, really hard for me. And I'm afraid my grief made me say and do things that weren't very complimentary. But I did the best I could.

VIC: You have to be honest with yourself. That's all that matters. For me, too. Honesty is the most important thing in life.

TANTOO: Just behave accordingly, right?

VIC: What was your first performance? Was it on radio? Stage? Television?

TANTOO: It was a school play in Anzac. That was my first time performing. It was just a Christmas play, but that's where I first discovered how it made me feel. And how natural it was. My teacher, Mr. Ted Walters—an amazing man—wrote the play. It was called "The Other Magi." The story was about the fourth Magi who never made it to Bethlehem because he was too busy doing good deeds along the way. When he cast the play, he named all the girls for their roles. My name wasn't on the list. Then he started casting the boys. Still nothing. I just sat there, blues hitting hard. I thought, "I'm heading into the bush and never coming back." I was maybe in Grade 7 or 8. Possibly Grade 9. Then he cast the Magi, the lead role. And that was me.

Boom. I was back. I could unpack my emotional suitcase. And that moment informed me, and him, and the community. Everyone in town saw that show. Everyone came out. And a star was born in Anzac. When Mr. Walters registered me in high school, he signed me up for drama. But things changed. In high school, I didn't get cast in anything. I was the kid sitting at the back, observing. I wasn't pushing forward among all those white kids. Then came the school play, *Pygmalion*, and everyone had to have a part. I was one of those who just walked through the scene. So, my dream of becoming an actor went into hibernation. I graduated at 18, and I got my first real role around 20 or 21. It was with the Native Communications Society. That's where I started making 10-minute films, 20-minute films, industrial safety films. I even did a half-hour film on fire prevention. Fire was part of my early life, I guess.

But I had hope. Hope that our stories could be told. Ironically, the first play I ever saw was *Waiting for Godot*. My husband took me to see it in Edmonton when I was very young. And there was something in that play that told me—we have a place in theatre. We can write our own stories.

And come to think of it, the women from the Air Force base near Anzac used to put on skits. Homemade material. So, I'd seen what it looked like to tell your own story, in your own voice. All of that gave me something to hold onto. When I ran into organic racism, and it was everywhere, I just kept pushing through. That was the only way. Keep pushing. Over time, I realized there were places we could meet. Shared spaces. And the people who were open, who recognized our humanity, those were the people who gave us a path. Who saw our perspective, our unique contribution. And thank goodness for them.

VIC: When do you think the door started to open for Indigenous performers to play real characters?

TANTOO: The first time I got a job in mainstream media was with CBC. They did a docudrama on Father Lacombe. They thought he was a hero—this noble figure. But they didn't know the truth of what he meant to my people—specifically the Métis. They didn't know about the land grabs. The trickery. The betrayal in Saint-Paul-des-Métis. So, there I was, playing a young "Native girl" who believed in Father Lacombe, who revered him. I had to perform that role, even though I knew the deeper truth.

It was hard. I really had to dig deep. I told myself: "There were people who truly believed in him. People who loved the priests." I performed that girl as one of those women—those who had faith, who revered the Church. That was the character I built. I fashioned her after the women I knew who truly believed. It was all shot on film, not in a studio, and everyone was wonderfully supportive. Especially my own people. They were so excited that someone from their world was getting that opportunity, someone representing them. We had Native newspapers back then, and there were articles being written. I still have a spread somewhere—me and Harry Daniels on that film. Someone saved it. It's in my archives.

VIC: Was that film with CBC?

TANTOO: Yes, it was. Jack Emack directed it. It was about Father Lacombe. That was back in 1971, I think. We shot it around Fort Edmonton.

TANTOO: It's time to share it. So much of what I lived through, younger filmmakers don't even know happened. The British mind, as you know, is very thoughtful—everything's pre-considered. I'm the opposite. I just go with a feeling. I don't think everything through. You're like those Métis fiddlers.

VIC: You mentioned your first role. Let's go beyond that. You did *Street Legal,* right?

TANTOO: Yes, I did some *Street Legal.* And I did *Spirit Bay.*

VIC: Ah yes, *Spirit Bay!* What year was that? How did it come about?

TANTOO: Goodness, I have no idea what year. I don't even remember if I auditioned. It might have just come through my agent. I travelled somewhere in the East—was it Manitoulin Island where we shot? It wasn't a Native lead. The kid was good. He was a good actor, but he wasn't Native. And you just live with that. You accept that the work is being done, that the stories are being told, and that things are moving forward. As an actor, you trade in your soul, in your spirit. That's your toolbox. You search through it and find the tools you need for each role.

Honestly, I don't remember the storylines or much about the producers. I mostly remember meeting people from the community. I recall this woman—we shot in her house—and her older daughter had some kind of health issue. That stayed with me. I never really dealt with producers. I avoided them, to be honest. I had a thing about people who handled money. I preferred to stay away. I let my agent deal with them.

VIC: Looking back now, do you think CBC or the Film Board, or any other Canadian institutions, helped you grow in your career?

TANTOO: Absolutely. Because they created the material. They stepped out and did it. They had a mandate to tell Canadian stories—that was from the CRTC. So, there was a marketplace for it. There was space for me to work and practice my craft. A place to build a career. I was inspired by that era—the '60s and early '70s. The world was waking up. New ideas were bursting through. People were making bold statements.

In our Indigenous communities, people were starting organizations, some with only a Grade 2 education, others highly educated. But all were demanding change. Creating what was needed We have a long history of humanitarianism—people doing what they can to relieve pain, poverty, illness. And we found allies in the South Side communities—people with those same goals. Those alliances happened naturally. They helped us take the next step, then the next, and grow together.

Many of the friends I have today came from that time. Independent filmmakers. My friend Mark Slipp—we built our friendship through his editing suite, back in the "splice it" days. He invited me in, and I learned so much about the industry, about storytelling, just through those friendships, those small kindnesses from technical people.

VIC: Public broadcasting is changing so fast now. Should public broadcasting go back to their cultural mandate? Or just focus on ratings and commercial appeal?

TANTOO: People often say, "The people know best." Especially during elections. And maybe, on some energetic level, that's true. But some thought patterns need to be left behind. Like outtakes—cut them, move on. From where I come from, we don't have a big voting bloc. What I think is valuable probably won't show up in the ratings. So, I can't say it should be about overall popularity.

In any community, it's not the loudest voices that matter most. It's the quiet ones—the ones barely speaking. Those are the people the community turns to when it needs to know: "What do you think? What are you seeing?" I think our industry should work more like that. Like a community. The loud ones—they've got TikTok, they've got platforms. They'll be fine. But the quieter voices—the ones with depth and wisdom—they deserve to be seen and heard too. Maybe that's the responsibility of those in the industry. Of journalists. You can't be lazy. You have to look deeper.

VIC: Looking back on your life and your career, what came about that you're proud of?

TANTOO: I feel really good about how Indigenous voices are finally being heard and seen across the board. I come from a time when we were voiceless. I remember arriving in the city for high school in 1965—there was nothing in the newspapers about us. Unless it was something negative: "no fixed address," "vagrancy," that kind of thing. Nothing positive. But now, we're everywhere. And yes, the hardships and the legacy of cultural genocide and colonialism are still with us, but so is the incredible resilience. I think of it as the Miracle Clan.

Look at what's happening in Indigenous fashion, in the environmental movement. There's incredible progress. People now understand that we have something to say, and that we have a deep connection with the earth. She speaks through us. She's been speaking through us for a long time, and people are finally starting to listen. There have been changes in the law. We have Indigenous lawyers now. The education system today is nothing like what it was when I first arrived on this planet in this life. And that excites me because the possibilities are limitless.

We're the missing enzyme. When the colonizers began building society, they took inspiration from the Iroquois Confederacy. Both Canada and the U.S. drew on that model. And that's good stuff. But they left out something essential: that the clan mothers decided who the leaders were. The women made the economic decisions. The decisions about the land. The men had their role, but it was the women who provided balance. That wasn't included in the colonial model. And that, I believe, is the root of so much of the sickness in society. We—Indigenous People—are the missing enzyme.

There were filmmakers who fought for us. Documentary filmmakers, all over the place, who insisted on telling stories from our communities. I did a lot of voiceover work with them. Every time I got to narrate something positive about our communities, about the land, it inspired me. It fed my taproot. You need things like that to keep going. Especially when you're burying grief. And sometimes, just when you think you're finally getting somewhere, when there's real possibility, your grief comes back out again.

VIC: What's important to you now?

TANTOO: I still want to act. But I want to act in stories that aren't limited to the worlds I've always been cast in. That means my allies, those writing and directing, will need to think of me in new ways. I'm back where I was when I started out. There was nothing. No roles, no examples, no map. Just this knowing that there was a creative force, a natural force, that had something in mind for me. I feel that again now. I don't know what's next. But I trust that creative force. I feel strong, and I'm finding the places that inspire me again.

For a while, nothing excited me. I was worn out. I didn't want anything to do with the industry anymore. I had to fight my way out of that. It was like a divorce—"Be gone, Beast!" But you save what was nourishing and carry it forward. Now, I'm creating a series—something I've never done before. It's what I want to impart, what I've seen, what I think matters now. And I'm trusting that the right people will come. People with healthy egos. Not the ones who will elbow me out of the way and say, "This is how it should be."

I want a respectful circle of creation. A space where we can do the work in a good way, and the work will be seen for its soul, not just its technical features. My friend Jay Craven, an independent filmmaker, a wonderful old socialist offered me a role. He adapted George Bernard Shaw's *Major Barbara* into a film. Gary Farmer and I had character roles. It was political satire. It was fun. That gave me hope. A new direction. A spark.

I just want people to see me as a human being. Include me in stories that aren't necessarily "Indian stories." When you invite me, you've already invited an Indigenous presence. That's a given. But understand, we're everywhere. There's an Indigenous woman who's been to space. We have astronauts, scientists, divers, pilots. We are underground, underwater, in the air. We are everywhere in society. And I think we've reached a point where we don't need to explain "the Indian" every time.

VIC: This acceptance is happening everywhere now. Not just for Indigenous people, but Black people, Brown people, Asian people—we're becoming one world. What could Canada's national broadcasters—the CBC and the Film Board—do to help with that?

TANTOO: Much of what they used to do. That's how I'd put it. It's similar to what we're trying to do at my school. If you're inspired by something out there, why? What is it that resonates with you? And where is it in your own life? We had students who wanted to make horror stories. But we didn't have a budget. We didn't know how to do Hollywood makeup. So, we said, "Back home, what's a horror story?" And they remembered the stories they heard as kids. Stories their parents told them—about little people, creatures, spirits. That became our first film. Whatever's going on in the wider society, find the root of it. Find the truth behind it. Then tell the story from that place. Even if it doesn't reach blockbuster ratings, the people who do see it will see something with substance. And of course, we want lots of people to see it. But I believe people want integrity. They want something real.

VIC: So these organizations can play a role in offering truth?

TANTOO: Yes. But they need confidence. Confidence that Canada is cool. That it's enough. They don't need to bring in American perspectives all the time. Maybe it's the U.S. that could learn from what we have going on. Canada has a lot to be proud of. Especially the space that has opened up for Indigenous voices. It's not perfect. Far from it. There are missteps. Crooked portrayals. But we're trying. We're finding our way. We're listening more. And that means not always listening to the loudest voices, but the ones truly connected to what's being discussed.

My friend Sharon Shorty was telling me how their community went back to a clan system, and it made governance smoother. Issues were represented by the people connected to them. The person at the head of the table changed depending on what was being discussed. That's a different kind of leadership. That calls on the CBC and the NFB to know their communities. To know where the voices are really coming from. To understand respect. Kindness. Integrity. To recognize when ego is driving. Because ego can unravel a circle.

The circle is our medicine. In Indigenous healing, we come back to the circle. It's how we see each other. It's how we understand all angles of a story. And I think all cultures probably start with a circle. So... can't Canada?

VIC: If you were to give CBC and NFB a scorecard over the last 40, 50 years, how would you rate them?

TANTOO: They've earned a place at the table. They've done well. But now it's time for reflection. They're not 20 anymore—they're 50, 60, maybe 70. It's time to look back. What did they do well? What nourished people? That's where they should recreate themselves—from their riches, not their ratings.

VIC: Do you ever miss anything from home, now that you're living outside of Canada?

TANTOO: I miss my little home at Kikino Métis Settlement. It's a beautiful place. I've worked so long to create it, to bring that dream to life—and now it's real. Living, breathing, nourishing. I miss that when I'm away. Where I am now is a kind of a harbour. It's a cave. No one here really knows me. I have real privacy, which lets me sit with the change I'm going through. As the world shifts, I'm deciding how I want to be part of it—how to stay in relationship with my ancestors and the guidance they give me.

VIC: It's been so interesting to hear about your work, your voice as an Indigenous woman, and your path as an artist. Any final thoughts?

TANTOO: Public broadcasters like CBC and NFB have been growing, just like we have. They're run by human beings, and we've all been maturing. We've all been doing the work. What they can do now is amplify what people are doing in communities. Support storytellers who are shining a light on everyday acts of care and strength. Right now, I'm working with a group of women who want to do a series on what older women are doing in their communities. That's where the real gems are. That's how we grow as a society, by learning how we're growing up.

There are so many people who give every single day, quietly, without recognition. The aunties, uncles, grandparents, working in clinics, helping the kids, showing up. These aren't dramatic stories, but they're beautiful, and they deserve to be seen. Too often, the camera only shows up for tragedy. I want to see it show up for healing. For creativity. For joy. There's so much change happening—in education, in justice, even in corrections. These are stories that matter.

VIC: As an artist, freedom is essential—to act, to write, to speak. How important is that freedom, especially when comparing Canada to and U.S.?

TANTOO: Freedom is crucial, but it depends on who you're working with. When you work with someone who thinks they know everything, there's no space. When you work with someone who's truly open, who wants to know what the actor brings, that's real collaboration.

Sometimes directors just want to fit you into a box. They don't see, or don't want to see, that there's a whole world inside that box. And if they're not interested, you're limited. But you learn from that. Because as artists, we take on the human experience. We become interpreters of it. So even when you're constrained, there's something to learn. And it's not just about Canada or the U.S., it's about human dynamics. Jealousy, envy, control—those things rob you of freedom, no matter where you are. That's why it's important to choose who you work with. The same way we choose our relationships: if someone treats you badly, you walk away. Work is no different.

VIC: I've been thinking about Ken Welsh a lot lately. The first time I saw Ken act was in *Riel*. He played the priest who gave last rites to Riel. I remember filming that scene—I was operating the camera myself. Ken was trembling while reading the Bible, and I was crying behind the lens. Not just because of the story, but because of him. That performance stayed with me.

TANTOO: He was powerful and yes, now he's gone. You know, he called me when the bodies of the children were found outside the residential schools. He was horrified. He wanted to talk about it. And then, I couldn't reach him anymore. I've thought about him a lot. After that discovery, so many people passed. I began to wonder if maybe some of them left to help those children on the other side. Spiritually speaking, that made sense to me. He was so concerned. Maybe he chose to cross over and guide them.

VIC: He truly was. You know, we've talked about a lot today about your journey, your voice, your artistry. The impact of CBC and NFB. Their role in creating space for truth and respect. I'd like to believe they've found the right path—and now, they need to keep going. Keep pushing further.

TANTOO: I've always felt I was meant to see these times. When I was a child, I'd hear stories about great changes coming. One night, the sky was completely red, and everyone stood outside watching. The Elders said, "A time is coming." And here we are.

VIC: We've covered so much excellent thinking. Thank you.

Chapter 3

DAVID SUZUKI

David Suzuki has long stood at the intersection of science, storytelling, and public conscience. A geneticist by training and broadcaster by calling, his voice has guided generations of Canadians toward a deeper understanding of the natural world and humanity's place within it. With unwavering clarity and moral conviction, Suzuki has challenged audiences to confront both the beauty and the fragility of the planet we call home.

VIC SARIN: So, you've retired now from CBC?

DAVID SUZUKI: Oh yeah. It has been an incredible opportunity. Well, I fell into a unit that educated the hell out of me. When I started with *The Nature of Things*, I was what I now think of as a shallow environmentalist. I thought the problem was people were taking too much from the environment and putting too much bad stuff back into it. I thought we needed laws to regulate that and enforcement to back them up. But reading Rachel Carson's *Silent Spring* in 1962 changed everything. It was about the unforeseen effects of pesticides, and it galvanized me.

The Nature of Things, already a beloved and respected series, was, to me, the first major show in the world that seriously tackled nature and science. I joined as host, but it was the people—Jim Murray, the executive producer, and John Livingston, the quiet force behind the scenes—who taught me about deep environmentalism. I'll always be grateful. They helped me understand that we humans act like we're the centre of everything, as if the world exists solely for us. That's not just arrogance, it's dangerous.

The CBC gave me the platform to share these ideas. I'll always be thankful for that. But the CBC has changed a lot. Back in 1972, when the first global environmental meeting was held in Stockholm, not a single government had an environment ministry. Carson's book had helped put the environment on the agenda. We'd interview people like Paul Ehrlich and their segments would run two or three minutes long. Today, that's unheard of. Everything is so rushed. We're chasing quick hits, and the result is shallower and shallower reporting.

VIC: What kind of support did you have from CBC leadership?

DAVID: Well, *The Nature of Things* was always trotted out whenever the CRTC reviewed CBC's licence. It was one of the pillars. But honestly, the execs didn't really know what we were doing. They just knew we had a loyal audience. The media always chases the hottest new trend. I remember when I started, during the height of feminism, burning bras and all that, a new show launched called *Some of My Best Friends* and its logo was a pig. It got all the attention and budget. I asked Jim Murray, "Why does that get the spotlight when science, applied through industry, medicine, and the military, affects every part of our lives?" He told me: "Hang in there. Stay on the air." And he was right. *Some of My Best Friends* was gone within two years. Meanwhile, *The Nature of Things* became the longest-running science series in CBC history. Survival of the fittest.

There were clashes. When I publicly opposed the development of the tar sands, all hell broke loose. CBC was strict about hosts remaining objective, especially in news and current affairs. They pulled me off the air and issued a statement saying I'd taken a leave to engage in political issues. Yet they kept paying me the whole time! They wanted me out of sight until the next election passed.

VIC: You've always been a bit of an outsider, but in the best way.

DAVID: I remember you saying that. And I was just doing what I thought was right—for Mother Nature. We're part of her, after all. When I started *Suzuki on Science*, I looked like a hippie. Scientists hated that. Someone like me representing science on TV! But it resonated with kids. CBC deserves credit for putting it on air, even though they buried it on Sunday afternoons, opposite football. Nobody watched it. We had no budget. After two years, I quit. My science was too important to waste like that. But it gave me my start.

Let me tell you something more important. I spent eight years getting my higher education in the U.S., and I'm grateful. I got a postdoc at Oak Ridge National Lab in Tennessee, where they processed plutonium for the atomic bombs. Meanwhile, the Russians were launching the first dog, the first man, the first woman into space. The Americans panicked. Suddenly, there was money for science—NASA, universities, you name it.

If you said you liked science, they just threw money at you. I attended a tiny fruit fly genetics conference in California, and days later had three job offers—Stanford, UC Davis, and San Diego State. I wasn't even looking! It was a golden time. But I deliberately took the first opportunity I could to come home to Canada. I was involved in the Black civil rights movement in the U.S., and even though Japanese Canadians had been interned during the war, Canada still felt different to me. Americans seemed to value everything in dollars. I was raised to believe you don't talk about money like that.

Canada had the CCF, which became the NDP, a respected Socialist party. In the U.S., that would be considered Communist. Canada had Medicare. Tommy Douglas was my hero. We had equalization payments, CBC, Quebec, the National Film Board. Those things mattered to me. They made Canada feel different. Not necessarily better, but better for me.

The CBC and the NFB let us see ourselves. With all the American media flooding in, those two institutions reminded us who we are. They're critical. Of course, politicians hate the CBC. If it's doing its job, it's going to criticize whoever's in power—left or right. So every government wants to rein it in. And just to clarify—despite being with the CBC for half a century, I was never an employee. I was always a contractor.

VIC: You've always been an individualist, David. I've followed you since the hippie days. CBC responded to that and gave you a real platform.

DAVID: Well, I wouldn't say they did because of me. It was because of *The Nature of Things*. But I was getting hammered constantly over the programs we aired. We did one on the use of animals in research, showing how much of it was wasteful and unnecessary. It wasn't an animal rights piece, but the backlash from science departments across the country was intense. People called for me to be kicked off CBC and even out of universities.

We also did an early show on organic farming. I thought people would love it. But the University of Guelph and the University of Saskatchewan were furious. They had deep ties to the chemical industry in agriculture. The CBC was scared stiff, and I get it. But Jim Murray, the executive producer, took the heat. He fought to keep me on air. Without him, CBC might've replaced me without a second thought.

Jim believed in science programming, and he believed I could promote the issues he cared about. He raised me, in a way, to become a spokesperson for nature. I started as a shallow environmentalist, but thanks to him and the show, I was educated. He fought the bureaucracy so I could stay on air.

VIC: Was there one area of science—like genetics or environmentalism—where you feel you truly made an impact? Do you feel proud?

DAVID: Looking back, I feel privileged to have been part of so many important issues. At one point, we were given special CBC funding to do two-hour documentaries. They were a big deal—Sunday night broadcasts, prime time. We did specials on water, food and agriculture, big dams, the economy, drugs. We did a whole series driven largely by John Livingston, a prophetic voice from York University. One was called *It's a Matter of Survival*, and there was another on radio: *A Planet for the Taking*.

Do I feel proud? Maybe, but more than that, I feel honoured to have been part of those stories. The tragedy is, so many of the problems we raised back then are now full-blown crises. Just last week I was in New York for the Planetary Guardians, a group of 15 leading environmentalists from around the world—Jane Goodall, Sylvia Earle, Robert Redford, Richard Branson, Mary Robinson. We were there to release a report based on Johan Rockström's work on planetary boundaries.

He's identified nine critical Earth systems—like the atmosphere, oceans, freshwater, the nitrogen and phosphorus cycles—within which humanity can survive. If we push past these boundaries, we face collapse. According to the report, we've already passed six of the nine—and we're about to cross the seventh. That means we're in what Rockström calls "the danger zone." If we cross those tipping points, we can't go back. We have five years to shift course.

So when people ask if I'm proud of what we did, I'm glad we did it. But have we had much impact? It doesn't feel like it.

VIC: It's true that awareness of environmental issues has grown, especially in the last 20 or 30 years. Were you always comfortable in front of the camera?

DAVID: Funny you ask. No, it wasn't natural at all. My parents were born and raised in Canada, but we were never considered Canadian. We were always "Japanese-Canadian." When someone from England or Germany moves here and has kids, those kids are just Canadian. But we—because we looked different—were always marked.

My dad couldn't vote, couldn't buy property in much of Vancouver. Many professions were closed to him. That was the world we grew up in. He used to tell me, "If you want to succeed in Canada, you have to work ten times harder than a white person." And he meant it. He also said, "You have to be ready to get up and speak, and fight for your ideas." He made me enter oratorical contests and trained me every night. I'd write my speeches and perform them in the basement while he coached me. If I messed up, I had to start again. "Slow down here," he'd say. "Emphasize this part. Move your hand." I'd be crying at the end of the day, but he trained me to be an orator.

The first time I was on television was in Edmonton in 1962. I did a half-hour on genetics, and the camera was nothing—it felt like I was just talking to my dad. The producers loved it. That turned into my first series on camera. It's not natural in Japanese culture to speak up like that, but my dad insisted. When I was in high school in London, Ontario, one of my nerdy friends said I should run for school president. I told my dad the idea, expecting him to laugh. But he got mad. "Why didn't you run?" he said. "There's no shame in trying. How will you know if you don't try?" That was a very important lesson to me. There's no shame in trying. And if you believe in what you're saying, you've got to stand up and say it. So, yeah—I thank my father for the shit-disturber I became in the media.

VIC: And how close are you with your kids now?

DAVID: At this stage, with ten grandchildren, I've come to realize something. The reason we go through all the trials of raising our kids is so they can give us the greatest gift of all—grandchildren. This is the most meaningful time in my life. I get to spend time with them, pass on the values my parents gave me, and they give me the motivation to keep going. I'm 88. I'll kick the bucket soon. But I've got to use this time to speak and act—for them.

During the Covid lockdown, I was at our cabin on Quadra Island with my wife, our youngest daughter, her husband, and their three kids. I'm a morning person, so I got the early shift. I'd feed them, dress them, and rain or shine, we went out. As a longtime activist, I'd grumble about the clearcuts, or a new dock going up. But the kids didn't care about any of that. They were in awe. If I found a frog, they acted like I'd won a Nobel Prize. We'd flip logs looking for lizards or snakes, and through their eyes, I rediscovered that the world is still a magical place. Despite everything we've done to it, it's still wondrous. And because of them, I'm more committed than ever to protecting what's left.

VIC: You've travelled millions of miles, touched millions of lives. But in the end, it's the human connection with you.

DAVID: Well, that's the only reason we're here. Strip away all the cultural constructs—books, songs, all the blah blah—and you're left with the fundamental biological imperative. Every species on this planet, for four billion years, has been driven by one thing: get enough food, avoid predators, and pass on DNA to the next generation. That's it.

Look at a beehive. Most bees don't reproduce. But every worker is doing their job so the queen can lay fertilized eggs. The whole structure exists to keep life going. We humans have built layers upon layers—politics, economies, corporations, legal systems—all based on the idea that we're exceptional, that we must keep going just as we are. But we forget we're just one species among many, utterly dependent on nature. From conception to death, that cycle is universal. Doesn't matter who we are. Nature runs the show. I've always had this respect, this awe for it.

At the end of my life, I'm asking: Why the hell have we failed? I mean, those of us in the environmental movement—we've failed. Fundamentally. You know, we all see the world through the lens of our upbringing, our profession. I once dated an opera singer, and at parties, everyone was trilling and performing. Dentists? They just stare at your teeth. I'm a biologist. I see the world biologically. And now, with DNA, we can trace human migration across the planet. If you follow those trails back, they all lead to Africa—150,000 years ago. That's where we were born. I'd love to be invited by the Ku Klux Klan to give a lecture—so I can say, "We're all Africans. What's your problem?"

Picture it: 150,000 years ago, grasslands teeming with more animals than the Serengeti today. Small groups of these hairless apes—us—roaming around. Not fast, not strong. Our advantage? A 1.5-kilogram organ in our heads. The human brain. Curious, observant, with a fantastic memory and, most important, the ability to imagine the future. That's our unique trait. Other animals can prepare for the future, sure. But we alone can consciously shape it. We tell stories about that—like in the Bible. I'm not Christian, but take Joseph in Egypt. He interprets dreams and warns the Pharaoh: "Famine is coming. Store grain." They survive because of foresight. Or Noah—just a carpenter—told to build an ark. His friends laughed, but he saved life from a flood. Indigenous teachings speak of seven generations. Honour those who came before, and consider those who will follow. That's real foresight, and it's what helped us survive.

In 1992, more than half of all living Nobel laureates signed a declaration: World Scientists' Warning to Humanity. It said, and I quote, "Human beings and the natural world are on a collision course... current practices put at serious risk the future we wish for human society." And they warned we had as little as ten years to change. That was 1992. Since then, the warnings have only grown louder. But we're not listening.

VIC: That echo of preserving nature—it's been there for a long time. Others have tried too. We talk about it, and yet we keep consuming more.

DAVID: There are so many reasons why. Since Covid, the garbage has gotten worse. Everything's delivered now. People don't cook anymore. Even on film sets, lunch comes in individual boxes. The waste is staggering. Take the vaccine rollout. A marvel of science. But look at all the billions of syringes, plastic, packaging. We create mountains of garbage, even as we're saving lives. That's the paradox. The deeper problem is that most of us no longer feel connected to nature. We live in big cities, artificial environments. Nature is "out there"—in parks or green spaces. But we are nature.

I tell kids: take a deep breath. Now hold it. I'll keep talking. Within seconds they're gasping. I say, "See? Air is so important, you can't even end your own life by holding your breath—your body won't let you." That air goes into your lungs, oxygen binds to surfactant in the alveoli, then circulates with every heartbeat. Half of that air stays in your lungs. You can't draw a line between you and the air. You are the air.

We're 60 to 70 percent water by weight. Just walking blobs of water with a bit of thickener so we don't dribble away. And yet we constantly lose water—through sweat, breath, urine—so we must drink more. We are part of the hydrologic cycle.

Our food? Once living. Grown in the soil. Sunlight turned into chemical energy through photosynthesis, which becomes our energy when we eat. Every bit of us is part of nature. Yet we act as though we're separate.

My greatest scientific claim? A genetic mutation in fruit flies that affects nerve signals and can be controlled by temperature. We got a huge grant to study it. Why? Because insects have the same nerve systems as humans. Studying flies teaches us about ourselves.

And yet we spread neurotoxins—pesticides like neonicotinoids—through our food system. These are nerve poisons. We soak seeds in them, and every part of the plant becomes toxic. Then we eat them. And we wonder about the rise in autism. It's madness. But we still don't get it. We don't think we're part of nature, so we believe we can poison the air, water, soil, and food without consequence.

The real crisis is that we think we're too smart. So smart, we believe we've transcended the limits all other species obey. That's why people like Elon Musk dream of Mars. It took four billion years for life to evolve on

Earth, and Musk thinks he can just terraform Mars to support us. That's delusion.

VIC: But, as you said earlier, we're living longer than ever. My grandfather made it to 55. My father to 65. I'm 80 now. And here you are, 88. Despite all the environmental doom, we're living longer. Yes, but we're also consuming more than ever. When I was born, the world's population was 2.5 billion. Now, in my lifetime, it's tripled—to 8 billion. The planet hasn't grown. Everything we need still comes from here—not from "out there." Everything that breathes needs space, and yet people still don't listen.

DAVID: You know, you hit the key point. The people on the "other side" of these issues—they're not idiots. They're human beings like you and me. They just see the world differently. For 95 percent of human existence, we were nomadic hunter-gatherers. Try to imagine surviving by finding your food every day—tracking animals through their migrations, following seasonal plants.

We carried everything we owned on our backs. That's how we lived for tens of thousands of years. Then, 10,000 years ago, agriculture changed everything. We had reliable food, permanent homes, the beginnings of society. And for most of that time since, we've been farming animals. Farmers understand that weather, snow in winter, rainfall in summer—everything is connected. They knew nature mattered.

But during the Renaissance, you had people like Descartes, Bacon, Newton saying, "We are the brain." Descartes gave us "*Cogito, ergo sum*"—I think, therefore I am. Bacon said, "*Scientia potestas est*"—knowledge is power. And with that mindset, we began to believe we were special. The Industrial Revolution amplified this. Machines could now do more than animals. We could fly faster than sound, live under the ocean, escape gravity.

Suddenly, we were no longer constrained by biology. If the air's polluted, we'll clean it. If we need water, we'll invent a way to purify it. We forgot we are one strand in a web of life. In that web, there is reciprocity—you give, you receive, you have responsibility. That understanding has been lost. We now live like we're at the top of a pyramid and everything below us exists for our use. That's insanity. The latest version of that delusion? We've only recently discovered planets beyond our solar system. And what's the first thing we ask? "Could it support human life?" We don't ask, "Is it beautiful?" or "Is life there?" We ask, "Can we live there?" The arrogance is staggering.

VIC: The contradiction of the human race—we're so brilliant, yet so fragile.

One insect bite and we're dead. Nature remains the great force. I've always come from that view. So, David, when you first started, you were a scientist, right? Genetics?

DAVID: I still think I am a scientist. But yes, I started in genetics. I went to Western in London, Ontario. Back then, with grade 13, if your grades were good, you could enter medical school after two years of undergrad. I was pre-med. I came back from the U.S. after two years and asked if I could apply. The dean looked at my grades—or maybe my race—and said, "No problem, you're in." But in my third year, I took a course in genetics, and that was it. Medicine was out the window. I fell in love with science. I would have done it for free. I was doing what I loved, and getting paid for it was a privilege. But I began to realize that science has enormous implications—not just my work, but science as a whole.

Look at the media. In the 1960s, the main sections were business, politics, sports, and celebrity. Science was always the tag-on. "Oh, look what scientists are up to now—threatening us with doom." Science wasn't seen as a foundational aspect of society. Even today, when I go to Ottawa, they treat me like a special interest group. "Oh, here comes Suzuki, with his environment stuff." We've marginalized science.

VIC: I'm sure you've wondered—if you hadn't taken the media path, but stayed in science—what discoveries might you have made?

DAVID: Honestly? Never thought about that. What's the point? You can't go back, and I did the best I could with what I had. Being in the media gave me a huge opportunity to share ideas. And it was the people in media—especially those on *The Nature of Things* and on radio—who made it happen. I loved radio. I hosted *Quirks and Quarks* when it launched. Diana Filer was the one with the vision for a science show. At UBC, they told us we'd run out of material. They said, "You can't do a weekly science program forever." Well, we proved them wrong. Eventually, I had to choose. Focus on *Quirks and Quarks*, or go all-in with *The Nature of Things*. To me, *The Nature of Things* reached a bigger audience, and the visuals were powerful. Television has that ability to touch people's hearts.

VIC: Do you ever weigh the pluses and minuses, or reflect on your legacy?

DAVID: Not really. I just feel grateful to have been part of it. We were putting ideas out into the world that weren't being said anywhere else. Look at David Attenborough—he's become a major environmental voice, and thank God for that. His shows are stunning. But when I met him in the '90s, he already knew *The Nature of Things*. I asked him, "Why don't you talk about the environmental consequences? A lot of these animals will be extinct by the time your programs air." He said, "When we do environment shows, the audience drops." So, they kept the focus on wonder, not warning. He's changed since then. He's become more vocal. I respect that. But I still think they could have done more to at least acknowledge that species were threatened. And now, the state of communication is dire. With so many channels and platforms, audiences are fragmented. But I believe *The Nature of Things* has never been more important.

VIC: Did you ever work with the National Film Board?

DAVID: Yes, I did two shows in the early 1990s that I'm proud of—one on insulation, the other on energy conservation. It was around the time of the Earth Summit. *The Nature of Things* wanted to show practical ways for people to reduce their energy use, starting at home. I was very pleased with those programs. But of course, priorities shift.

VIC: From my perspective, David, I call you a globalist. You've travelled constantly, your message is international. Are there any countries you feel have really gotten it right—who are on the right environmental path?

DAVID: The only country truly attempting it at the national level is Bhutan. Others have taken serious steps—Norway, Denmark, Sweden, Germany, the Netherlands, even the UK after hosting a COP meeting. France and Spain have made progress. The slow food movement has gained traction. There are examples. But at the core, most countries still prioritize their economic systems and political institutions over nature.

In Canada, it's especially troubling. The Premier of Alberta has outright said environmentalists have no business speaking up. But air doesn't respect borders. What happens in Alberta affects the entire planet. Jason Kenney, Stephen Harper, now Danielle Smith—they've fostered a political culture where climate change isn't even discussed as an existential crisis. That's a tragedy. Our legal and political systems are part of the problem. Nature doesn't care about human boundaries. A salmon born in British Columbia may pass through Alaskan waters, swim to Japan. Whose fish is that? We can't legislate ownership of nature. People applauded when Quebec granted legal personhood to the Magpie River. But think about that—who are we to "grant" rights to a river?

Nature existed long before us. Rights should begin with nature. We should be the ones adapting to its limits, not the other way around. Just today, I heard Anthony Fauci—whom I admire—say the most destructive animal on Earth is the mosquito. And I thought, come on. Yes, they spread disease. But the most destructive animal in Earth's history is us.

My granddaughter Makena understood that better than most. Her mother's a marine biologist, and one day Makena got covered in mosquito bites. A visiting professor said, "I wish we could just get rid of mosquitoes." Makena, six years old, replied, "But frogs and birds eat mosquitoes. I wouldn't want to live in a world without them." She got it. That's the perspective we need.

We fought for years for the right to a healthy environment. But really, it's the environment that deserves the rights—and we should be the ones adapting to those rights. I told Mark Carney the other week: "All the economic indicators are rising, but every planetary health indicator is in decline. Something doesn't compute." That's because our economy is not connected to nature—it just uses nature as a resource. It's insane.

VIC: Do you miss working now that you're retired?

DAVID: Sure, I miss the camaraderie—being out with the crew, filming in the field. But do I want to go back? Hell no. I'd wanted to retire long before I actually did. I told *The Nature of Things* for years: "We need to find a successor. I shouldn't be the show." But it took a while. Eventually, they accepted that I was just getting too old to travel. And my carbon footprint from all that travel? It's indefensible.

When I finally refused to fly for filming, they said, "But there's this Harvard professor you have to interview in person." I said no. Then they said, "He's coming to Calgary." So, I agreed—but took an 18-hour bus ride each way from Vancouver. That wasn't fun anymore. I've had my chapter in TV. It's closed.

VIC: If I remember, it was Knowlton Nash who brought you in?

DAVID: Nash played a role, yes. But it really started with Jim Murray, the long-time executive producer of *The Nature of Things*. He was seconded to produce *The National Dream*—a big CBC project meant to show off our ability to produce high-quality film after *The Whiteoaks of Jalna* flopped. *The National Dream*, based on Pierre Berton's books, was a hit. Jim could have done anything after that—become a VP at CBC—but he chose to return to *The Nature of Things*. Nancy Archibald, his partner, was executive producer at the time. Jim said, "I want to do a science series." So CBC created *Science Magazine*, which was meant to be different: two to four stories per half-hour, no host.

Midway through production, Jim realized the show needed something to stitch those segments together. That's when he brought me in as host. It took off immediately. Young people loved the shorter segments. We got a 50 percent larger audience than *The Nature of Things*, which was already doing well. But after one season, Knowlton Nash said, "It's a one-time thing." On the final episode, I signed off thinking it was over. But the audience backlash was so huge, they demanded the series continue. That's the power of public response. But let's be honest—the only reason CBC supported the show was to reward Jim Murray. It wasn't because they cared about science programming.

VIC: I travelled across the country with Jim and Pierre Berton. Did winter and summer trips with them. I once asked Jim, "You've never done drama—how did you get this?" He said, "Vic, I don't have to know everything. I just need to find the right people to do the right things." That was his gift.

DAVID: That may be. Jim saw something in me. I'm forever grateful to him for bringing me into *The Nature of Things*. And the producers—they did the real work. They pulled the crews together, organized everything. When the show aired, I got the credit. People would say, "Oh, that Suzuki show was great." But it was Tom Smith's program, or Carol's, or someone else's. It upset a lot of producers, justifiably. Mind you, I got all the blame too. If a show was controversial, I was the one getting hammered. But Jim never resented my visibility. He never once said, "Hey, I'm the exec, I made this happen." He was humble. That humility meant a lot to me.

VIC: What about public broadcasting? The pressures are very different compared to commercial TV.

DAVID: As a scientist, my whole motivation for being in media was simple: science shapes our world. More than politics, business, or entertainment, it's science—especially when applied through industry, medicine, and the military—that dictates how we live. But in our media, science is marginalized. When the internet first launched, what did people go to? Porn, shopping. Information? Science was a tiny sliver. Now, social media is the main way people learn, and it's full of half-truths and misinformation.

A single image—a turtle with a straw in its nose—sparked a ban on plastic straws. But that's not the issue. The issue is plastic, full stop. We get our knowledge in fragments, through algorithms that reinforce our biases. That's where we are. There are PhDs who claim evolution is fake. That the moon landing was a hoax. We've lost the ability to discern what's credible. Social media spreads information, but there's no accountability.

And forget civil discourse. I once told a protester during Covid, "Look, the air you breathe out is going right into my face. Don't you think we have a responsibility to each other?" He said, "I used to think you were great. Why are you such an asshole?" That's what passes for conversation now.

VIC: That honesty—it's vanishing. When the Lumière brothers first showed a film of a train coming toward the screen, the audience jumped back. Now we see CGI wonders and feel nothing. The image has lost its authenticity. With phones and AI, we can't even trust what we're seeing.

DAVID: Just before coming here today, I was listening to Ziya Tong talk about microplastics in film production. You know that plastic water bottle over there? It likely contains a quarter of a million invisible microplastics. It's terrifying. She's scarier than I ever was!

She showed a still from Barbie—everything was plastic. And the sets? Often made of Styrofoam, a deadly material. She showed a worker carving a Styrofoam sphere, covered in white dust. He wore a mask, but when he went home, he brought that dust with him. Now many of them are dying of cancer. Her solution? Use CGI instead of physical sets. But as you say—what is real anymore? That's the conundrum.

VIC: You're still in great physical and mental shape. What keeps you going?

DAVID: Love. That's it. If love for your children and grandchildren isn't enough to motivate you, go play golf. Do whatever. But for me, love drives everything I do. A reporter once asked me, "What do you want people to say about you after you're gone?" I said, "You mean when I'm dead?" He said, "Yes." I said, "I don't give a shit what they say—I'll be dead. Say whatever you want." But I do want to be able to say to my grandchildren, "I did the best I could—because I love you." That's it. As long as I can walk and talk, I'll keep going. For them.

Chapter 4

ADRIENNE CLARKSON

Adrienne Clarkson is a distinguished Canadian figure whose career spans journalism, literature, and public service. From her groundbreaking work as a CBC broadcaster to her role as a cultural advocate, she brings elegance, intellect, and insight to every endeavour. Her lifelong connection to public broadcasting reflects a deep belief in storytelling as a force for understanding. This portrait captures a life shaped by curiosity, conviction, and a commitment to excellence.

VIC SARIN: In the mid-'60s, CBC's and NFB's dramatic output was incredible, wasn't it. I worked on so many brilliant projects and with brilliant people. The CBC nurtured homegrown talent: Catherine O'Hara, Dave Thomas, even Lorne Greene, who started in CBC radio. Adrienne, you have been and still are a vital part of Canadian creative energy.

ADRIENNE CLARKSON: There was a real, vibrant relationship between those two institutions. Both were created with a combination of idealism and practicality. We needed a national broadcasting system. In the 1930s, during Prime Minister Bennett's time, private broadcasters had no interest in creating a national network. They didn't think they could make money doing it. So the government stepped in. A Conservative government, no less, created the CBC. And I've always believed that without the CBC, we wouldn't be a country.

People sometimes say to me, "You had a career in television," and I say, "No, I had a career at the CBC." I never worked for a commercial network. Never wanted to. And when I wasn't at the CBC, I worked for the Ontario government or, later, as Governor General.

Public broadcasting was conceived as a tool to unify the country—to make sure people in Moose Jaw, Toronto, Kelowna, and Montreal could all participate in the same national conversation. And that, to me, was the essence of the CBC: a national conversation. It wasn't just journalists. It was also artists, storytellers, actors. Some informed, some performed, but everyone was contributing to this vast, shared dialogue.

When television arrived in the early 1950s, it became a new way to extend that conversation. My first program was *Take 30*, from 1965 to 1974. It was live. Black and white. No videotape. We'd arrive at the studio at 7 a.m., review scripts, write or revise segments, check the lineup. We did a half-hour show—live—every single day. I remember you, Vic, pulling cables in that studio. It was small, maybe three times the size of this room, but it held about 30 people. It was alive with purpose.

Recently, I was in what they now call *The National* newsroom. It felt cold. Sterile. One presenter, three robotic cameras, no lighting crew. No human touch. Back then, we had a lighting grid. A real crew. Two lighting professionals on hand every day. I learned quickly that lighting isn't about vanity, it's about humanity. About being seen clearly, as a real person.

I remember Johnny Grizzle, who was head of lighting when we transitioned to colour in 1979. Because of my complexion—not white, not Black, but beige—they used me in all kinds of lighting tests. Floor scoops, backlighting, you name it. I worked closely with Nicky Balch, the best makeup artist I've ever known, to see how makeup could compensate for lighting shifts. Every detail mattered. Television is a craft, so is film. Every frame, every element that seems effortless is built on technical mastery.

I recently re-watched some early episodes of *The Fifth Estate* and *Take 30*. Even in our humble little studio, the lighting was meticulous. The way my co-host Paul looked, the way Madame Benoît glowed while teaching us to cook—there was attention, craft, and care. And afterward, the whole crew would eat the food. It was joyful.

And that 1966 black-and-white interview I did with Leonard Cohen? The lighting on his face, every shadow, every contour, was carefully sculpted. That wasn't accidental. We had run-throughs. Lighting rehearsals. Directors tweaking setups. Even with little money and basic sets, there was art in the detail.

Those old kinescopes—they weren't even videotapes—still show the depth of skill behind the scenes. Now everything is automated, and yes, that has its advantages. But there was a human warmth to those days. A sense that people were constantly thinking, reacting, contributing.

When I moved to *The Fifth Estate* after ten years, the work shifted. We were mostly in the field, with only intros and outros done in studio.

Suddenly, you're thinking like a filmmaker: considering angles, sound quality, the location itself. I always cared deeply about where I stood for a segment, what was behind me, how the sound would come through. There were no teleprompters. Everything was memorized. You had to know your material—feel it—because that's what made it real.

VIC: Exactly. What you're describing, the studio environment, the crew, it was never just technical. It was deeply creative. For live television, that engagement mattered. Everyone was connected to the outcome.

ADRIENNE: Live television. There was never anything like it. I keep waiting for the day when someone finally says, "You know what? This is all a bit dull, doing everything mechanically. Let's bring back live shows." I loved live broadcasting. The producer would say, "This person has seven minutes," and within those seven minutes, you did the intro, conducted the interview, and wrapped it up, all while the studio director was counting you down. "Thirty seconds... fifteen..." and you'd know to say something like, "I've enjoyed this conversation very much. Thank you, Mr. Loudon. We'll see you again." People often complain that the news gives someone only one minute to speak, but I always say: one minute is enough. You can say a full paragraph in one minute. You can make a clear, compelling argument. It's about discipline.

In the ten years I did live television, I can't recall anything that went so wrong you wished no one had seen it. The worst was once when an alarm clock went off during an interview, someone had left it on set. Otherwise, we simply did the work. Everything was live. It was the best training I could have had, for anything.

I truly loved the CBC, especially the CBC I first knew. I don't look back on it with nostalgia so much as with reverence. It was an ideal. People kept thinking that as technology improved, television would improve too. But that's not necessarily true. Editing on a machine isn't better than physically cutting and viewing film. I remember hanging film strips during *The Fifth Estate* edits. There was something deeply connected about that process.

VIC: Technology has its place, but it's also distanced us. We're glued to our phones. People don't know how to say hello anymore. I'm old-school—I can talk for hours because I genuinely enjoy seeing the person in front of me. I love people. A machine will never give me that feeling. And what we had, back then, that was human.

ADRIENNE: Yes, that's exactly what I'm saying. That human touch wasn't just between people on-camera, it was behind the scenes too. Everyone worked in a human way. We all reacted to each other. Do you remember Fergie, the cameraman? Tall guy. I'd see him shake his head behind the camera if he didn't like the direction he was being given. Then someone else would whisper back to the director, giving a bit of pushback. You could hear it. There was a conversation happening.

I started at a time when women weren't welcomed at the CBC. There were no women producers. The first one to get a credit was Cynthia Scott. Before that, there were three women producing, but they were called "story editors" and were paid less, just because they were women. I once heard an executive producer justify not giving a raise by saying, "Helen lives with Beth. She doesn't need more money—they share expenses." I remember in 1976, one of our secretaries told me she was going to ask for a raise. I told her to say her rent had gone up. She came back in tears. The response? "You don't need a raise. You dress well. Your husband has a good job."

When I told my executive producer in 1969 that I was pregnant, he didn't even look up. Just said, "That's great. If you're not back in six weeks, I'm breaking your contract." There was no maternity leave. No protections. So I made the best of it. We turned it into a series on pregnancy—one episode each week while I was expecting. We covered each stage. It was fun, and meaningful too. But don't call it a golden age for women. We worked incredibly hard and often got no credit.

VIC: You're right. But we've come a long way. I think I was the first Southeast Asian person to work at CBC.

ADRIENNE: And I was certainly the first Chinese Canadian.

VIC: That's why I admire the CBC and Film Board so much. How did this vast country—with three or four time zones, multiple languages, and a harsh climate—stay connected with so few people?

ADRIENNE: Because CBC invested in the technical infrastructure. Private broadcasters in Alberta or Saskatchewan had no interest in building a national network. But the government did. Public broadcasting already existed in places like Britain, France, Germany. We weren't the first—but we did it well. And during that golden period, from the beginning of television through the transition to colour, it was extraordinary.

Take *The Fifth Estate*. It's now 50 years old. I was there at the start. You were there as a cameraman. It had a mandate and ideals, and for a long time, it kept them. We travelled. We reported internationally. We interviewed the Shah of Iran. I interviewed Mrs. Thatcher and Edward Heath during the

1981 election in Britain. We chased Thatcher to a factory where she was campaigning. There were no handlers, no PR wall and she spoke freely. It was fascinating. And Harold Wilson. We got him too.

The goal was always to show Canadians the world through Canadian eyes. Ireland. Bill Cran and I reported there during the Troubles. I worked with David Hannington too. Now, *The Fifth Estate* no longer does international stories. That limits what stories they can tell. Are we drilling down into personalities? Are we focusing on trivial items?

Back then, the format mattered. You'd have three stories, each getting a fair share of time and weight. An item on the U.K. miners' strike, a lighter story from Hollywood, and another about misordered toilets in Stephenville, Newfoundland. All of it mattered. Sometimes, we'd do a full hour, like we did on the Shah of Iran. But the balance was always intentional.

VIC: That was the strength of public broadcasting. It served everyone across the spectrum. *Man Alive*, *This Land*—programs with huge reach, even when the populations were small.

ADRIENNE: Yes, and *The Fifth Estate* had real viewership. We considered under a million to be disappointing.

VIC: How much creative freedom did you have?

ADRIENNE: Total freedom. We never saw the bosses. They were in the Public Affairs Department somewhere, but they never interfered. No one ever told us, "Don't do that story," or, "Pull that episode." Never. We were left alone to do our work.

VIC: I remember working with you and being amazed at your memory. A researcher would brief you, and next thing, you were on mic, saying everything perfectly. It was incredible.

ADRIENNE: Yes, I've always had a good memory. That's been a real asset. It's better to speak naturally than to rely on a teleprompter. Honestly, I think many people aren't served well by teleprompters. I've seen so many presenters, often young women, struggle with them. Staring blankly at the screen, disconnected.

Even teleprompters have a script—you should read and internalize it. I could teach them how to do it properly. But it's not just memory. I don't consider myself especially brilliant. My husband, John, is the real intellectual. A philosopher, always thinking in new ways. I'm more practical. My strengths have been speed, memory, and the ability to get the story clear in my mind—and get it out. That's been my creative contribution.

VIC: You also have remarkable taste in art. I didn't realize it fully until we worked on *Artemisia*, the film you directed. But it seems art has been a thread running through your whole life.

ADRIENNE: It has. At university, I did an honours degree in English, Philosophy, and Art History. So really, my academic background was completely unsuitable for television. My entry into the CBC was serendipitous. I had just completed my M.A. in English and was teaching part-time at Victoria College for $3,000 a year. I wasn't enjoying it. I didn't like teaching—I'd rather be taught—and the students weren't particularly interested either. I was 25 and already disillusioned. Then I ran into Sheila McKenzie, at a party, whom I'd known at university. She told me she was working at CBC as a script assistant on a daily show. I was amazed. No one I knew worked at CBC. I'd grown up listening to CBC Radio and I loved it.

When I was nine, my parents gave me a little maroon Bakelite radio because they thought CBC was good for my English and my thinking. I listened religiously—to the news, to *Stage 47*, to radio plays produced by Andrew Allan, even to soap operas after school. So when Sheila said they were looking for someone to do book reviews on the show—alongside interviews and segments like Madame Benoît's weekly cooking spots—I jumped at it. I prepared a segment, memorized it, and delivered it straight to camera.

The moment I walked into Studio 6, I loved it. I'd never been in a studio before. I loved the darkness, the quiet movement of people in the shadows, the enormous, cozy cameras. I sat at a table and did my review. They called me back. Every few weeks, I'd come in and review three books. Then, after a few visits, the producer, Leo Rampen, asked if I'd like to try conducting an interview. Anna Cameron, the host, was away. I did the interview and loved it. Soon after, Anna said she was planning to leave. She was 37 and wanted to return to the stage while she still had her looks, as she put it. She encouraged me to audition for the host position, as did Paul Soles. So I did. It was one of CBC's last big "cattle calls. "Forty-eight women auditioned. My test interview was with the head of textiles at the ROM. I had to discuss Egyptian versus medieval fabrics. We got the research minutes beforehand.

Everyone else seemed to have TV experience—models, dancers. I felt completely out of place. But I went on vacation, and when I came back, they called to say I had the job. When I negotiated my contract, Eric Koch, who had a sharp tongue, said, "If you don't make it in a few months, we'll toss you back in the gutter where you came from." I told him I hadn't come from the gutter.

I'll never forget my first week. I walked up the stairs of the old Havergal College building, where the offices were. At the top stood Peter Campbell, head of current affairs. I didn't know who he was, but he greeted me, took my hand on that crisp October day, and said, *"Che gelida manina, signorina."* It's the opening line of the tenor's aria in *La Bohème*. I thought I'd died and gone to heaven. Peter had been in Foreign Affairs, even an ambassador. In 1959, during the Cold War paranoia about homosexuality, anyone suspected of being gay was purged from the Canadian civil service, just like in the United States. Peter and others from that Foreign Affairs world came to the CBC. They were brilliant men. I only saw Peter a few times after that, but that greeting stays with me.

We never saw the "bosses." The only time I had a direct interaction with a president was after a trip to South Africa. I went there during apartheid with Gordon Stewart. Our South African cameraman turned out to be a spy. The show we made was powerful—and critical of apartheid. The South African High Commissioner wrote to CBC's president, Al Johnson, demanding I be fired, claiming the program was unfair and didn't understand "how apartheid was good for Black people." Al's response was brilliant. Just four lines: "Thank you for your letter. The CBC is an independent broadcaster. While I am its president and report to Parliament, I do not interfere in content, which is managed by our trusted producers." That was it. No rebuke, no reprimand. Al never mentioned it to me. That kind of quiet, total support was everything.

VIC: Can you talk a bit more about that kind of freedom—the independence to tell the stories you believed in?

ADRIENNE: It was astonishing. I don't know how it works now, but in my time, no one ever interfered. We had full creative freedom. No one questioned our content. And it's not just about avoiding scolding—interference can come through budget cuts or withheld support. But I never experienced any of that. We did some very contentious pieces. One of the most important was on the 1976 Montreal Olympics cost overruns. I worked on it with Brian McKenna. It named Mayor Drapeau, his close friends, the developers—people in power. The piece led to the Malouf Commission. It won awards. And not once were we told to back off, tone it down, or pull it. Never. Not once.

VIC: What about a story that was particularly difficult—something you had to really deal with?

ADRIENNE: I think doing the Olympic story was quite difficult—and also quite dangerous—because I believe there were criminal elements involved in that story. You just don't want to think about that, and nobody ever protected me. You were in it by yourself, and you took the risk because you were the journalist.

VIC: Was there any story where you just felt really good afterward—on a creative level, I mean?

ADRIENNE: It's hard to feel good about a story like that, but proud, yes. I'm very proud of the fact that we did our Hebron story when we did, which was in 1982. And of course, that's still a major point of contention in Israel. But they were just starting to build a settlement then—in the holiest of holy places to Muslims and to Jews. I'm very proud of that work, but I wouldn't say it was something I liked, or would want to revisit. You know, when someone asks you what your favourite show is, you tend to think it should be something you enjoyed. I didn't enjoy it. In fact, I was gritting my teeth.

You weren't my cameraman on that one—my cameraman was Eric Derschmied. He's the only other living cameraman I've worked with who I'd say had "the eye." He's still alive, he's 94 now, and he had a charmed life. He was one of those people who, before you could even say, "This is the shot," he'd already seen it, jumped off the truck, and started setting up. Derschmied just knew. He would get the shot without needing direction. You didn't have to tell him anything. He had instinct.

But he was a terrible person. Bill Cran—who was our producer on *Hebron*, and whom I absolutely loved—said to me, "You have to drive with Derschmied." I asked, "Why?" He said, "Because Stephanie and I can't stand him." Stephanie was our script assistant. So I said, "Okay, I'll do that." Then Bill added, "And he doesn't smoke." I was so grateful. Everybody smoked in those days. It's horrifying now to think about how polluted I was by all that smoke. The script assistant smoked, the cameramen smoked—you didn't smoke, but most of the others did. The sound people smoked, the producers smoked out of every available orifice. And if we were having a contentious moment in the car, they'd roll up the windows—so I'd be stuck there with four people puffing away. It was horrendous.

So, yes—I had to babysit Derschmied. What kept me going was the belief that I was perfectly safe with him because he had such a charmed life. He was already legendary. He'd been in Israel during the wars, and there was this story that he'd been on a bus that was bombed. Everyone else was either killed or maimed, and he walked off—camera on his shoulder—completely untouched.

Bill said, "He's not going to get killed. We may get killed, but not him. If you're with Derschmied, you'll be fine." So I just went into a sort of neutral zone and listened to Derschmied talk all the way there and all the way back. "Uh-huh... and then what happened?" I'd say, just to keep him going. But the moment we arrived, he leapt out and started shooting. He just saw things. Like you do. You and Derschmied are the two greatest cameramen I ever worked with. And I don't say that out of kindness—I say it objectively. Because it wasn't just about visualizing something, it was being in it. Understanding that what you get visually as a cameraman, the sights, are really the heart of the story. You're inside the story without needing to be told the narrative. That's what a great cameraman is.

VIC: But what's so remarkable, sitting here from my side, is how you—as a journalist, and an intellectual person on so many levels—are so sensitive to the visual side of things. That's rare. Most journalists don't see it. They're focused on their pen, what they write or say. How did you find that balance?

ADRIENNE: I've always said to young people—be realistic about yourself. If your body is telling you something, listen. Once, during my second or third year on *Take 30*, I got a letter from a high school girl. She said, "I really want to do what you do. I think I'm good at it. We have a little TV studio at school. But the problem is, every time before I go on camera, I have to go throw up." I wrote back: "I don't care how good you look or how strong your desire is. If you're vomiting before every taping, don't do it. Your body is telling you this isn't for you."

People used to say to me, "The camera loves you." And I think that's true. And I loved the camera in return. You don't have to play to it, but there's something about being in sync with it. Recently, I had to review some old footage for the 50th anniversary of *The Fifth Estate*. Watching myself back, I could see the difference. I don't mean to sound critical, but I can't watch many of today's presenters. There's no intuition.

What I did—it was intuitive. I was lucky. I had an intellectual background, a photographic memory, and I found a medium that suited me completely. I never wanted to be an actress. I never wanted to play anyone else. I've always believed your role in life is the one you've been cast in. So you play yourself. I've always felt very connected to th the camera. Maybe it's because my father loved taking pictures of us from the time we were little. He had a Pentax, a Contax, even a little Bell & Howell movie camera. Sadly, all our home movies were stolen in a house robbery while I was in university. But I came from a family that valued looks, not in a shallow way, but as part of presence and self-respect. My father was a very handsome man. My mother was beautiful. They both paid attention to appearance—our appearance. Before we went anywhere, even just on a picnic, my father would stand us in front of the hallway mirror. "Oh, we are so good looking," he'd say.

We didn't have much. He was building his import-export business after the war. But he still said to a friend working in government, "I want a really good photo of myself for the company brochure. Who do you recommend?" He was referred to three names. One was Yousuf Karsh. So he went to Karsh's studio. It was near our house. This was before Karsh was famous. This was 1946 or '47. And I have that portrait: Karsh's photo of my father from 1947. You can see how handsome he is.

My mother made wonderful clothes for me. She cared about how we looked—she cared about how she looked. So I never grew up needing external validation. No boss, no man, no stranger ever defined me. My family gave me that. I realize now, in my later years, what a gift that was. That's the basis of self-confidence, especially for a woman. Not having to rely on anyone else to tell you your worth. Not needing approval from someone who might give you a job. Because I brought it with me.

VIC: I feel that many of the world's problems come from people holding things in, controlling everything instead of opening up. When people open up, you can find dialogue. You had that ability. You could get the most guarded, respected people, especially in the '60s and '70s—when things were so conservative—to open up. Do you think that came from being a generalist? Or maybe because you weren't Anglo-Saxon? Did being a bit of an outsider help you?

ADRIENNE: I *was* an outsider. But at the same time, I had people I admired. When I first started watching television, there was a nightly show at 7 p.m. called *Tabloid*. A woman named Elaine Grand did the interviews, and I thought she was just fabulous. I didn't aspire to be her, because I didn't see any path into that world. But I admired her deeply. The way people revealed themselves to her—it showed me what interviewing could be. That's the real goal: revelation.

Whether it's investigative journalism like *The Fifth Estate*—getting people to show who they are—or more reflective interviews, the goal is always the same. Cynthia Scott and I used to go to England and interview historical figures—people who'd written important books, or lived through war. To get that kind of deep, personal insight was marvellous. Those are still my happiest moments: talking to someone and not knowing what the result will be. Not knowing what they'll say, and then seeing where it leads. It's like throwing an ice cube onto a black wood stove. It hits, then rivulets run off in different directions. You follow the most interesting one. There used to be a show called *Close-Up* where the host interviewed one person at length for a full half hour. I always dreamed of doing a show like that. And I did get to do that, on *Take 30*. Some of those interviews were extraordinary. I'm very proud of them. They were amazing.

VIC: Is there one interview or segment you look back on and feel especially happy about? Your absolute favourite?

ADRIENNE: I've re-watched some of the interviews I did for *Take 30*, in black and white, when we went to England. Talking to people like Arthur Koestler and Rebecca West—people I read while growing up—those were very meaningful to me. To sit with them, talk about their writing, their lives... that was wonderful.

VIC: Was there ever a story you refused to do?

ADRIENNE: Yes. I told both the senior producer and the executive producer: "I can't do a story on child abuse." And because of that, I probably wouldn't have been able to do stories on residential schools either. I'm not saying those stories shouldn't be told—they absolutely must be. But I couldn't be detached enough to do them myself.

When John N. Smith did *The Boys of St. Vincent*, I was able to watch it. Because when something is transmuted into art, it becomes bearable. But in current affairs, we deal with the raw reality. I couldn't have done that. There's no other topic I feel that way about. Maybe torture, maybe waterboarding, but certainly child abuse and the residential school legacy. It's an important story. I admire those who have told it. I just couldn't.

VIC: What's been your biggest challenge, professionally? You've done it all—interviewer, director. And what's brought you the most satisfaction?

ADRIENNE: When you're a perfectionist, you never actually find perfection. You're always on the road toward it. But the one thing about being a perfectionist is, you should only impose it on yourself. Never expect it from other people. That's how I've lived my life. I don't expect them to meet the same standards I set for myself. That wouldn't be fair.

But it's never stopped me from pursuing perfection. There are moments—little ones—when I feel it. Like when someone answers a question and I get to follow up with something unexpected. As an interviewer, you can't back down if someone doesn't answer your question. Ask again. And if they still don't answer, ask a third time. In my experience, if you're cool and patient, they will answer the third time.

It takes nerve. Interviewing takes guts. People will put you off. Often, they don't even know the answer. They've lied to themselves—or to others—or no one's ever asked them that question before. You're helping them uncover something they've never articulated. But it's a delicate line. You're not a police interrogator. Though I have watched police interrogations and they're fascinating when done well. I once saw footage of the first interrogation of a suspect, and it was riveting. No force, just repetition, tone, patience. It's a skill. In interviews, especially on television, you have to make it palatable to the viewer. You can't come across as hostile. I never wanted to make anyone feel attacked.

Even when I asked the Shah of Iran about his secret police—about torture—it wasn't about "beating up" on him. He was the Shah, the King. I wasn't going to intimidate him. At most, he'd be embarrassed. He was dethroned later for other reasons, soon after our interview, actually. You once said in your memoir that he looked like he was being interrogated—sweaty. But I think he was already very sick with cancer. He had a greenish pallor. Shortly afterward, he began travelling for treatment. Our research suggested he'd been to Switzerland several times, even before we met him. But I never approached interviews like police work. I like to watch how others ask questions. I find that interesting. But that was never my style.

VIC: Over the years, do you think journalism has changed? Has it shifted in any way?

ADRIENNE: Oh, sure. I think it's changed a great deal. When I started, a lot of people hadn't gone to journalism school—I never did. Many learned on the job, starting in newspapers with lowly positions, or in television as researchers, then moving up to story editors and eventually producers. Education in general, I think, isn't as strong as it used to be. But in our time, if someone was a good researcher, they could become a good producer. Many of our researchers became senior producers. They either had the goods or they didn't. I think of someone like Susan Foulci—she was an excellent researcher who went on to become a senior producer.

And the truth is, even though investigative journalism carries a sense of social responsibility, it's still show business. You're only as good as your last show. You're on a tightrope. And that's what I always liked about it. I never had more than a yearly contract the entire time I worked at CBC. It was always 39 weeks. I felt that was how it should be—they should be able to walk away from me, and I should be able to walk away from them. To do what, I didn't know? Maybe grow apples? But I never wanted, nor did they offer, anything more long-term than that.

VIC: You left CBC for a good period. Then you came back and had your own show as a producer.

ADRIENNE: Yes. What brought me back was Avram Sam, who took me to lunch and said, "We haven't had an arts program on CBC for 25 years. Would you consider doing one?" And I immediately said yes. It was something I had always wanted to do. The last CBC arts program had been done 25 years earlier by Vincent Tovell, who was a wonderful filmmaker and producer. He was about ten years older than I was when I first joined the CBC. I felt it was really important to showcase Canadians doing art, architecture, literature—all the creative work that shapes our life in Canada. So I accepted, and I had a wonderful time. For 10 years, I worked with an amazing team of producers. *(Ed's. Note. The show's title was* Adrienne Clarkson Presents.*)*

Each producer would do maybe two shows a year, if that, because each episode was an hour long. We committed a lot of resources, and CBC, despite being funded annually by Parliament, always acted as though it would go on forever. People planned shows years in advance. For example, Frank Gehry, the great architect, wasn't well known here when we started. In the third year of the show, we began filming with him, knowing that he wouldn't finish the Bilbao Museum in Spain for five years.

So we filmed a bit every year. And when Bilbao opened, we had the beginning, middle, and end of that project. That kind of long-view storytelling is almost gone now—from CBC and from most television networks in the world, except in places like France and Germany, where they still do that kind of work.

It was a privilege to be able to unleash that kind of talent—the camera people, the researchers, the producers—all of whom deeply loved their subjects. A show like *The Fifth Estate* is filled with hyper-tension: lawsuits, people not liking you—often with good reason, because you were criticizing them in the exercise of their function. But with the arts program, we were revealing beautiful things to Canadians about other Canadians. It was a joy. It was a fabulous time. I couldn't have been happier to have that as my last show before I left CBC.

VIC: Is there anything left that you still want to do?

ADRIENNE: I'm still doing quite a lot! Now that I'm 85, I've become very interested in what's happening to older people in Canada, and in what the government is doing about it. When you and I were starting out in the '60s, the average life expectancy was around 70 for women, 65 for men. Now, as Honourary Chair of the National Institute on Ageing, I follow these trends closely. The average life expectancy for women is now 89; for men, it's 82.

I'm asking: what are people going to do with the rest of their lives when they retire at 55 or 60? How is society going to support that? Will they have enough money to live well? My granddaughter Talia is 22 now. Her life expectancy may well be 91 or 93. That's a lot of life to plan for. People still ask me to do various things, and if I think they're worthwhile, I say yes, especially things related to aging.

There's so much that hasn't been thought through—particularly in our healthcare system—and around what people do after they retire. I find it fascinating that people don't want to go into offices anymore. They want to lounge around in sweatpants, on Zoom or Teams.

Even honours and awards ceremonies are done on Teams now. Nobody wants to go into the office to celebrate a few retirees. I don't understand the alienation from human contact. At CBC, we were always together. Of course, we travelled, but when we weren't, we were in the office—talking, seeing each other. I was even trying to get people to stop smoking in my office! But there was that energy that only comes from being around other people. We're animals—we're meant to be in herds.

When I hear that office buildings are being abandoned because people won't go in, or that legal battles are happening over it, I think, Why? Is it because people don't want to work? Don't like their colleagues? Don't want to commute? Sure, commuting is terrible—an awful waste of time. But shouldn't that lead to decentralizing offices, not eliminating them altogether? It worries me. But yes—I'm still very involved. And if someone asks me to do something meaningful, and I think it's worthwhile, I'll do it.

VIC: You've had an amazing journey—broadcaster, writer, generalist, filmmaker, author. Thank you so much for taking the time to talk.

Chapter 5
PETER MANSBRIDGE

Peter Mansbridge became one of Canada's most trusted voices during his long tenure as anchor of The National. *With his signature calm and clarity, he helped shape the way Canadians understood their country and the world. From breaking news to historic milestones, Mansbridge brought journalistic rigour and a deep sense of public service to every broadcast. This portrait captures the quiet authority and enduring influence of a true broadcasting icon.*

VIC SARIN: Peter, where were you born?

PETER MANSBRIDGE: I was born in London, England, and I was only there for a couple of years. My parents were British—my father had been in the Second World War. He flew Lancasters with the RAF. When I was about two, he left the RAF and started working for the British government. He was transferred to Kuala Lumpur, which was then Malaya before it became the Malaysian Federation. We lived there for about three years. It was a difficult time. There was an insurgency, and British colonialists were targets. So eventually, we moved to Canada. My father took a job with the Canadian civil service, and we moved to Ottawa. That's when my Canadian life began. I was about five or six years old when we arrived.

VIC: What do you remember about early Ottawa?

PETER: Cold winters! But we were excited. My sister and I had lived on the equator so we'd never seen snow. We had help around the house in Malaya, so we'd never done basic chores like mowing lawns. I was so eager that the first thing I did was go out with scissors and try to cut the grass. I was five years old. It was a whole new world. I traded my crooked cricket bat for a hockey stick and became a Toronto Maple Leafs fan. The rest of my family were Canadiens fans, so that sparked the classic Canadian rivalry. At that time, there were only two Canadian teams—Montreal and Toronto. But it was exciting. The weather, the people, the country—everything felt new.

VIC: What did your father do in Ottawa?

PETER: He was an organizational expert in the civil service. He started near the bottom, but he worked his way up to First Assistant Deputy Minister of Health. Eventually, Peter Lougheed hired him to go out west, where he became the Chief Deputy Minister of Health and Social Services in Alberta. He held that role until he retired.

VIC: You were exposed to government and public service at an early age.

PETER: Absolutely. Ottawa is a government town, and my father was very much a government man. He believed deeply in public service. He admired the people he worked with and the role of the civil service. Back then, in the '50s, '60s, and '70s, the public service was held in high regard. Not so much today. After retiring from Alberta, he ended up teaching public administration at the University of Victoria. My older sister became a nurse, and my younger brother followed in my father's footsteps. He has strong organizational skills and worked in labour negotiations for major companies.

VIC: Was your family close at that time?

PETER: We were fairly close, but I was always a bit apart. I never finished high school and didn't go to university. I joined the Navy after junior matriculation, but that didn't work out either. Eventually, I ended up working out west with a small airline, and that's really where my career began. During that time, I wasn't close with my family. I think they were disappointed. To them, success meant becoming a lawyer or a doctor. And that was never going to be my path. I took my own road. And it worked out.

VIC: Did you have any friends at the time? Anyone you were close to?

PETER: Most of my friendships were formed through work—first at TransAir, the little airline I started with, and then over 50 years at the CBC.

VIC: Where did you go when you first moved out of home?

PETER: Initially, I went out west with the Navy. Then I was stationed at Camp Borden in Barrie, Ontario, where I took flying school. From there, I went to Portage la Prairie, Manitoba, for advanced flying. Then it was Winnipeg, Prince Albert, Brandon, Churchill, Manitoba, up on the shores of Hudson Bay. And that's where I got my start.

VIC: That cross-country journey must have given you a pretty good sense of Canada.

PETER: It did. And I had a strong interest in current events. That had come from the dinner table. Every night, we'd sit down and talk about the news. The '60s were an incredible time—The Great Train Robbery, Kennedy's assassination, the Vietnam War, the Cold War, discussions about nuclear weapons—all of these things were happening. We talked about these issues every night. My father encouraged us to take sides, then switch sides to argue different points of view. While I'd never thought about the news profession, I was learning about it at that table, every night.

VIC: Was radio a part of that world too?

PETER: Absolutely. We listened to radio all the time. In Malaya, it was the BBC World Service. When we moved to Canada, it became CBC Radio: *The World at Eight* in the morning, *The World at Six* in the evening. Programs like *As It Happens, Radio Free Friday*, and then there was television, still in its early years. But it was mostly CBC for us, both on radio and TV.

VIC: If you look back now, were you critical of the news at the time? Were you conscious of it? Did you have your own opinion, or did you just accept what was being told?

PETER: You accepted it. The standard of broadcasting at that time was generally accepted as the best it could be. The attitude was, "Give me the facts, and I'll decide how I want to feel about it." I was young, and I was impressionable, so good journalists made a real impact on me, especially in how they told stories. Storytelling is such a huge part of good journalism—being able to tell the story in a way that pulls your audience in, that makes them listen or watch or read, and come away with a deeper understanding of the issue. If you can do that, you're taking your audience along with you.

VIC: Is there any story that left a huge impression on you at that time?

PETER: Keep in mind, I was up north for a lot of it, when I was in Churchill, Manitoba. In Churchill, you got radio at the same time as everyone else, but television came a week later. So, you didn't watch much TV in real time. It became a town-wide secret not to spoil the hockey scores because you wanted to watch the game when it finally aired. But still, the development of the Vietnam War had a big impact.

The assassination of John Kennedy had an even bigger one. I was in school when it happened. They announced it over the PA system. I rushed home and sat in front of the TV for three or four days straight. In those days, CBC just plugged into CBS, so you'd watch their full coverage.

Walter Cronkite was my hero. But even then, I still didn't have the slightest idea I'd end up in broadcasting myself. The Kennedy story, the escalation of the Vietnam War, the protests—it all had a huge impact on me. Canadian politics had an effect too, but not quite on the same level. Still, I watched the Liberal Party of the mid '60s closely—the Pearson era, then Pierre Trudeau's arrival and election in '68. And then, not long after that, I found myself suddenly in the world of journalism.

VIC: So, how did you go from that interest to actually getting into journalism? What made you take that step?

PETER: My introduction to journalism has become a bit of a legend, and it's especially hard to explain to journalism students today, because mine was a complete fluke. I had never considered journalism. I can look back now and see that I was kind of primed for it because of those dinner-table conversations and the interest I had in current affairs.

To me, there are three things you need to be a good journalist, before anything else. First, you have to be fascinated by what's going on around you. Second, you need to ask questions of the people who understand what's going on. And third, you need the skills to communicate what you've learned to others who are equally interested but don't have the same access. If you don't have those three traits—almost as if you're born with them—it's going to be tough. So, I had those going for me, even if I didn't realize it.

One day I was working at the airport. I was 19 and I did a bit of everything: loaded bags, moved freight, sold tickets. One day the ticket counter was really busy because they'd oversold a flight. There was chaos. They needed someone to start boarding passengers, so they asked me to make the PA announcement. So I did: "TransAir Flight 106 for Thompson, The Pas, and Winnipeg, now boarding at Gate 1." We only had one gate, but it didn't matter, it was still a big deal. There was a man in the waiting area who came over to me after I made the announcement. He said, "You've got a good voice. Have you ever thought about broadcasting?" I said no, I hadn't. He said, "I'm the manager of the CBC Northern Service station here in Churchill. I can't get anyone to work the late-night shift. Would you be interested?"

He didn't ask me about my education or experience. Nothing. Total failure of the CBC's HR department! But I said I'd be interested. I could work TransAir during the day and I could come over to do the night shift. I started the next night. That became the first building block in what turned into a 50-year career at the CBC. I remained in that chief correspondent role until I retired in 2017.

VIC: So you were in Churchill for three years?

PETER: Three years. And I enjoyed it so much, it was almost hard to leave. When they offered me a job in Winnipeg, I wasn't sure I wanted to take it. That job was in both radio and television, while Churchill was radio only, but I loved that job. And I was nervous. Winnipeg meant moving up to the big leagues with people who were trained as journalists. People who'd worked at newspapers, or had gone to journalism school, such as it was back then. There weren't many programs. But I took the job. I had a young family by then, and one thing led to another... and the amazing career that followed.

VIC: So, from Churchill—where did you go next?

PETER: From Churchill, I went to Winnipeg. I was there for almost five years. Then it was Winnipeg to Regina, where I covered Saskatchewan for *The National*. I was only in Regina for about a year before they moved me to Ottawa. From there, I went to Toronto, then did some overseas reporting, filling in for correspondents in places like London and Washington. Eventually, I began anchoring. And by 1988—20 years after that airport announcement in Churchill—I was appointed Chief Correspondent when Knowlton Nash retired. I stayed in that role until I retired in 2017.

VIC: Let's talk about your move to Winnipeg.

PETER: When I arrived in Winnipeg, the rest of the newsroom looked at me like, "Who is this kid?" And they were right to wonder. I didn't know anything about journalism. I hadn't taken any courses—I was self-taught. Back in Churchill, I used to sit and listen to shortwave radio to study how reporters did things: how they conducted interviews, how they wrote stories, how they kept people engaged. So, when I got to Winnipeg, there was understandable concern from the other journalists. And quite frankly, they were right. I didn't know much.

My first assignment was to cover the annual report from Great-West Life Insurance Company. Totally wrong assignment for someone like me with zero training. I had no background in business or finance. I went to the assignment editor, Jake O'Donnell, and said, "Mr. O'Donnell, I don't know anything about this." I'd just arrived. He said, "Don't worry, I'm sending you with Dalton the cameraman." And I thought, "What would he know about business?" But Jake said, "He'll look after you."

So we headed out, and when we got to the press conference, Dalton picked up the annual report, flipped through it quickly, and said, "Just a minute." Turns out, Dalton was a business whiz—he loved the stock market, understood all the figures. He scanned the report, gave me a two-minute briefing, took a pen, circled a key line and said, "This is your story. Ask about this." And that's exactly what I did.

It got me through day one and I learned a lot. First and foremost, it taught me the value of teamwork. I had assumed reporters worked alone, camera people worked alone, maybe you were lucky enough to have a sound or lighting tech. But I learned that when you work together, you do a much better job. Jake knew that when he assigned Dalton to go with me. I was absolutely petrified. I can still remember standing there at the press conference, asking a question I didn't fully understand, but it led to a great answer. In fact, that answer was picked up by other news agencies.

VIC: At that time, were you comfortable in front of the camera?

PETER: Not initially. I mean, I wasn't nervous, but I wasn't yet comfortable enough to have what you'd call an on-air presence. I was lucky enough to be born with a voice, apparently. The rest of it, you've got to work at.

VIC: It's much more than just the presentation. It's the content, the substance.

PETER: Listen, I was a reporter. It wasn't all about appearance or sound. It was about understanding. It was about writing and developing a story in a way that people would find compelling and want to understand. That takes time. You don't walk out of Churchill, Manitoba, knowing how to do that. I was lucky in Churchill. There were great stories to tell—polar bears, icebreakers, the rocket range up north. They were captivating stories. But Winnipeg was a different challenge. There, I dealt with stories about finance, social assistance, tensions between Indigenous and non-Indigenous communities. It was a much broader and more difficult landscape.

I had a bit of that experience in Churchill, but not enough. So it took time. I was in Winnipeg for five years. I tried for promotions and didn't get them. I wanted to be the national reporter job in Newfoundland and later in Manitoba, but I didn't get those jobs. And I learned from not getting them. I wasn't ready. That was tough, but it taught me what I needed to work on to improve. So when I hear young journalists today say, "I got turned down, maybe I'll just quit," I tell them, "Wait a second. You got turned down once. That's just the beginning." I always saw rejection as part of the process, and I was better for it.

VIC: Youth is impatient. You think, "I'm as good as anyone else. Why not me?" You don't always see the bigger picture.

PETER: Oh, I was impatient too. I remember sitting up in Churchill, already hooked on the business. There's something about it. It pulls you in. You fall in love with the passion, the storytelling, the way you can craft something others will understand and respond to. And once I got hooked, I said okay, "I want to go to the top. I want all the way top in television." At the time, that meant Stanley Burke or Lloyd Robertson—I said, "I want that job." I knew it would take years, but that was my goal. I never wavered, even thought there were setbacks along the way.

VIC: So you had that sense early on—that vision. That drive.

PETER: Absolutely. I had the confidence that I could get there, if I worked hard enough. And like so many in this business, I worked very hard, sometimes at the expense of other parts of my life.

VIC: But maybe the patience you gained, and your time in Churchill, gave you a kind of foundation. You learned about the country. You learned about Indigenous culture. You learned about weather, isolation, independence. You weren't being controlled. And then you looked at these anchors—Walter Cronkite, Earl Cameron—icons. You said, "I want to be one of them." But what was it exactly that drew you in? The idea of being on television? The storytelling? The presence? Because people really listened to those guys.

PETER: It was the sense of trust. There was immense power in that era. People believed what the anchors said—Cronkite, Cameron—because they trusted them. And that trust was everything.

VIC: The news was the heartbeat of the nation.

PETER: Exactly. And in many ways, that trust is what we've lost today. There are many reasons, but credibility isn't what it used to be. Back then, it was everything.

Walter Cronkite was the epitome of this. One of the greatest thrills of my career came when CBS needed a piece out of Canada. A spacecraft had crashed in the Northwest Territories late in the day, and they couldn't get anyone there in time. There was also a debate happening in the House of Commons about it. They asked CBC, "Can you supply someone to cover it?" And the response was, "Sure, Mansbridge can do it." So I got in touch with their desk in New York to find out how much time they needed and so on. I wrote the script, sent it to them and they loved it. I put the piece together and did an on-camera close. This was all happening late in the day. Then at 6:30 p.m., *The CBS Evening News with Walter Cronkite* came on, and this story was the lead item. Cronkite read the intro and said, "Peter Mansbridge of the CBC has our report."

My heart was pounding, Walter Cronkite said my name. And it's funny, because I've had young reporters come up to me after hearing their names mentioned on *The National*, and they've told me how much it meant to them. And while there's no comparison between me and Cronkite, I understood exactly what they were feeling, because I had felt it too.

VIC: In the '60s and '70s, people truly looked up to the anchors. They trusted what they were being told. Has that changed?

PETER: It's changed a lot. In the '80s and early '90s, we began to see the end of that era. Back then, if you asked someone on the street who anchored the big U.S. newscasts—ABC, NBC, CBS—they'd answer without hesitation: Tom Brokaw, Dan Rather, Peter Jennings. Try asking that today, and most people wouldn't know. It's not because today's journalists are any less talented, it's because people get their news in so many different ways now. Most young people get everything from their phones.

VIC: It's all fragmented now. The digital world has changed everything.

PETER: Exactly. And news organizations are scrambling to figure out how to get their audiences back. Some think the solution is to mimic social media formats—like Twitter, or X as it's now called—but that's not what the audience for traditional newscasts wants. They want credibility, truth, and responsible journalism. They want stories that matter, stories that impact their lives. Sure, there's room for lighter stories near the end of a broadcast. You want people to feel that life will go on. But when the trivial stories are leading the newscast, that's when your credibility starts to erode.

VIC: There's a huge responsibility in being an anchor. What you say matters, people believe it. So behind the scenes, what did you do to ensure that what you were delivering was accurate? Were you checking the content?

PETER: Two things. First, I never fully appreciated how much people trusted the anchor until after I retired. People still come up to me—just recently, in Winnipeg—and say things like, "I used to sit with my parents and watch you at 10 o'clock. My father would say, 'Listen to him. He's telling the truth.'" That really struck me. Second, yes, I was deeply involved in the process. I was one of the senior editors of the program, as well as the chief correspondent. I saw all the scripts, not just the ones I read on air.

I sometimes reworded things if I thought the phrasing could be improved, though the writers were excellent, often better than me. I also reviewed the reports sent in from journalists around the world. They had to be vetted. I was part of the editorial discussions, what story goes first, how much time to give it, whether a complex issue needed a second piece, and what we'd have to drop to make room. If you're going to be the face of the organization, you should know what you're saying, and be accountable.

What puzzles me is when anchors are just a face and voice, not involved in the content. That's a failure. And part of the problem today is a lack of transparency in how decisions are made. If people don't understand the editorial process, they begin to question everything—why some stories are covered and others aren't, why certain sources remain anonymous. Without transparency, trust erodes.

We weren't a hundred percent transparent either, but times are different now. Journalists are under attack, and we're losing credibility. We have to earn it back. One way to do that is by helping the public understand how decisions are made. Right now, many people believe we're biased, that we make things up, that we're fake news or pushing disinformation. Those are serious issues, and if we don't address them, we risk losing everything.

VIC: Especially in the U.S., it's remarkable. You can watch three different networks report on the same event in completely different ways. They can't all be right. So where does personal bias come in?

PETER: Well, listen, journalists aren't neutered at birth, they do have feelings, and they have biases. But the idea is, when you're on the job covering an event, you check those at the door. You tell the story in such a way that you lay out the facts as best as you can find them, keeping your own opinions out of it. You aim to be fair and accurate, and you let the viewer, the listener, the reader decide how they want to feel about it. But first, you've got to lay out the facts, all the relevant ones.

This issue of bias has haunted journalism forever. There have been times when bias has crept through. But in my experience, the overwhelming majority of stories done by fantastic journalists—at CBC, CTV, Global, and among my American colleagues—have been reported without bias. They present the story as it happened. It's up to the audience to interpret it.

These days, people question almost everything they see in the news, and some of that questioning is healthy. But I tell people: you've got to do a little homework. Watch a number of different programs and figure out which one you trust, not which one tells you what you already believe, but which one demonstrates solid journalism. That's the one that should become your home base. Sure, look around occasionally, but you need a trusted source, because navigating today's complex world requires good information. And that's what professional journalists are offering: answers.

As critical as I can be of what I see in today's media—and I don't want to sound like one of those old guys going on about how things were better in the "golden era"—we do have to be honest about what's being lost. When I was young, I used to roll my eyes at the older folks saying the same thing, but now I understand where they were coming from. The bottom line is: audiences should demand better, and journalists should be accountable. That's how we get to a more informed public.

VIC: You worked at CBC for a long time, and of course it's funded by the government. Was there ever any pressure on you, direct or indirect?

PETER: Here's where I take issue: it's not funded by the government. It's funded by the people, through the Parliament of Canada. All parties vote on those budgets. Of course, governments influence the amount of money allocated to public broadcasting, and that does affect the CBC's mandate to some extent. But in 50 years at the CBC—and 30 of those at the top levels of editorial decision-making—I can honestly say I never experienced any forced pressure. Were we aware of what politicians were saying about us? Sure. We heard it. But that never changed how we approached a story.

There was only one time I can recall forced pressure, and that was before my time in senior editorial roles. It was during the October Crisis in 1970, when the government forced the CBC to broadcast the FLQ manifesto. CBC management at the time gave in to that pressure, and many of us thought it was the wrong decision. But I never saw anything like that happen again. Were all our decisions perfect? No. Did we make mistakes? Yes. But here's the thing: you gain credibility by admitting when you're wrong. Even if it's a tiny error, you correct it. Some outlets don't bother, they think it's not worth it. But I believe it's always worth it. If your audience sees you correcting something small, they're more likely to believe you care about getting the big things right.

I have enormous respect for journalism. It plays a critical role in helping us understand the world. But we have to protect it. Part of that is being transparent about how we do our work.

VIC: Looking back over your long career, journalism has clearly changed. Where do you think there's room for improvement or correction?

PETER: It's absolutely changed. The news landscape is nothing like it was 5, 10, or 20 years ago. There are far more players now—more news organizations, more so-called news shows that are really just opinion programs dressed up as journalism. And that has an effect. For traditional, trusted news programs to regain their prominence, they need to take a hard look at how they do the work and how they deliver it. Legacy broadcast platforms—cable and traditional TV—are fading. It's all about streaming now. It's all digital. So we have to find new ways to tell stories that still uphold the best of our values.

One example is a CBC digital show called *About That*. It's only available on YouTube and other digital platforms. It already has a huge audience, even though you don't hear it talked about much. But people have found it because it answers that fundamental question: why does this story matter? And that's what more of us need to do. It's not just about the headlines. It's about explaining why things are important, where they came from, and what they mean. That's what audiences are crying out for—understanding. Some of us are doing that. Others need to catch up, or they'll be left behind entirely.

VIC: Should we continue to work hard to build Canadian identity, this feeling that defines us?

PETER: Well, I think identity is incredibly important. Like you, I've travelled a lot of the world. Thanks to this job, I've been lucky enough to visit every continent except Antarctica. I've met thousands of people in incredibly tough situations, war zones, natural disasters, political upheaval. And you know what? They have no trouble identifying Canadians. They know what being Canadian means. In fact, they often have a better grasp of our national identity than we do.

Here at home, we do polls trying to define what it means to be Canadian, and we often land on something like, "Well, a Canadian is not an American." But when you ask people abroad, the answers are far more meaningful. First of all, they're incredibly envious. Many would give anything to be in our shoes. But beyond that, they'll say, "A Canadian is someone who cares, and shows it."

That's been our history. We've shown up when it matters. Think of the First and Second World Wars, Canadians volunteered, and tens of thousands never came home. They believed in helping liberate others. In natural disasters—floods, tsunamis, hurricanes—it's often Canadians who are remembered for coming to help. Children in those places don't forget.

So, no, people around the world don't struggle with our identity—we do. And I think that's partly because we live in such a diverse country. We're diverse in language, culture, geography, and sheer size. And with that diversity comes disagreement, on big issues. So we sometimes convince ourselves that we're not all truly Canadian, because we're constantly arguing over this or that.

But we are Canadian. And in many ways, that tension is healthy. Disagreement is okay, as long as we work toward compromise. That used to be part of who we were: a country of compromises. Are we still that today? I'm not so sure. But if someone could help bring us back to that idea, to valuing compromise as part of our identity, it might answer a lot of these lingering questions.

VIC: Public broadcasting is really at the heart of what we're talking about. Do you think it's still valuable to have, or is it time we let it go?

PETER: I think it's always good to have a discussion and a debate—a vigorous one—about the state of public broadcasting. I'm a great believer in it. Especially in a country of our size and diversity, I think it's essential that we have those discussions, that people offer their opinions and that political parties, if they have a better way of doing things, put those ideas forward. We don't spend anywhere near as much as other countries on public broadcasting, but we still spend a lot, about a billion and a half dollars. That's significant, especially when there are many competing demands for public funding. I understand the debate. But shaping a country's identity often comes through a good public broadcaster.

Have I been critical of the CBC? Yes. I was, even while I worked there. I love hockey, but I got tired of it knocking us off the air two months out of the year. That said, there are far bigger issues than hockey, like management decisions about the CBC's mandate, programming priorities, and its focus. Those kinds of discussions should always be front and centre, because they can make the public broadcaster better.

VIC: You never worked for the Film Board, did you?

PETER: No, well, actually, I shouldn't say that. When I was 10 years old, I was in a National Film Board film. I was the star! My sister and I starred in a short film called "Michael and Mary Visit the Parliament Buildings." We got a week off school, toured the entire Parliament, and ended up meeting Prime Minister John Diefenbaker in his office. That was an NFB production, so yes, I did work for the Film Board, but only when I was 10.

VIC: I want to get a clip of that! Honestly, I give so much credit to the CBC and the NFB for holding the country together, for connecting the voices. These two institutions really worked to unify the country. Don't you think?

PETER: Absolutely. That makes perfect sense. There have been times when all three major cultural institutions—English CBC, French CBC, and the NFB—were healthy and doing great work. But to truly unify the country, they need to work together. They've tried, but it never quite worked. I remember doing co-productions with Radio-Canada, my friend Bernard Derome and I would talk about doing more, but it didn't really happen. There were language barriers, budget barriers, and differing interests. They were drawn to stories we weren't, and vice versa. That's unfortunate, because to achieve what you're describing, you need that kind of collaboration.

VIC: I worked on environmental stories in the late 1960s, before it was a mainstream issue. We were the first to talk about air pollution, water pollution, and pesticides. I'm proud of that. I just want Canadians to feel good about where we came from—to have our own voice and not always feel second to the U.S.

PETER: There are great journalists in the U.S. and some are friends of mine. But the best journalists I've ever met are Canadian. That's why American networks keep trying to hire them.

VIC: They scoop them up in no time. So how do you feel about your retirement?

PETER: I feel great. I always said I didn't want to be doing *The National* with a "7" in front of my age, so I retired at 69, and I was happy for it. That decision opened the door to a new and fulfilling chapter in my life. I thought stepping down might be painful, but it wasn't. I was over it in a couple of days and already looking for new opportunities.

Since then, I've written books—I'm now working on my fifth—and I host a successful podcast four days a week. It gives me space to ramble, reflect, and speak freely without the constraints of a newscast. I occasionally share opinions, and I love doing it. I also travel across the country giving speeches, and I now spend nearly half the year living in Scotland. None of this would have been possible if I'd stayed on.

In many ways, I was lucky to leave when I did. The business was going through a transition, and still is. There are a lot of good people trying to rebuild the kind of public trust we once had. I hope they succeed, because there's too much at stake, especially here in Canada. People need to trust their news organizations, and those organizations must exist in an atmosphere where good journalism is both valued and allowed to flourish. That's our journalistic tradition in Canada, and it should be our future too.

VIC: It's an honour to hear your stories. Thank you Peter.

Chapter 6

LOUISE LORE

Louise Lore is a veteran producer with a distinguished career at CBC and the National Film Board of Canada. She played a pivotal role in shaping public broadcasting with a focus on Canadian identity, cultural inclusion, and narrative innovation. Her projects often centred on social consciousness, amplifying stories that reflected the diversity and complexity of Canada. Lore's work helped define an era of documentary and dramatic programming that resonated across the country.

LOUISE LORE: You know, Vic, I remember sitting on a plane with you. I don't know where we were going. I think it was just across Canada, or maybe overseas. You were sitting beside me with your camera on your lap. I said, "Put your camera away. You're going to be very uncomfortable."

VIC SARIN: And I said, "It's worth it cause this way I knew the camera would work when we landed." I always travelled light. Let me ask you, where were you born?

LOUISE: I was born in St. Catharines, Ontario. In the 1940s, we were the only Chinese family in town. St. Catharines was a very small town. The only thing that was probably unusual was that my best friend went on to become very well known, Barbara Amiel. She became a national figure on CBC television. I came to Toronto after I had travelled around the world and had no job. So Barbara talked to her boss at the CBC, Ross McLean.

He interviewed me. I don't think I impressed him very much. I think the interview lasted about two minutes. Back then, everybody wanted to work at CBC. They had the pick of the best and brightest. And I wasn't very impressive. A high school teacher who knew nothing about the medium. But then he found out I had been hired by CBC Sports as a researcher. So I think he must have thought, "Oh, I must have missed something." Next thing I know, he called me and offered me a job in current affairs, which I knew a lot more about than sports. Anyway, my first job was literally as a gofer—go for coffee, go for tea. I did that for about a month. Then I became a researcher, and by the time that show ended two years later, I was a story editor. That was my on-the-job training.

VIC: Let's go back a bit more. I want to know about your parents and your early life. What did your dad do?

LOUISE: My father was a chef, a cook. We had a Chinese restaurant, like every other small town in Canada.

VIC: What was it like for you, going to school?

LOUISE: I had a very happy childhood. We didn't have much money. The restaurant wasn't very successful, it was near the General Motors factory, so most of our business came from factory workers. I grew up in a very small town. There was just one high school. I was a shy child, but in high school I found my feet. I got involved in everything at school. I think I had a very happy, maybe even uncharacteristically happy, childhood.

VIC: What did you do for fun as a child? Anything that might have prepared you for film or radio?

LOUISE: There were lots of movies. I probably spent more time in the library, though. I worked there and read a lot, that was my main pleasure. We also watched television. That was the era when TV was just being introduced.

LOUISE: You know, I can remember, I was of the generation when there was one television on our street. They would allow all the neighbourhood kids to come in for one program. We'd all sit in little rows and watch this amazing thing called television. I think it was *The Howdy Doody Show* or something like that.

VIC: So that was like magic back then. And it was the only game in town, right? On television?

LOUISE: Yes, CBC began in the '50s: 1952. And originally, it really was important. I remember watching late-night television. Some of my happiest times were watching NHL hockey games with my dad. That was something we did together, when television was still where the family gathered. It was good for social interaction in a sense.

VIC: You mentioned you were Roman Catholic?

LOUISE: Yes. I went to a Roman Catholic school early on. There wasn't a Roman Catholic high school then, but I went through the Catholic system when I was younger.

VIC: As a girl watching all this, did you ever think, "Maybe one day I want to work in television?"

LOUISE: No, none at all. I mean, if you lived in a small town at that time, working in television felt like saying, "I want to be a star in Hollywood." It was so glamorous, far away, exotic. I was quite content. After my father died, I went back to St. Catharines and taught high school. They had just established a Roman Catholic high school, and I taught there for two years.

Getting into television at CBC was pure accident. After two years of teaching, I got itchy feet and travelled around the world with my girlfriend. When I returned to Canada, it was already summer and all the teaching jobs had been filled. So I stayed in Toronto and spoke to Barbara Amiel, who was working at CBC then as an on-camera star, very glamorous. She said, "I'll get you a job at CBC." And I thought, "That's impossible. How would I ever get a job? I don't know anything." Sure enough, I got an interview with Ross McLean, who was launching a new big current affairs show for the network. Eventually, I was hired. I'd run errands, deliver scripts to the studio, that kind of thing. And I remember people were incredibly kind. I was totally ignorant of how it all worked. But the area head gave me a tour and said, "I suppose you're wondering what this building is all about." He showed me the videotape system and the editing process—I'd never seen it before. It was all magic to me. Anyway, I ended up being promoted to researcher.

VIC: Was that promotion because of your academic background?

LOUISE: I think it was because I worked hard. Honestly, this was the '60s. We were the generation discovering marijuana and pop music and all of that. There weren't any union rules or formal boundaries then. You were just expected to do the job, and it was all fun. It was all about discovery. We'd think nothing of pulling an all-nighter. That was absolutely normal. "You have to edit till four in the morning?" Okay. You just did it.

VIC: So there was a sense of magic. You were excited?

LOUISE: Yes. It felt like a gift. We were working together on projects, spending all our time together because there wasn't time for another social life. The job was your life. And I've always said, I'm so grateful to have had a job where I kept learning. Every story, every project taught me something new. That's such a great gift.

VIC: By the way, I remember Barbara Amiel so well. She was a script assistant. She wasn't just physically striking though, she was also incredibly smart.

LOUISE: Yes, very smart. She could really write. We still keep in touch—not close anymore—but, you know, she's still married, still... she registers. She recently wrote a book called *Friends and Enemies*. I'm still listed as a friend.

VIC: Let's go back to your early days. What year was it when you started?

LOUISE: In 1967 with *The Way It Is*—not *This Hour—The Way It Is* was the show, and it was an incredible one. Ross McLean was the executive producer, but the key producers were Patrick Watson, Moses Znaimer, and Ken Lefolii—who had been editor-in-chief at *Maclean's*.

VIC: That's quite a team.

LOUISE: They were all unbelievably intelligent, talented people—each very different. It was an incredible learning experience for me.

VIC: What did you learn?

LOUISE: Everything—because I didn't know a thing about production when I arrived. I learned by example. I remember the first time I cut a piece that was going to air. I had edited the sentence at the end, but the director beside me said, "No, no, that's the ending." And he cut it off before my version finished. I was a bit put off, then I realized he was right. It was a better ending. That's how it was back then, you learned by doing.

VIC: A lot of it was live television, right?

LOUISE: Yes. Very scary. We'd run scripts onto the studio floor with seconds to go—very tense, very alive.

VIC: Any particular episodes or stories that have stuck with you?

LOUISE: Yes, during the rise of Quebec nationalism, we did a show with interviews featuring all the leading figures in Quebec. I remember the CBC brass were not happy with it. We all took a stand, either the show aired as it was, or we walked. We really felt strongly about telling the full story. It was an exciting time.

VIC: How much interference did you deal with in those days?

LOUISE: This was post-*This Hour Has Seven Days,* so the CBC executives were very cautious. There was a lot of nervousness around producers and the rebellious energy of current affairs. It was the same brass who had dealt with *Seven Days,* and it created a tense atmosphere. But over time, that relationship changed for me.

VIC: I remember *This Hour Has Seven Days,* what a show. I was one of the cameramen. There was so much tension when we went live those days.

LOUISE: Yes, the whole country would watch. The next day, people would talk about it in their offices. It was that important.

VIC: One of the most successful shows at 10 p.m. every Sunday. The whole country would come to a stop just to tune in. It was ground-breaking for investigative journalism and current affairs, and yet it was cancelled.

LOUISE: As a producer, I always took the production side. But there were issues—editorial control, studio dynamics—and people don't realize how many innovations came out of Canada.

VIC: I remember working with the producer Larry Gosnell on three stories in California about air pollution, water pollution, and pesticides and we were the first to bring these stories to the forefront of the world.

LOUISE: Yes, and nobody really talks about them now. They were pioneers. VIC: I even remember *Time Magazine* had a cover story on air pollution — a few months later! Awareness of the issue caught on like wildfire, but the seeds were planted by a producer at the CBC.

LOUISE: What's so rare now, and was so precious then, was that people at CBC and the NFB really believed in their mission. We believed we had a mandate to educate, inform, and illuminate. That was the CBC's stated purpose, and we truly believed in it.

VIC: So it wasn't just entertainment.

LOUISE: Exactly. Yes, we made entertainment programs for after dinner, but we were also commissioned to educate Canadians—to bring light to world events. I really believed in that. I swallowed the Kool-Aid, as they say. Even now, retired for decades, I still open the paper and think, "That would make a good *Man Alive* show."

VIC: You were working in ethics, values, and religion?

LOUISE: Yes, broadly speaking. We wanted to reflect on important ethical or spiritual questions, without promoting one institution over another. It was about illuminating ideas so everyone could engage in reflection. That was always a joy. It was all about ideas.

VIC: And now?

LOUISE: Now, I think the tragedy is we've lost appreciation for the gift that television and communication can be. You don't need to pander. You don't need to only tell people what they already know. You can explore new ideas, what someone else thinks, especially if it's different from what you believe. That's not easy today. The vehicles for that kind of dialogue are rare. But at the CBC, that was our mission, and we did it regularly.

VIC: Yes, you're right. From my perspective, it feels like the media gives viewers what they want instead of opening new doors to invite them to look at things differently or learn something new about the world. It's not about informing now, it's about attention and ratings.

LOUISE: That's exactly it.

VIC: Which raises the question: How important is public broadcasting?

LOUISE: I think it's super important. We need a provider of information that doesn't have a fixed editorial bias, something that isn't Fox News or CNN or MSNBC. A trusted perspective that, while not entirely without opinion, isn't operating with a vested interest in any one point of view.

VIC: That would've been unthinkable.

LOUISE: Exactly. There's a rising belief that public broadcasting has no value, that a voice outside of the commercial world isn't needed. I find that terrifying. Especially if you think about the role of education in society. In schools now, civics and citizenship aren't even taught. Children grow up without a sense of the greater society, or their role in it. You can stream shows from all over the world, but none from your own neighbourhood, your region, or your country. If you only watched Netflix, would you ever even know what it means to be Canadian? All of this makes me deeply worried. We're a country five thousand miles across. Without a national broadcaster, how would we communicate with each other?

VIC: The natural lines of communication run north–south, don't they?

LOUISE: Yes! People in B.C. have more in common with Seattle. And in the Maritimes, it's Maine or Vermont. Without something like CBC, what kind of country do we have?

VIC: Even though I'm an outsider, I was born elsewhere.

LOUISE: But most Canadians are, in a way. We're hyphenated—Pakistani-Canadian, Chinese-Canadian, Indo-Canadian. We've encouraged multiculturalism, and we cherish it. But we also need something that creates a national identity. That identity must come from our environment, and from our national media. We don't have that kind of aggressive patriotism like Americans do, so we need this even more.

VIC: Especially now, when many people in Canada aren't Canadian-born.

LOUISE: Yes. That makes the role of public broadcasting even more important. People who've come here made a choice to be here. They want to be part of the country, of the culture. They need someone to expose them to the values of this land. But what happens instead? It's easier to learn about California or Florida than it is to learn about Saint John's or Regina.

VIC: Yes, we're overwhelmed by social media and global streaming. It's hard for young people to develop a strong Canadian identity.

LOUISE: Exactly. And don't forget, local and regional newspapers have vanished. Even papers like the *Globe and Mail* are struggling. There are no local sources anymore to help communities understand who they are. If you don't have a sense of where you come from, how can a society truly flourish?

VIC: Think about it. The NFB started in 1938. CBC started in 1952. This country stretches five thousand miles, across three cultures—French, English, Indigenous. Half the year, it's frozen solid. And yet, these two institutions gave a voice to the people.

LOUISE: Yes, the NFB especially. It might be the best model. When I was there, there were studios across the country. They worked independently. So, at the Film Board, there was a French division and an English division. The English division was further split into regions—East Coast, Montreal/ Quebec, Ontario, the Prairies, and the West Coast. Each of these worked independently with filmmakers, mainly emerging talents, though there were some veterans too.

VIC: And a big part of the mandate was working with local talent?

LOUISE: Exactly. The idea was to support local voices—stories from those regions—and most importantly, to offer training. To give young filmmakers the tools to tell stories from their own communities.

VIC: The Film Board trained so many filmmakers.

LOUISE: Yes. Of all kinds. They provided an amazing platform, top-notch facilities, encouragement, and crucial guidance. Producers would work closely with directors, offering mentorship, but always with the understanding that it was their film. There's a big difference between offering advice and taking over.

The Film Board was always clear: "We're here to assist you. We want to help you make the best film you can, but it's your film." When I was there in the '90s, we launched the first diversity program, so that filmmakers of colour had a dedicated fund. At the time, there really weren't many, and they needed extra support to tell their stories. We also launched the first Indigenous program. Those initiatives were early and important. Some of today's big names came out of those programs.

VIC: Alanis Obomsawin being the most well known?

LOUISE: Yes, Alanis is probably the most recognized, but there have been many other talented filmmakers who emerged from those programs too.

VIC: It's a wonderful thing—because Canada saw so much postwar immigration. You had newcomers and people born and raised here. The Film Board helped both tell their stories.

LOUISE: Absolutely. And that builds understanding. That's where the tension often comes from, when we don't understand each other. Whether it's Muslims, or any other group, just understanding why people live or believe as they do makes a huge difference.

VIC: Exactly. It's a wonderful role the Film Board played. And CBC was often the outlet.

LOUISE: Right. Racism, homophobia, all kinds of fear and hatred, they often come from ignorance. When you don't know someone who's different from you, it's easier to fear them. But when you see someone on film—someone you can relate to—you start to think, He's just like me. That fear becomes smaller. That strangeness begins to disappear.

VIC: One thing we all value—especially in the so-called free world—is choice.

LOUISE: Yes!

VIC: Having the CBC or the Film Board gives us that. In a commercialized media landscape, at least we can choose something different. You don't have to watch CBC if you don't want to.

LOUISE: Exactly. It may not be for everyone, but it serves a purpose. Not every CBC show is entertaining to me either. Not every project I worked on was perfect. But the bigger picture—the mission—is what matters. It's about having the option to engage with content reflecting our values and identity.

VIC: That's what I love about Canada. In the best sense of democracy, we have a choice. If I want to hear one voice, I can. If I want to breathe the air I choose, I can. Isn't that a joy?

LOUISE: Yes, and it's at risk of vanishing. Everything becoming commercialized, like in the U.S., where every show feels the same. One person says one thing, another says the opposite. But in public broadcasting, you can listen, reflect, and seek honesty.

VIC: Honesty really is the most important thing, isn't it?

LOUISE: Yes. Honesty, knowledge, values. That's the richness that public broadcasting offers. And we should never take it for granted. BBC was the instigator for a lot of us.

VIC: I actually started working for ABC in Australia, which at that time was very similar to the BBC. That's really where I started. And in my own films, I've tried to express that idea, that waiting isn't always the answer. Sometimes you need to act, even when things feel uncertain. It's a small denominator to judge the bigger picture by. Can we talk a bit about some of the truly interesting things that came out of CBC or the Film Board? Any shows or personalities that brought something important to Canadians or to the world?

LOUISE: Well, yes. One that really stands out: we went to Iran to film a segment for a documentary I was directing on Islam. It was the 1970s. Back then, people in North America knew nothing about Islam. It was still seen as this strange, distant religion. We made a one-hour documentary—I think it may have been the first of its kind in Canada. I can't say that definitively, but it was certainly among the very first. I even took that film to the Aspen Institute in Colorado. They were beginning to study the developing Arab world, and our documentary offered an early insight into that. This was long before Islam became part of the nightly news cycle. At that time, no one had any real understanding of that part of the world.

That project really showed me what *Man Alive* could be. The title itself—*Man Alive*—was an invitation to cover anything and everything. I used to say, "It's about religion, which means it's about everything in the world." I wouldn't let anyone tell me, "That's not a topic for your show," because of course it was. The title comes from Saint Irenaeus, a 16th-century bishop from Lille. He said, "The glory of God is man fully alive." So our goal was to explore everything that makes a human being flourish. Anything that made us fuller, richer humans, that was our territory.

One of the first films I did for *Man Alive* was with the United Church. It was about Ralph Edwards, a homesteader in the Rocky Mountains. He lived on a remote property, three days by mule track to get in or out. He became a key figure in saving the Trumpeter Swan population. At the time, they were nearly extinct. But he had a lake on his property where some swans had taken refuge, and he fed them—hauling in chicken feed over three days by mule. He was one of the unsung heroes of conservation, and we told his story on national television.

VIC: That's incredible. Was *Man Alive* explicitly Christian in orientation?

LOUISE: No, not at all. People assumed that because it came out of the religious programming division. But it wasn't limited to Christianity. We did episodes on Islam, Buddhism, you name it.

VIC: I remember the Dalai Lama coming in.

LOUISE: Yes! We interviewed him twice. He came to the studio with his entourage of old monks. We couldn't get him to sit down, he was fascinated by the technology—he kept chatting with the cameramen, looking at all the equipment. And the monks just stood there—we had set out chairs, but they said "We can't sit down until His Highness sits down." He was just like a curious child, full of delight. It was so touching and funny at the same time.

VIC: I spent nearly a week with him. He was more curious about what I was doing than anything else! Yes, his wisdom is deceptively simple. I remember one of his metaphors: Chinese flowers are beautiful, but then they become dandelions. His point was that beauty and impermanence are intertwined. It was profound. There were so many stories like that. And CBC allowed us to go find them. You'd have an idea, pitch it, and then go do it. That kind of freedom—at 33rd Avenue in Toronto—you don't find that often. It opened doors, and that is what makes life rich, not money, not fame, but experience, knowledge, connection. And for me, the camera gave me access to those experiences. But it was CBC that gave me the camera. It wasn't just about the filmmakers—it enriched viewers too.

LOUISE: Exactly. CBC allowed creative people to explore the world through a Canadian lens. And in doing that, they enriched Canadian viewers. They introduced them to places like Dharamsala—places they might never see, but could come to understand just a little bit more through the screen.

LOUISE: You know, some people would say CBC creative types are self-indulgent, just going off and doing whatever they like. Well, yes, that can be true. But it's reciprocal. Those explorations—the films, the stories—they're shared. They come back to inform the public. They aren't just indulgences. And that's where choice comes in. The audience always has the choice. Don't want to watch? Turn the dial. But it's about having that choice.

VIC: Exactly. But critics look at CBC and say, "They're just self-important arty types."

LOUISE: Right. And for people like that, the bottom line is everything. They don't put value on things that aren't easily measurable, things that don't have a price tag. But not everything that's valuable comes with a number.

VIC: I agree. People can question CBC, sure. But the real value lies in the freedom to explore ideas that aren't necessarily commercial.

LOUISE: I'm not against the commercial side, don't get me wrong. If you want a bigger house, fine. But I should also have the freedom to do more meaningful, less commercial work. That's the ultimate freedom. We talk a lot about democracy, but I don't think everyone understands what democracy really means in the broadest sense, for humanity.

VIC: Is there a particular CBC or NFB project that stands out, something you're especially proud of?

LOUISE: I recall we did a documentary for *Man Alive* about a young man who was blind and faced mental challenges, but who had an extraordinary gift—he could play any piece of music he heard. That little story became the most awarded film from CBC. It won prizes all over the world and generated an outpouring of mail. It was so simple, just one family, but so inspirational and beautiful. That's one of the projects I'm proudest of.

David Cherniack also did some really important work with Indigenous communities. We followed one particular community over many years, documenting their challenges. It was one of the earliest sustained efforts to show, through a personal and human lens, the realities those communities face. It helped viewers see that these were people just like us—struggling, surviving, resilient.

VIC: And you've worked on both sides—CBC and NFB. Is there a common vision between the two?

LOUISE: When I was at the Film Board, one of my key tasks was to build that relationship with the CBC. I had just left CBC, so I still knew people in the right positions, people who could help. As a result, a large number of Film Board productions aired on CBC during my time. That was significant, but not always easy. The organizations have very different mandates.

VIC: How so?

LOUISE: CBC is broadcast-oriented: focused on ratings, strict formats, station breaks. The Film Board is about creative freedom. A film might be 45 minutes, or an hour and 45, and the filmmaker might not want to cut even a second. So, there were tensions. But at the heart of it, both institutions were committed to Canadian stories and Canadian concerns.

VIC: Now that you've retired, what's the takeaway for you? How do you look back on it all?

LOUISE: I feel incredibly fortunate. Honestly, I feel grateful to have had a career where I looked forward to going to work every day. I was constantly learning, surrounded by smart, interesting, sometimes difficult—but always stimulating—colleagues. Yes, I feel very lucky. I miss the intellectual challenge. I miss the pleasure of working with ideas every day—of telling stories. I always loved my job.

VIC: And do you still believe in creative freedom in both organizations?

LOUISE: Yes, I do. But I'll also say—some people have really dumb ideas. At both CBC and NFB, we were public institutions. Our doors were always open. So I'd get young people coming in with ideas, and I'd listen. Then I'd point out—filmmaking is expensive. I'd say, "When was the last time you walked up to someone and asked them for $150,000?" Because that's basically what you're asking me for.

VIC: That's a fair point. There has to be responsibility. It's public money.

LOUISE: Yes. And to your question about whether either CBC or the Film Board needs to change—well, yes. When I worked there, any suggestion of change felt threatening. We'd dig in, argue, defend. But the world is changing fast—too fast for us to stand still. I try to keep up, but I'm not 20. And maybe the CBC hasn't adapted quickly enough.

CBC Gem is great, but young people increasingly get their news and content from a wide array of sources different than the ones their parents and grandparents grew up with. So we have to ask: are we really serving the next generation? These decisions are being made by a head office full of older people. I don't know exactly what changes are needed, but I do know this: the ground is shifting beneath us. CBC and NFB are old institutions with rich histories—and they should be cherished. But to stay meaningful, they have to adapt.

When it comes to wishes, things I still want to do, I don't think I've written the final chapter yet. I just came back from a trip to Australia and Papua New Guinea. I was determined to see the birds of paradise. Last year, the trip was cancelled because Canada put Papua on the no-fly list. But this year, I did it. So yes—my checklist is definitely not over.

VIC: So far, the journey's still ongoing. How do you feel about your life journey?

LOUISE: I'm lucky enough to have had some pretty remarkable experiences. One time, I did a one-hour documentary on Ingmar Bergman. I flew to Sweden to interview him. Everyone I spoke to there warned me,

"Oh no! You're interviewing Bergman? Be careful. He's terrible. He once threw a chair at someone!" I was terrified. Here I was, about to meet one of the greatest directors of all time—and I was directing him, which made it worse. I thought he'd find me completely unworthy. He was late, of course. We were filming at the *Svensk Filmindustri* offices. He walked in, looked at me, grabbed me, kissed me on both cheeks and was completely charming. He'd said he only had time for a half-hour interview. But he started talking and didn't stop. It went on for over an hour. What no one told me was… he loved women. So I think I had an advantage. He was warm and funny, not at all the monster I had been warned about.

VIC: So much for the furniture-throwing!

LOUISE: Exactly. He was just a temperamental person—in a society like Sweden, where people do not express emotion. By my standards, he was perfectly normal. I'd been terrified, but in the end, it was a wonderful experience. That film is now in the Museum of Modern Art. Not because it's a cinematic masterpiece, but because it's a record of him.

VIC: That had a lot to do with you, though—the chemistry.

LOUISE: Maybe. That's what we do as filmmakers. We find the human connection.

VIC: In '69 I was working for *The National* news and John Lennon, prior to his conviction for marijuana, wasn't allowed in America and had a stop in Montreal. John and I connected and he invited me to go to Montreal for his bed-in and gave me exclusive rights to film it. I did go to Montreal but didn't stay, as I wanted to go bring it to the news. Looking back, what a regret of mine.

LOUISE: Oh wow. That's extraordinary. And yes, it's those little stories—those gems—that make life so interesting. It's not that we exploited them. It's that they became part of our lives. Another one, Mother Teresa. I interviewed her several times. The first time, I didn't know much about her. It was the early '70s. She spoke at Convocation Hall. It was packed. I was so moved. When I went backstage to interview her, I didn't even start with questions. I just blurted out, "Mother Teresa, I want to come work with you." I meant it. I was ready to follow her to India as a volunteer. She looked at me, sized me up, and said, "My dear, there are many doors we can walk through in life. You are doing more good where you are." So I've been turned down by Mother Teresa. She didn't want me as a volunteer. Mother Teresa didn't want me!

VIC: Being of an ethnic background—did that ever lead people to see you as "exotic" in those days?

LOUISE: If they did, I wasn't aware of it. Honestly, I wasn't. I grew up in a small town, and my mother taught me never to apologize for being different. She used to say, "Louise, when our ancestors were sitting on silk and eating with chopsticks out of China bowls, these people were still in caves." She grounded me in the dignity of our culture—Chinese civilization. I never felt ashamed of who I was. In fact, I think looking different probably helped me. I stood out. There weren't many other Chinese people at CBC at the time, so I was memorable.

VIC: Is there one person in your life who made the strongest impression or had the greatest influence?

LOUISE: I wasn't prepared for that question! Well, probably my mother. Absolutely. She had the strongest influence. I grew up in the 1950s, a very traditional time, but she insisted that I get an education, that I live a full life before marrying. That was radical before feminism arrived. Because of her, I didn't follow my girlfriends into traditional roles. Instead, I travelled. I made it a goal to explore cultures. That's how I chose to spend my money—and my life. It's been a life of exploration and learning.

There's still so much I don't know—so much I still want to learn. And I know I'll never get to it all, but that's okay. The effort is what counts. I grew up in a devout household, taught in Catholic schools. At the time *Man Alive* was on air, most Canadians listed a religious denomination. Now? Very few people go to church. Probably Muslims are the most observant now.

Our society has changed so much. The community bonds from churches, synagogues—they're gone. People used to check in on each other, help the elderly, take you to the doctor. That's vanished. The only communities left with strong bonds are the fundamentalist ones—and I think that's out of a desperation for community. We've lost a lot of the ties that made us Canadian. CBC used to be central. The church was central. Local newspapers connected us too. Now, those anchors are fading.

VIC: We could talk for hours but I know you have a tai chi class to attend. Thank you so much Louise.

Chapter 7
DENYS ARCAND

Denys Arcand is a cinematic provocateur whose films have stirred minds and sparked debate, both in Canada and abroad. From The Decline of the American Empire *to* The Barbarian Invasions, *Arcand brings a sharp eye to the hypocrisies and hopes of modern life. In this conversation, the Oscar-winning director reflects on his early days at the NFB, the collaborative magic of documentary filmmaking, and the intellectual ferment that shaped Quebec's cultural awakening.*

VIC SARIN: You've done so much extraordinary work, and you've brought Quebec to the forefront of world cinema. People didn't really know much about Quebec before. How did that all begin? Why did you feel it was necessary?

DENYS ARCAND: Oh, I never felt anything was necessary. I just went from day to day, strange as it may seem. I came to the Film Board by chance. I had studied history at university, and they needed someone to make short educational films about history for schools. That's how I got hired—otherwise, they weren't hiring anyone. They were full, and everyone from Halifax to Vancouver wanted to be a filmmaker. At that time, it was the only place in Canada where you could actually make films.

So I got in because I had this specialty in history. I did three medium-length films about historical topics, and from there I just moved from project to project. Honestly, each time it just happened. I had no vision of becoming a feature film director—I was doing documentaries and I was happy doing them. They were fun, and we worked in small crews of four or five people. We had two station wagons, we went everywhere, it was absolutely wonderful. Then, at some point, Jean-Pierre Lefebvre said, "Why don't you make a feature?" And I said, "Really? I don't know how to do that." I'd never even been on the set of a feature film. But I told him I knew someone who could write. I'd met a good writer at university. We came up with a story and pitched it to a producer who said, "That's great, why don't you do it?" So I shot it without really knowing what I was doing. A woman showed up one day and said, "I'm going to be your script girl." And I asked, "What does a script girl do?" I really didn't know anything. I just filmed it the way I thought best. Then I was invited to the Cannes Film Festival, and they said, "This is a new way of shooting—a new style." And I was the first one to be surprised.

It all just kept going from there, never with a plan. I never once said, "I want to win an Oscar." I never thought of that, ever.. I just said, "Okay, that worked. Let's do another one." And then another one. It was all serendipity, basically. It just happened to me.

VIC: That desire to make films—that love and passion for it. Let's go back a bit. Where did you grow up?

DENYS: I grew up in Montreal. My family was originally from a small village, but my parents moved to the city so their kids could get a better education. I went to one of the best colleges in Montreal, and then to the Université de Montréal to study history. But honestly, I wasn't that interested in history—I was more drawn to writing, theatre, and of course, movies. But movies felt so far away. They were made in Hollywood or Paris or London—not in Canada.

I loved them. I went to the movies as often as I could. I was mesmerized by the images, the storytelling. But it seemed unrealistic to think I could ever work in that world. Then I got hired to make short films, and from there I moved on to longer films. It all happened quite naturally. I didn't dream of becoming a filmmaker—I just knew I was good at writing and photography, and I was drawn to theatre. I staged plays in college, but at the time it didn't seem possible to make a living doing that. My father had made huge sacrifices to get us to Montreal and give us a good education. He was hoping for a brilliant lawyer or a successful doctor in the family. He was very disappointed when I became a filmmaker—disappointed his whole life, really. Even when I had some success, it didn't change how he felt. But I kept going anyway, almost haphazardly.

VIC: What did you do for entertainment when you were very young?

DENYS: When I was really young, I had no entertainment at all. I lived in a village of about 800 people, and there was nothing—not really. I had an uncle who was an agronomist and owned a projector with 16mm films, mostly about agriculture. They were somewhat boring, but now and then he'd show something about a classical singer or something more artistic. So we'd see flickering images on a bed sheet, but it all felt very distant.

Once I moved to Montreal and went to school downtown, things changed. There were theatres nearby. I could go see plays, concerts, and films. I naturally gravitated to all of it and saw as much as I could. At the time, I didn't know what I was watching were masterpieces. I'd watch Westerns by John Ford or Howard Hawks and just think, "What great stories!" It wasn't until ten years later, when I read *Cahiers du Cinéma*, that I realized those films were major works of art. The same thing happened with music. Someone once told me, "There's a pianist coming from Toronto—Glenn Gould. You should check him out." I had no idea what the *Goldberg Variations* were, but I went to Her Majesty's Theatre and was blown away. It was so beautiful. So my cultural education happened like that—just following my interests and living downtown where it was accessible. That's how I refined my tastes.

VIC: What about radio? Did you listen to CBC Radio?

DENYS: Not really. It wasn't part of my world then.

VIC: So your entertainment was mostly Hollywood?

DENYS: Hollywood films, yes, but also French films. Because we spoke French, there were a few distributors that brought in films from France. There were two downtown theatres that specialized in them. So I saw a lot of French cinema, and some Italian and Mexican films as well. I remember seeing Luis Buñuel's Mexican-period films in Montreal. Don't ask me how or who distributed them, but somehow, they were shown.

VIC: Any film that left a big impression on you?

DENYS: Oh yes, tons. One that stands out is *Hamlet* by Sir Laurence Olivier. I saw it because of the poster outside the theatre. It showed Olivier with a sword, and I thought it was some kind of Errol Flynn swashbuckler. But I discovered Shakespeare that day and was absolutely astonished. The story, the final duel—it was unforgettable. And *The Robe*—do you remember *The Robe*? It was one of the first CinemaScope films. Incredible. Romans and epic storytelling. So many others made an impact.

VIC: So what drew you in? The technology, the magic of it all, or something more—the political, the social themes?

DENYS: I was just immersed in the experience. I can't say exactly what fascinated me—maybe it was the aesthetics, maybe the story, or maybe I was just dreaming about the actresses. I fell in love with some of them, especially the foreign ones like Lucia Bosé, the Spanish actress—she was stunning. It was everything at once, really. I was just absorbing it all. I wasn't thinking about technique at all back then. Absolutely not. I was just receiving the experience like a child being told a magical story or a legend. I simply took it in.

When I got to the Film Board, that's when I started becoming aware of specific techniques, because people talked about them. I remember the Board had a print of *Triumph of the Will* by Leni Riefenstahl. They said, "You have to see this—it's horrible in content, politically repugnant—but the images, the editing... just look at that." So I did. And that's how my education began, shaped by the people around me.

I learned a great deal from the other young filmmakers—people who were much more aware than I was about who the important directors were and how they worked. I remember once, we all left the Film Board one afternoon to see *The Birds* by Hitchcock because it was opening downtown in Montreal. Everyone said, "You have to see this—look at the editing, the way the birds are introduced, the first image, the final shot…" So yes, my education really took shape there.

VIC: There seemed to be more passion for making films in Quebec—in French Canada—than in English Canada. Why do you think that is? Is it cultural? The English are often more reserved, while the French are more open, passionate. Or is it just perception?

DENYS: Hard to say. Talking about national psychology is dangerous territory, it often leads to absurd generalizations. Still, there were differences. For English Canadians, Hollywood was always an option. It wasn't too far culturally, so some of them just went south. For us, that wasn't an option, it felt out of reach. So we made films here, out of necessity. But yes, French Canadians are a bit more open emotionally, a bit more willing to experiment. I remember in the camera department at the Film Board, the British approach dominated at first: key light, fill light, back light, very classical.

Then Michel Brault came along—an extraordinary director of photography—and said, "That's not how an office looks." We were doing a shoot in a studio meant to represent an office, and he said, "Offices are lit with neon." So he flooded the whole studio with harsh neon lights. The head of the department was scandalized—wanted to fire him. But Michel stood his ground. "This is how an office looks," he said, "cold, inhuman, unflattering." And years later, Gordon Willis did the same thing in *All the President's Men*—flooded the newsroom with practical, overhead lights. But Michel had done it 10–15 years earlier. So yes, we experimented. We pushed things.

VIC: The Film Board being in Montreal… that must have been an advantage.

DENYS: Oh, absolutely. Quebec cinema was born because the Film Board chose Montreal. Originally, it was based in Ottawa. When they were deciding where to move, it was between Montreal and Toronto. By some miracle, they chose Montreal. Because of that proximity, we could slip in, find our way, get our start. That's how we became filmmakers. That's how Quebec cinema came into being. If they had chosen Toronto, maybe it still would have happened, but it would've taken 25 or 30 more years.

VIC: What was the first project you did for the NFB?

DENYS: *Champlain*, a film on Samuel de Champlain, the founder of Quebec City. It was a very, very simple film, mostly made with maps—geographical maps, old drawings—and the little we actually know about Champlain. That's what I had to work with, so it was quite basic. I made it with one cameraman and myself, and that was it. I edited it with that same cameraman. But then I needed to work with an animation camera because I had added some drawings and needed to create movement. They told me, "You've got to go to the animation department." The Film Board was like a mini studio—like a little Paramount. It had a studio, dressing rooms for actors, and also an animation department. Norman McLaren was the king of that world. The head of animation was Colin Low, and these people were extraordinarily kind to me.

I had no idea what I was doing. Colin said, "Come every day at five o'clock, and I'll give you 45 minutes of my time." And he did—for about a month. Every day, he taught me how to make the animation camera move, just because he wanted to help. He wanted to teach. It was absolutely amazing. He was a master of animation, and he shared that with me. Throughout my life, whenever I had a specific technical problem, I would go to him for help—and he was always there, always open. So there was this real collaboration between English and French people. On the level of filmmaking, we had a perfect understanding of each other.

But at the same time, for some bizarre reason—and I always wanted to make a documentary about this—if you went into the cafeteria, there were English tables and French tables. No one told you to sit anywhere. There were no rules. But you just wouldn't sit with the English people. You'd sit with your own. The same for them. We'd say, "Hi, how are you? Good, I saw your film—lovely, very good," and so on. But that was the extent of it. This was the famous "two solitudes" that Canadians often talk about. It was absolutely real. You could see it, feel it. It would have been a very difficult documentary to film because it was so subtle. But I always wanted to make it. I thought about it for a long time, but I never did.

VIC: How much connection was there with the rest of Canada at that time? Was it a strong connection, or were there really two solitudes, as you say?

DENYS: Well, at the beginning, there were no real films being made outside the Film Board—French or English. Everything was being done there. And then these unusual characters started making films outside the Film Board: David Cronenberg, for instance, with *The Fly*. And then it all started to sprout. You still had some vague connections, but not organic ones. You'd maybe run into each other at film festivals—that's when we'd see each other. Later, when my films became better known, I'd go to the Toronto Film Festival, the Vancouver Film Festival, and the Atlantic Film Festival. That's where I made friends, had conversations. But beyond that, there wasn't much connection.

VIC: I was thinking that the Film Board being in Montreal helped French filmmakers find their voice more easily. Otherwise, it would've been harder.

DENYS: Definitely. It was a blessing for us. For my generation, the Film Board was where we learned to make films, where we discussed ideas, where we grew. We were always together—someone had just seen a new film, someone else was back from Paris with new stories. When Michel Brault, for example, worked in Paris, and Claude Jutra too—they'd come back and say, "We saw this," "We tried that," and so on. People don't realize that in the early '60s, the Film Board was famous worldwide. I remember seeing John Cassavetes, François Truffaut, Bernardo Bertolucci walking the halls. These people came to see what we were doing, because it was absolutely unique. We were working with small Arriflex 16mm cameras, handheld, doing things no one else was doing. So it was a magnet for young filmmakers around the world who wanted to know, "How do you do this?"

VIC: I remember my first trip for the CBC in 1968. We travelled around the world and ended up in Kenya. Back then, Africa was still considered dark and distant. Every time we set up to load the camera, kids would come running, asking, "Where are you from?" I'd say, "Canada," and they'd have no idea. But then one kid said, "Film Board of Canada!" And I said, "Yes, that's Canada." They knew about the Film Board in the 1960s—but not Canada.

DENYS: It's true. We didn't even get a flag until 1965. The Film Board was around long before that.

VIC: The Film Board was kind of a guiding light for creative filmmakers in this country. Whose vision was that?

DENYS: I don't think it was one person's vision. It was a series of happy accidents. The Canadian government needed to make films during the war—training films for soldiers, because they didn't have enough instructors. So they brought in Scots and British filmmakers to start the Film Board. Those people taught others how to make films. When the war ended, you can't just fire a civil servant, so they kept them. What do you do with them? "Make films about agriculture." So they made films on potatoes, on avoiding insects, that kind of thing. Then someone said, "Can I make a film about my church?" And they said, "Okay." Then someone else, Colin Low, for instance, said, "There's nothing more beautiful than a horse being trained in a corral by a cowboy. Can I film that?" And they said, "Alright." It grew, slowly, organically. There was no master plan, thank God! If the government had imposed a plan, it would've ruined everything. But the people there loved film. They kept asking, "Can I try this?" and someone always said, "Okay, do it." And that's how it blossomed. That's how real creativity happens. It doesn't come from the top.

VIC: What I'm very interested to know about is the freedom you had as filmmakers in the early part. And how much of that freedom is necessary—how much do you need to be allowed to do what you do?

DENYS: Exactly. I think the secret of the Film Board was that, at the very beginning, there was no bureaucracy at all. The whole French unit, for instance, was run by two guys—two producers, Fernand Dansereau and Jacques Bobet. And under them, they had two ladies: one was the budget officer, and the other was a sort of general production assistant. That was it. There was no director of production, no planning department—absolutely nothing. So you'd go into the office of one of those two guys and say, "I've got an idea for a film. Can I do a film on lumberjacks?" "Lumberjacks?" "Yeah, it'll be about half an hour long." "How much will it cost?" "Roughly this much." "And when can you shoot?" "Next month." "Okay. Go do it." That was it. There was no need to submit your idea for script review or project assessment. It was a personal relationship. That was the deal. You just got the go-ahead. And that was the secret.

Another part of the secret was trusting the right people. And as you know, being able to judge talent is very rare. If you're a producer, can you identify someone who truly has talent? Can you find it? It's terribly difficult: in sports, in filmmaking, in everything. Can you recognize the individuals who are going to become great filmmakers? How do you judge that? How do you sense it? In those days, they just knew. I don't know how. It was magical.

VIC: From my experience with *Hue*, a film I made about skin colour, the sense of freedom has changed. The question to you is—do you think we need breathing room?

DENYS: More than breathing room! A documentary is a discovery. And you try to explain this to civil servants, and they don't understand. You say to them, "Okay, I'm going to go into the textile industry. I want to know how these people live and what they're dreaming of. I have no idea yet. So, I can't tell you. Give me money, give me a camera, and I'll go there for a year and come back." Nowadays, that would be impossible. They want you to give them a script. "What are you going to say?" "I can't tell you yet—I don't know these people." I'm going to discover them, and my film is going to discover them with you, and with me. It's a whole discovery. That's the whole idea of making a documentary. This is impossible in the field of civil service. You must know what you're doing. You must know in advance what you're going to find. But you never know. In a documentary, you're fishing for marvels. Sometimes you're lucky—you find them. Sometimes you're not—but it's still interesting. That spirit—that approach—has disappeared from the landscape. That's why so many great documentary filmmakers aren't doing it anymore. Because it's been stifled.

VIC: What made that change?

DENYS: It's the invasion of bureaucracy. Bureaucracy is the worst thing for creativity. It kills it. As soon as you have committees and meetings and paperwork, creativity dies. People go elsewhere to make other stuff.

My last documentary film was about the first referendum on Quebec independence. It's called *Comfort and Indifference*, which to me was exactly the essence of the debate. I spent four years doing that, from 1976 to the referendum in 1980. And I'm quite happy about it. It was received badly on both sides. The independentists in Quebec thought I wasn't militant enough. And the federalists thought I was too soft on the independentists. But I think that's exactly the position the filmmaker should have.

I'm independent. I'm just telling you what I saw. And what I saw, through my lens, is that Quebecers are primarily concerned with their comfort. And once that's settled, they're mostly indifferent to the rest. People were scandalized by that. And I was attacked by both sides. Which told me I was right. If you're attacked by both sides, you probably did your job.

When I did that film, I said: "There's a referendum coming. I'm going to shoot for four years. I don't know what I'm going to find. It could be the end of this country, or not. Whatever happens, I'll film reality. And you'll have to live with what I come up with." And they agreed. But I think it was one of the last big documentaries the Film Board did—at least on the French side. After that, it disappeared.

VIC: Did you do anything for CBC at all?

DENYS: Yes, I did a big series for CBC called *Empire Inc.*, just after the referendum—so, 1981 or 1982. I did it here with Mark Blandford, for CBC in Toronto. It was fairly popular, and I think it worked well. It was my first time directing a big Canadian drama, with lots of extras, big sets, and Stratford actors. It was a new experience, working with all those people. I loved it. I really enjoyed it. But it was an entirely different process—more like a job, a real directing job. I wasn't emotionally involved. I just wanted to do a good job, technically. And it helped me a lot with my later films. It was a really good experience. The actors were wonderful—Ken Welsh and others.

VIC: Wonderful actor. Yes, really. Let's come back to your work. Which film are you most proud of?

DENYS: Well, okay, I'll say something that might sound preposterous, but I'm in love with all my films. I was lucky. All my films are happy stories, for me, at least. I enjoyed making all of them. They were totally enjoyable. I worked with people I loved—actors, crew. The memories are very happy for each one. So I can't say, "This one is my favourite." Okay, yes, my claim to fame is *The Barbarian Invasions*. I won an Oscar. I won a prize at Cannes. What more could you ask for? But to me, it wasn't different from the others. Some were popular, some were not. Some failed, some did okay. To me, that's irrelevant.

What I enjoy is the process of making films—writing, shooting, using the camera, editing. Finding the right cut. Working with the composer. I love every step. And when I get to the answer print—*la copie de réponse*—I say, "Okay, that's the best I could do on this one." And then I go home and forget about it. Truly. I'm not anxious about whether it will be a success. I just hope for the best. But my mind is already on the next thing. I don't dwell.

Even when I shot commercials, for practical reasons, of course, I enjoyed it. Not the subjects, obviously, but how to shoot something with precision in six seconds. What kind of camera? How do we make it efficient? That kind of problem-solving, I was passionate about that too.

VIC: What changes have you seen among crews and colleagues?

DENYS: What I miss is the incredible sense of community. We were smaller crews. We barely knew what we were doing. The camera was still a mystery. It was a miracle to shoot all day, watch the rushes, and see an image that was in focus and adequately lit. It amazed us. Every day was a party. We were young. We'd shoot all day, watch rushes at night, then go out to restaurants, then nightclubs, sleep at 2 a.m., start again at 6. The energy was unbelievable. Today's crews are much more professional. They're excellent—because they work all year, on American films, international productions. So the quality is better. But we've lost that wild sense of adventure and tight-knit camaraderie. Now, we don't even have rushes. Everything's on a monitor right away. Crews are working constantly. At the end of the shoot, there's no wrap party, just a handshake and, "See you on the next project."

For my last film, I had to do a camera test in a cemetery, but there were no grips available in Montreal—everyone was booked. Finally, my DOP called two guys and begged them. They said, "We've worked every day for 60 days, and we start another job tomorrow... but we'll come, because it's you." The subtext was: "We think this is probably your last film. We wanted to be there." So that was touching. Sweet and sour. And I don't know—maybe it is my last film. I used to always have the next idea, the next story ready. But this time? Nothing. I finished the film, went home, and... nothing came. Maybe that's a sign from the heavens. Or maybe tomorrow I'll have a new idea and start again. That's why I'm writing. I'm trying to write a little book. Anecdotes from making films. I don't know if it'll be any good, but that's the creative thing I'm doing now.

VIC: Very nice. You don't stop.

DENYS: No, you should never stop.

VIC: When you make a film, what gives you the most satisfaction? Is it the audience reaction, the money, the box office… or something else you feel inside?

DENYS: If I'm doing a feature film, what I like most is this: one year before the actual shoot, I wrote something. I worked very hard on writing dialogue I thought was the best I could do. Then, on set, these spectacular actors come in and say my lines—and it works. That's the deepest satisfaction. It's, "Yes, that's what I wanted to say." And they bring it to life. That moment is absolutely perfect. There are other moments too. For example, in *The Barbarian Invasions*, I wanted to shoot one scene in a single take, one frame. The same frame throughout. It was the scene where the dying man's friends come to say their goodbyes. Each actor enters the same frame, one after the other. I wasn't sure it would work, but in the editing room, my editor said, "I think I can do it, but I need total concentration—please leave." Two days later, she called me: "I've got it. Come see." I sat down, watched, and it was perfect. That kind of moment makes life worthwhile.

VIC: What's been the most challenging thing for you?

DENYS: I don't know if one thing stands out. Everything is a small challenge, incremental. The first time I did a film, it was just me and a cameraman. Then, doing *Empire Inc*, I had extras, period costumes, horses and carriages, big cameras. I remember being extremely nervous. Then my first time walking up the steps at Cannes, I thought, "What if they boo me?" It was all challenging, just in different ways. What I'm happy about, looking back, is that I made a living making films in Quebec. I didn't have to teach, which I dislike. I did it twice when I was broke, and I hated it. But I was able to earn my living doing what I love, and that's a gift. I worked with a group of people—actors, crew—many of whom are still friends. That warmth matters.

VIC: You write your films?

DENYS: Always. And I direct, of course. I edited a couple of films myself, but once the technical side shifted to digital, I started working closely with editors. I'm in the editing room every day, watching every shot. I don't just drop in once a week—I'm there, breathing down their neck, in a good way.

VIC: You're very clear?

DENYS: Not always at first. I become clear once I start working with the actors. I remember a moment during *Empire Inc.* I gave some direction—"You walk here, you turn there"—and a young actor said, "Do you decide this on your kitchen table the night before, with salt and pepper shakers?" And he added, "We're more than salt shakers. If you give us some freedom, maybe we can offer something you hadn't thought of." That changed everything for me. The next day, with Ken Welsh and another actor, I just said, "Do what feels natural." I sat in a corner and watched. Then I framed the shot around what they did. Since then, that's how I work—unless it's an action scene, which needs to be very precisely planned. But for human interaction, it's better to let it breathe.

VIC: Can you think of a scene that still stays with you?

DENYS: DENYS: Yes, several. The death scene in *Barbarian Invasions* is one. Everything aligned—no wind, perfect light, the sky… the gods were with us. For *Jesus of Montreal*, we had six weeks of beautiful weather, and on the last night, I needed a storm. At midnight, during our break, my assistant said, "A storm's coming." We rushed outside, got the actors on the crosses, and it rained. Torrents. It was perfect. We all said, "Jesus is with us."

VIC: And any scenes that didn't work?

DENYS: In *Jesus of Montreal*, I wanted to include the scene where Jesus multiplies the bread. You remember that story—people are hungry, and Jesus creates bread for the masses? I wanted to do my own version of that in the film, and I had written a scene I really loved. The scene was short. The actors are rehearsing the Passion, and they're hungry—they're poor, they have no money. The guy playing Jesus says, "I'll try to find something." So he walks into a pizzeria and talks to the Italian owner. He says, "Okay, we're six actors. We're basically starving. We're trying to put on a Passion play. It would be great if you could make us a pizza, but we have no money."

The guy flies into a rage: "What do you think I'm doing here—feeding the world? I've got a family to support, rent to pay, ingredients to buy. I can't just give pizza away!"Jesus smiles and says, "Okay, I understand," and starts to walk away. Just before he exits, the man calls out: "Okay—cheese and tomato. That's it." Jesus comes back, smiles, and says, "The smell is perfect. Thank you." The man begins making the pizza. Then he says, "Okay, mushrooms—but nothing else," and adds mushrooms. A moment later, "Okay, pepperoni—but not too much," and he adds that too. And of course, after ten minutes, he says, "Ah, fuck it. I'll dress the whole thing."

I loved that scene, I was in love with my own writing. But we couldn't find a good Italian actor in Montreal. So I cast someone who had never been in a film but had done some amateur theatre in the Italian community. He was very good one-on-one with me, but as soon as the camera rolled, he froze. Completely froze. He couldn't say his lines. I tried for half an hour to make him feel at ease—to get him to relax—but it was impossible. I had to scrap the scene. That's one of my big regrets. I would have loved to have that scene in the film.

There were also a few times I had issues with actresses—not because of the film itself or my relationship with them, but because of things going on in their personal lives. Sometimes they had just broken up with a boyfriend or were in emotional distress, and they'd show up in tears. Their performance became almost impossible to manage that day. So yes, I had a few problems—not many—but a couple of times I remember clearly. There were scenes I didn't shoot, or had to cut short, or shoot around entirely, because the actress simply wasn't able to work that day.

VIC: Let's talk a little about the relationship between the director and actors.

DENYS: It's very delicate. A very, very delicate subject, but fundamental. Actors and actresses have to trust you. Completely. They have to be ready to go to the ends of the Earth for you. How do you establish that trust? Sometimes it's through explanation, if they're more intellectual. Sometimes it's just something basic, something instinctive. You feel good around each other. You have to establish that.

It's like a maestro conducting an orchestra. A friend of mine was a concertmaster. The first time he worked with the New York Philharmonic—which over the years had been conducted by Mahler, Toscanini—he told me: when you stand in front of them, you have two or three minutes to establish your authority. If they don't trust you, it doesn't matter what you do. They'll follow the first violin instead. But if you earn their trust, then they'll follow you. Someone in the wind section nods, that's the sign. "Okay, this guy knows what he's doing." It's very subtle.

It's the same thing on a film set. I've seen it happen when a crew loses faith in the director. I've been there, sometimes just as a bit actor or visiting the set. And it's awful. The whole set becomes like a zombie production. People go through the motions, but they don't believe in it anymore. That's a disaster. Nobody says anything, but you feel it. So you must maintain trust. Bergman, for example—he was terribly macho in his time, and this would be absolutely unacceptable today—but someone once asked him, "How do you build that extraordinary relationship with your actresses?" And he said, "It has a lot to do with how you pat their bum when they come into the studio." Now, obviously, if anyone said that today, they'd be fired immediately. But that was Bergman—and people allowed it then. And while the comment itself is completely inappropriate now, the essence of what he meant was about familiarity, ease, trust. There's something deeply human about that connection. You have to build it.

VIC: I want to go back into your personal life. How did your parents feel about your career once you started to make films?

DENYS: My mother went to see a few films. My father never saw any of them. He just wasn't interested. He was a river pilot—before that, a sailor. He spent 15 years in the South Pacific in the merchant marines. To him, filmmaking was a despicable occupation. He hated movies for two reasons. First, he believed cinema was a diversion for idle people. He remembered the Great Depression—walking past theatres in the 1930s and seeing long lines of unemployed men spending their last fifteen cents to see a film. That was his idea of what filmmaking was. He also had moral objections. He and my mother both believed movies were full of immorality—women undressing and kissing men who weren't their husbands. They saw films as morally questionable. Like *Cinema Paradiso*, in a way. They never reconciled with my career. They had almost no understanding of what I was doing, how my films were received. I never got any encouragement, no feedback.

VIC: So you really never had any strong support?

DENYS: None at all. In fact, the opposite. They never liked what I was doing. Not a single word of encouragement, ever. It leaves a mark. You start to doubt yourself. You don't have the certainty of, "I'm a genius—this is my vision." For example, I've made changes to films at the suggestion of festival directors or distributors—shortened endings, cut scenes—because I lacked confidence. Some of those cuts I regret to this day. I would say, "Oh, you think it would be better that way? Okay." Instead of saying, "No, this is my film. I won't change it." I wasn't that kind of director. And I think that comes from never having been supported by my family. It stays with

VIC: Do you have close friends?

DENYS: Yes, but most of them came through sports—tennis, mainly. They're not really involved in filmmaking. They're happy for me, but we don't talk about it much. We rarely talk about filmmaking—mostly tennis, Federer, Nadal, that sort of thing. I have a few friends from film, like some first ADs I worked with who are still close, but not many.

VIC: Did you ever do a film on tennis?

DENYS: No. I've never done a film about sports. It's difficult, although with today's technology, it's getting easier. But my issue was this: elite athletes are so physically distinct. The way they move, sit, stand—it's so particular, so poetic—that actors can't replicate it. It's the same with dancers. You can't fake Baryshnikov. You can't fake Nureyev. Their bodies move in ways actors can't emulate. So I've always believed it's impossible to make a good film about sport. The poetry of the movement can't be recreated.

VIC: Do you have favourite films?

DENYS: Oh, tons, tons of films. Luis Buñuel's *The Discreet Charm of the Bourgeoisie*—to me, that is absolutely perfect. It's great. What else? *The Seven Samurai*, Kurosawa. It's just immense. It's absolutely... and when you think he shot that for a year, 360 days of shooting—it's unbelievable. But the result is like the Sistine Chapel. It's overwhelming. What else? Tons of other stuff.

John Huston's *Fat City*—absolutely magical. He knows what he's talking about. He'd been a boxer, so it's beautiful. I could go on, I mean—so many.

VIC: Are there any of your own films that really stay with you?

DENYS: A lot. They all stay with me, but for absolutely personal reasons. You know, it's not the same as admiring a masterpiece by a grand master. For me, maybe I was in love with that actress. I'll die still loving her. So when I see her on screen, everything comes back to me.

VIC: Do you feel the CBC and NFB are still important for this country.

DENYS: They were extraordinarily important. They were a major part of Canadian cultural history. But I don't know how to recreate that flame that was burning when we were there in the early '60s. They are still necessary in Canada—because we're not in the U.S., where private money can be enough to sustain creativity. There's enough money there that you can get by without government support. In Canada, it's impossible. So yes, we need government money, but that money has to be used in the best possible way, and that's not happening now. How do you plan a policy that would work?

VIC: What do you think that policy should be?

DENYS: It's about trusting the artists—trusting the people who are creative. They know the answer, not the bureaucrats in the various departments. They don't know what they're talking about. Individual filmmakers know. You have to let them create, let them practice their craft. They'll come up with the good films, they'll come up with the solutions. But creative people are usually met with distrust because they're... bizarre. They don't conform. They refuse to give you a pre-approved script for a documentary, and stuff like that. So it's a very difficult situation. Very difficult problems to solve.

VIC: Do you have any wishes?

DENYS: I wish to see better Canadian films. Better Canadian shows on television. That is what I wish for.

VIC: Thank you so much Denys.

OUR LES GÉANTS

R LES GÉANTS

Chapter 8

ALANIS OBOMSAWIN

Alanis Obomsawin is one of the most important documentary filmmakers of our time. A member of the Abenaki Nation, she has dedicated her career to telling the stories mainstream Canada too often ignores. With more than 50 films produced through the NFB, her work has illuminated the struggles and triumphs of Indigenous communities across the country. Her voice is clear, courageous, and unforgettable.

VIC SARIN: I'm very honoured to be listening to you and speaking with you. How did it all start, Alanis? Where were you born? How did everything begin?

ALANIS OBOMSAWIN: I was born in New Hampshire, on Abenaki territory. My parents are from a community here in Quebec called Odanak. I was brought there when I was six months old and raised there until it was time to go to school. Then we moved to a town called Trois-Rivières, here in Quebec. That was the worst part of my life. I was the only Indigenous person there, and it was very bad. That's where I developed this feeling—that something needed to change. There had to be a change in the way they were teaching.

VIC: What was so bad about it?

ALANIS: Across this country—and in the U.S. too—the history books used to teach children were mostly written by the church. Not all of them, but many. And they were full of lies and racism. That did so much damage to our people and our nations, for generations. I won't go through all the horrifying things, but when you're a child, you don't understand what's happening—you're just in it.

At some point I realized, if children could hear another story, they wouldn't hate me so much. Simple as that. So I turned to books. As I grew older, I began singing—mainly about our People, our Nations, our history.

That's where it came from. The more I did it, the more I understood how important it was. Because teaching is the root of everything. If you teach children to hate, that damage carries on for generations. But if you teach them to love, well, there's a good reason to be alive. That became my mission. I went to a lot of schools across Canada, in the U.S., and even in Europe.

VIC: What kind of support did you have to do all that?

ALANIS: At first, none. I had to fight for everything. But every time I went to a school, they'd ask me to come back, or to go to another school. So I built it myself. Eventually, a few people in the school tour business reached out to help me organize and get to different places.

VIC: What about your parents—what role did they play?

ALANIS: It was a different story for them. My father was a guide. He worked in the bush, hunting and fishing. He died very young, at 42. I was 12. My mother lived much longer. But life wasn't easy for a long time.

VIC: Did you have any siblings?

ALANIS: I had two sisters and one brother—but they all died as infants.

VIC: Was the feeling you had—of isolation, or rejection—something other people experienced too?

ALANIS: Oh yes, absolutely. Many people went to residential schools. I didn't, although I went to school outside my community, and that was bad.

VIC: How did your journey of singing and expressing yourself begin?

ALANIS: It just came naturally. I was a child, and I sang all the time. I'd rock in my rocking chair and sing. So it wasn't some big thing, it was just normal.

VIC: So your voice became the way you expressed that pain?

ALANIS: Yes. I wrote a lot of songs myself—in my language, in French, and in English. And there was always a group of people who followed me, who wanted to listen.

VIC: Did you move around much as a young person?

ALANIS: At first, I stayed mostly in Quebec. But I started travelling quite early, in the early 1960s. One day, someone said to me, "Do you know that in Canada, the prisons are mostly filled with Native people?" I was surprised. I said, "Really?" They said, "Yes." And I thought, well, that means my relations are in jail. I'm going to visit them. So I toured a lot of prisons across Canada. That was another side of life—not an easy one—but I'm so glad I did it.

VIC: Were there other areas where you felt Indigenous people were having a really hard time?

ALANIS: I knew from the beginning, from my own experience. And in the 1960s, the situation for our people was terrible. You have to understand, 1960 was the year the government officially said we were Canadian citizens. Not before that.

VIC: That's hard to believe.

ALANIS: There were parts of the *Indian Act* that changed that year. Before then, we weren't even allowed to hold ceremonies. No powwows. We weren't allowed to gather more than three people at a time, just in case we were plotting revenge against the government.

VIC: Given all that opposition, did anyone come to your side?

ALANIS: Many of our people were writing, creating, trying to make change.

VIC: So music was your way. That was your path?

ALANIS: It was the only way I had. And I was right.

VIC: Did you get encouragement for your singing, back then?

ALANIS: Yes, I was invited to many places. I performed in many of our communities, and I visited a lot of residential schools too—they were still very much active in the 60s.

VIC: Besides singing and expressing yourself, did you listen to the radio, or find other sources of inspiration?

ALANIS: No. It was pretty plain and simple. Everything I did came from everyday life. I didn't discover big influences, and no one really helped me that way. When I started touring prisons, someone did help me, because no one had done that before. I was the first person to go into a prison to perform. If you want to call it "entertain," I guess that's what it was.

VIC: Could you recall any incident from your prison visits—something that stayed with you, maybe where you felt you helped with healing?

ALANIS: Oh yeah, there were lots of funny things. Like one time, I was going to this prison, and the person who helped me set it up said, "I'm warning you, Alanis—this is the worst one in Canada. There are 500 guys there." He told me a lot of prisoners ended up there from other prisons in Canada because they were tattletales, or troublemakers. He scared me with all the things he was saying. I started to worry—I was afraid I might look sexy or something. So I wore a nun's dress. Not a black nun's dress, but a cotton dress like the kind worn by someone who washes the floor or cleans. It had puffy sleeves and greyish stripes—just a big dress. When I arrived, the guards at the front said, "Oh, Madame Obomsawin..." They didn't know if the population—they used to call them that, I don't know if they still do—would come. They said, "No one's ever come here to entertain. And they make fun of each other if they go see someone like that." I said, "Look, it doesn't matter. I'm allowed to stay from, let's say, two to four. If they don't come, I won't be insulted. I'll just leave. That's okay."

So we were supposed to start at two or three—let's say two. At 2:30, no one. Quarter to three, still no one. Maybe ten minutes before, the guys started coming in. The sound was loud—I think the floor was cement, and they had these folding chairs, so it was very noisy as they set themselves up. Then the guard brought me to the front. There was a table, and on it, a microphone on a pole. I was supposed to sit behind the table, but I thought, "This is stupid. I can't do this." So I took a chair and put it on the table. Then I took another chair, climbed up on it, then onto the table, and sat down. That way, I could see everybody. There I was, in my nun's dress with my drum. Two French Canadian guys in the front were laughing so hard their shoulders were going up and down. They couldn't believe it.

I sang one song and said, "You think it's funny, me coming here to sing for you?" I turned it into a bit of a story. I said, "There are two guys here, killing themselves laughing. Well, I'll sing another song, and if they're still laughing, they can take my place. I'll take theirs. We'll see how funny it is." Then there was silence. And I thought, "Oh my God, they're going to get beat up."

So I said, "Me, nobody needs to stand up for me. I take care of myself. I can do it." But I was scared—scared they'd be punished for laughing. So I kept singing. They were still laughing, but less. Then I started teaching them words in my language. They were tapping their feet, singing along with me. There I was, on my stage.

Then the guards came and said, "Okay guys, back to your cells." Not one of them left without touching my hand, kissing me on the cheek, saying thank you. It turned out to be fun—and something I always remember. It could have been ridiculous, but in the end, it was very loving.

VIC: So that reception you got—it must have encouraged you.

ALANIS: I wasn't thinking about it that way. My roots—my reason—was change. You do everything from that. I felt that through my storytelling and singing. And I was right. It was powerful. It helped people see who we are.

VIC: So most of your storytelling—through music, through song—was about your culture?

ALANIS: Some of it, yes. But when I look back now, I realize something. When I was growing up in Odanak, we didn't have electricity or running water. We had a well, and one dirt road. At night, there were oil lamps. And sometimes someone would stand up and tell stories. All the stories had to do with animals—because everyone was a guide in the bush. The stories came from their experiences with people they were guiding, and the animals they met. I realized much later that the animals had rights—just like human beings. The same.

In those stories, the animals acted like people—doing annoying things, or vice versa. That was important. Because in those days, the church was trying to change everything. Ceremonies—if they happened—were always hidden, underground. I heard all my young life that my language was Satan's language. That was the kind of world it was. They did everything they could to make sure we felt we were less than they were. I wasn't consciously thinking about all of that at the time. But I knew there was a lot of hate. And that it was very wrong. I wanted to change that.

VIC: Was there a big difference back then between French and English attitudes toward Indigenous people?

ALANIS: There were differences in some ways. But when it came to racism and prejudice—and feeling superior—they were pretty much the same.

VIC: Is there one incident that really stands out to you—something that made you feel the weight of all that?

ALANIS: Yes. One time, I was in school—maybe grade 4. The school was run by nuns, except for one teacher, a regular person named Roman. She really hated me. When she'd walk past me, she'd pinch me. I always had marks. One Friday, she told us to read a story from a book called *Lives of the Saints*. It was like a Bible storybook. Probably written by the church.

She told us to read a particular story and learn it. Monday came, and we were all lined up. She started going down the line, asking each child to tell the story. It became clear that none of them had looked at the book. They didn't know the story. They were stammering, guessing—word by word. She was yelling at them, getting angry. And I thought, "I hope she asks me, I know it."

She finally got to me, and I told the story as if I had the book in front of me. And do you know what she said? She said, "Well, you little savage. Get out of my classroom. I never want to see you again. Go back where you came from. You have no business here." She insulted me right in front of all the other kids. So I picked up my books and my things and went home. My parents asked, "Why are you home so early?" I said, "I got thrown out of school."

My mother's first reaction was, "You must have done something. Maybe you said something you shouldn't have said." She always blamed me first. My father asked me to tell him what happened. So I did. The next day, a child came to our house—because we didn't have a phone—to see why I wasn't at school. My father took me to the school inspector.

In those days, the inspector had a very important job. He worked in another building. My father told me, "Tell your story." So I did. The inspector said, "She'll have to go back to school." But my father said, "That teacher insulted my daughter in front of all the kids. I want her to apologize in front of them." And the inspector agreed. So I went back to school, and the teacher did apologize in front of everyone. But that was my life. I knew my lesson—and yet, I got thrown out of school. You can imagine what I must have thought. How was I supposed to make sense of that?

VIC: At that age, to be isolated and feel so alone—it must have been difficult.

ALANIS: Whenever the teacher brought out the Canadian history book, I knew I was going to get beat up that day. I would just run and run. I used to fall down on the sidewalk all the time, and they'd kick me. But I didn't hate anybody. I just felt it was because of what the teacher said. It was pretty simple, my way of thinking. Then I came to a point where I thought, "They just don't hear the right story." I figured that out. And I was right.

VIC: How did you learn all that so fast? You were so young.

ALANIS: You learn to defend yourself. I was getting beat up all the time. Insulted. It was bad.

VIC: Did you have support from anyone besides your family? In school, or elsewhere? I've had a few stories like that, because of my brown skin. There weren't many of us then, and of course, things are very different now. But there was opposition. So, there must have been some on your side as well?

ALANIS: It took a long time. When my father died, I was totally broken. I was 12. And in those days, we were living within French culture. In that town, when someone died, the coffin was kept in the house. They'd hang something on the front door—it was called a crêpe. Crêpe is a kind of material from France, very expensive. It didn't wrinkle. You'd make it into two flower-like shapes at the top, and two long pieces hanging down like curtains. That meant someone in the house had died. It was like an exhibit, people would pass by, see the crêpe, and come in, even if you didn't know them.

My father was in one of the bedrooms. I was in the kitchen, rocking in a chair. I'd sit with him for a long time, then come back into the kitchen. And I remember saying to myself, "Nobody's going to beat me anymore." I made all these rules. And I did it. And it worked. I told myself, "When it's recreation time, you don't leave the wall. Stay near a brick wall." And when they started insulting me, I'd say, "Could you come closer? I can't hear you." That's exactly what I did. And then I started beating people if they insulted me. Man, they were really sorry. I became a real fighter.

VIC: Did you have a difficult time with men growing up? Especially as a teenager?

ALANIS: It was bad at that time. In all the communities, women were disappearing—raped, killed, chopped up. Terrible stories. That went on for many generations. I wasn't protected from it. I came very close to it many times.

VIC: How was the legal system back then? Was it also biased?

ALANIS: Yes. It was known that the police were doing the same things to the women. It was not a good situation. It was bad.

VIC: Did you have any good friends back then?

ALANIS: There was one family I was very close to, on the same street. They were French Canadian.

VIC: So you were able to have some closeness, at least. But still, with everything going on, did you ever think maybe you should stop resisting—stop pushing back?

ALANIS: No. I just found ways to defend myself. When I was younger, I was afraid all the time. But I became stronger.

VIC: Did you finish school?

ALANIS: Not really. I went to school there for a while, then to a private school. I was learning stenography. I couldn't understand it.

VIC: What I'm trying to understand is how you stayed so focused—how you weren't distracted by all the hurdles you went through. You held tightly to that vision, to the treatment of Indigenous people. Song was your way of expressing yourself—of connecting with people. Did you write your own lyrics? Were they meant to uplift, or were they simply honest about what was going on?

ALANIS: Yes, I wrote some songs. I gave a concert in Vancouver, and it was to redo an album I had done called *Bush Lady*. It tells the history of how women were treated like that.

VIC: At some point, you must have realized that the treatment of your people was wrong, that you had grievances to share. How did you begin making others aware of that? And then—how did you move into film? Was it to reach a wider audience?

ALANIS: I knew nothing about film. It happened in the '60s, in my community. One day I was teaching the children a game, and we were playing when these two little girls came crying. I asked, "What's wrong?" They said, "We went swimming next door, and they said, 'No savages here.'" And they had their 25 cents or whatever the entrance fee was. Right away, I thought—because I was already quite well known as a singer—I should expose those people and show how racist they were. But then I said no. Why should we send our children where they're not wanted? So I told the kids, "Don't worry. We'll get our own swimming pool." I thought it would be easy. I have news for you. It was very, very difficult.

But I did a campaign, and we built a swimming pool. That was almost 60 years ago. And this year, on my birthday—August 31st—I turned 92. The community held a ceremony for me, and they celebrated around that very pool. It was raining a bit that day, but they had built new facilities—new change rooms. I hadn't seen them yet. They even added water jets around the pool. When I arrived, some friends came with me. It was such a beautiful moment. I think it was the best day of my life.

They invited me inside to see the new buildings—there was a door that led from the change rooms right to the pool. And from that doorway, it looked like it had just been built. I couldn't believe it. It was so beautiful. And they didn't cut corners—you know how sometimes people say, "Let's do it this way, it's cheaper." Not here. It was the best of everything.

And I just stood there. Almost 60 years later—look at this pool. I was so happy for the children. And then—maybe three years ago, I'm not sure—the government asked the band from my community to expand the *garderie*—the children's kindergarten. So now we have more children there—55 kids, from babies to five. The mayor and directors from the next town came to meet with the chief and council, and they asked permission for their children to swim in Odanak—because they don't have a pool anymore. Isn't that incredible? And the council said yes. I'm glad. You're not going to be nasty to children. Children are children.

VIC: You transitioned from performing to making films!

ALANIS: It started with a man named Ron Kelly. He made a film about the campaign I was doing to build the swimming pool. It aired on CBC during prime time, on a show called *Telescope*.

VIC: I worked on *Telescope* for two years!

ALANIS: Well, people at the National Film Board saw the program and invited me to come in, to speak to directors and producers, like I used to do in schools. And I was shocked. I saw films that were supposed to be about our people—but they never spoke. It was always this British voice narrating. And I said, "Did you know they can talk?"

I was appalled at what was missing. I told them, "Our people can speak. We have a beautiful language. We have many stories." I sounded like a preacher. That's how it began. They asked me to work with them as a consultant, to give ideas, to be what they called a "person see this," which they meant as someone who helps shape content. That's how I started. And I've been there ever since.

The pool was built around 1965 or '66. The film appeared, I think, in '66. I started at the Film Board in 1967. That's how it all began.

VIC: So you didn't really shift away from music—but you added filmmaking to your vocabulary. Did you feel film could reach the masses faster?

ALANIS: Not exactly. First of all, they invited me—and I knew nothing about film. So learning was exciting. But my main goal was always to reach the classroom. There was a studio at the Film Board called "Multimedia." Everything they did there was for schools, film strips, mostly. That's where I started. I was so excited because it went straight into classrooms. It changed the way things were being taught. And it meant our people could be heard—our voices, our stories. The real history, from our perspective. That was the change I wanted. I felt like I was in paradise.

VIC: What kind of support did you get from the CBC or the Film Board?

ALANIS: Well, the Film Board at that time—it was difficult. It's an institution, and a very important one. And like any institution, everyone who works there holds some power. If they didn't like you... well, you can imagine. I was at the very bottom. It was really a man's world, first of all. Back then, it was almost all men making films.

Kathleen Shannon fought hard—she created the The Women's Film Studio. She and I were very good friends, but I never wanted to be part of that Studio. She was upset about that. She'd say, "That's terrible, you're a woman. You should be here." But I told her, "No. I'm not here to make films just about women. I'm interested in men, women, and children. And I'm not going to go into a space where people tell me what I should be saying or doing." We remained friends—I always supported her—but I stood on my own. It wasn't easy. Now, I have so much support, but that has nothing to do with how it was when I started. Back then, it was very difficult.

VIC: What role do you think the Film Board played in your larger quest?

ALANIS: Well, at first—I'm sure they thought I was the wildest thing that ever walked in there. One time, a producer even told me I wasn't allowed to speak to white people—I could only speak to Indians. The trouble was, they got the wrong Indian. But the Board itself—it was created for the right reasons.

Think of John Grierson, who founded it. He did something extraordinary, and not just for Canada, but for three other countries too. One man, one mind. He went to India, Australia, New Zealand, and Canada. He influenced Mackenzie King, who was Prime Minister at the time. They used to call it the Film Unit. I was lucky, because in the 1970s, John Grierson came back to Montreal and was teaching at McGill. We became very good friends. He was such a brilliant man.

He used to say he felt uncomfortable going to the movies, because it was always Hollywood stories—the rich, the chandeliers, the glamorous people coming down staircases. And poor people, or people of different nations, would sit there watching something they could never attain. Grierson coined the word "documentary." And he said that people should be able to go to the movies and see themselves on the screen. That's where it comes from. It's so beautiful.

And that's the National Film Board of Canada—created with that kind of thinking. I feel so proud of that. I travel all over the world, but I'm always happy to come home to Canada. Not every country has so many institutions like we do. And now, it's a different time. Our people are respected in schools. I do a lot of mentoring with young people, and if there was ever a time when everything is possible for our people—it's right now.

I feel so rich because I'm 92 years old, and I've lived long enough to see the change. Today, in all these institutions, there's space for Indigenous people. There's money. There's opportunity. Whatever discipline you want to pursue—look into your heart. You can do it. That's where we are now. This is why I feel so great. The change has been so tremendous. People are curious. And when they learn about all the terrible things that were done to our children—over generations—they don't feel good about it. They feel bad.

They want to see change. I think most people want to see justice done for our people. And I'm a witness to that.

VIC: So, thinking about the tide that has turned, how much credit would you give to institutions like the CBC or the Film Board?

ALANIS: I give a lot of credit. I love the CBC. I love the Film Board. I love Telefilm Canada. I think it's tremendous what they've done. Yes, there was racism in those institutions for a long time. But now, it's the opposite. I'm so excited about the way people think today. How they talk. People say, "Oh my God, we never knew about this." It's a different time. I'm not saying there are no problems, that's not true. But the change is so big.

VIC: From my perspective, I call these public broadcasters—funding's drying up. CBC isn't what it used to be. The Film Board too, maybe?

ALANIS: Yes—but I don't see it the way you do. I don't think it's losing something. I think it's creating something new. There's so much possibility. Just a couple of nights ago, I attended an awards celebration organized by the CBC. I was so impressed. The discipline, the professionalism, it was incredible. They had to change the stage many times, and even the stage changes were choreographed like a play. It was all so beautifully done. It was a long evening, and I was deeply impressed.

VIC: These institutions you're talking about—you've seen their entire history, from where they began to where they are now. Their independence—financial and creative—how important is that?

ALANIS: They do have independence. CBC, the Film Board—they never have enough money, when you count all the things they want to do, and all the people who want to come make films. But yes, there is independence. It's not the government that decides what film you can or can't make. Maybe it was like that at some point, but not now. They have their own ways of creating, and I'm very impressed.

VIC: What was the first film you did?

ALANIS: It wasn't actually a film, it was educational kits for kids, with film strips. And me, I was so excited, just the idea that children would be in a classroom and hear the voice of a family or a community. That's all I was interested in. I wasn't thinking in any grandiose way. And to this day, I'm still excited about those educational kits I made. It's funny, because I taught a class not long ago, and later on the Film Board reproduced those kits on DVDs. But before that, it was just film strips. You had a long-playing record for sound, and a little projector for the strip. When I started, the teacher would tell a child to go sit next to the projector, and a voice would say, "There were twelve chiefs here," and the student would move the frame by hand. That's how it was.

It took me a long time to finish the first one, because I was always working in three languages. Eventually, they made a little progress—the record would say, "There were twelve chiefs here—boing," and the sound would trigger the student to change the frame. But I thought, "Oh my God, when I go back to the community, they'll say this is retarded—'boing' after every sentence." Still, the stories were so strong. It was so wonderful.

I did one in Quebec and I did one in B.C. with the Interior Salish in Mount Currie. There was a woman there who did something called "Puberty One and Two." She was the last woman in her community to go through the traditional practice for when a girl begins menstruation. It was very beautiful. Her name was Marie Leo. It's funny, just a little while ago, I was talking to a group of children here. And I'm sure it's the same across America, not just Canada. When a child starts menstruating, they're told it stinks, it's ugly, it's disgusting. But in that little film strip, Marie talked about it in a way that made it sacred. So beautiful. I mean, is there any power greater than giving life? If you menstruate, you can be a mother.

So I flipped the narrative. I told students: it's not dirty, it doesn't stink. What they're saying isn't true, and it's not right. I repeated that. I showed the puberty film at the private school where my daughter was going—kids were around 10 or 11, that age. I spoke directly to them. Even the nun stayed to watch. When the bell rang for lunch, the children stood up and asked the nun if I could stay. They said they weren't hungry. I think it was the first time they realized how sacred menstruation is. And how wrong it is to shame it. This world that puts down the most beautiful things—it's another kind of hate. That's what made me not care whether it was just a film strip or a record. What mattered was what it said. How it helped children learn. How it made them feel included.

VIC: Who sponsored that film?

ALANIS: The National Film Board.

VIC: So the Film Board played a huge role for you.

ALANIS: Yes. And I'm very, very *reconnaissante*. I'm so happy I ended up there. I kept singing, but I was making films—I'm up to 65 films now. All the films I made are used in universities, in colleges, everywhere. I feel like

I've won. Because it was all about changing the way they talked about us. The way they taught us. About making it clear our language wasn't wrong.

Vic: Do you have any dreams or goals left—something you still want to do?

ALANIS: No, I'm just making more films. I think it's so powerful. Just the day before yesterday, I was in a classroom with 78 children—grade 1 and grade 2. I sang, I told stories. I just love listening to children. Their questions are so incredible. And I haven't changed. I'm still doing the same thing—just more and more. It's about giving *la parola*—the word—to all the people. That's what the Film Board does. It gives people the chance to speak. That's what it's about. And as long as I have my health, I'm going to keep working.

Vic: Why not! And looking back now on your whole journey—you feel good?

ALANIS: Oh yeah. There were some very dangerous places I went to—covering stories—but I'm glad I did it.

Vic: Are there people you'd like to acknowledge? People who helped you?

ALANIS: At the Film Board, Bob Verrall was very helpful to me. I don't know if you know him. He was there from the beginning. He's retired now. Along the way, there were a lot of difficulties. I had a hard time getting the money to do what I wanted. That's for sure. It wasn't for the reasons you were talking about, but I had to collect money myself, and the Board would match what I brought in. After the '80s, life at the Film Board got better for me. And I'm just so thankful. What they did, what they could do—it's unbelievable.

VIC: And what about the CBC—did you work with them too?

ALANIS: Oh yes. CBC was also very good to me. Right now, there's an exhibition on my work in Montreal called "The Children Have to Hear Another Story." It started in Berlin, went to Vancouver, then Toronto, and now Montreal. It's going to New York next. It's wonderful—it covers about sixty years of my work.

VIC: How do you feel about your life now, at this point?

ALANIS: Well, I feel good because of the chances I've had to influence other ways of thinking—especially when it comes to traditional teaching.

VIC: And how do you feel about this country now, compared to when you first started out?

ALANIS: Well, you know, it was very difficult for a long time. And not just for me, but for all of us. We were all feeling the racism and how damaging it was. But it's better now. I find that people talk differently about us. People who used to think we were so much less than they were—they've started to think differently. And our people are strong. We have lawyers, doctors, judges. It's a different time.

VIC: Could you share with me a few people—whoever they may be—who played a significant role in your journey? People you're grateful for, or whose contributions you're especially conscious of?

ALANIS: Well, it's not just for me, but for our people. Right now, we just lost someone very important to us—Senator Murray Sinclair. I made a short film about him a while ago. He was someone who started out studying law, became a lawyer, then a judge, and then a Senator. He's made a big difference in this country regarding the rights of our people. He was part of the Truth and Reconciliation Commission, along with Chief Wilton Littlechild and Marie Wilson. The changes they made—just incredible. The truth is out there now, and the changes are big.

VIC: Let's talk about your film *Kanesatake*.

ALANIS: Yeah. Well, one day, I was driving to the Film Board, and I heard on the radio that there had been a shootout in Oka. So instead of going to the Board, I went to Oka. I saw exactly what was happening—chaos. You couldn't get in. The police—it was a terrible mess. Then I drove to Montreal, back to the Film Board, and I said, "I'm changing my story. I've got to go right now. I want a crew." But there was hardly anyone there, just one camera person and one sound guy. And the sound guy said, "Alanis, I'm warning you. I hate guns. If I see one, I'm out." And I said, "Don't bother coming. The Mohawks have guns. The police have guns. The army has guns."

So I did the sound myself for the first one or two weeks. We were there at the camp, and no one was allowed into the village. The press was complaining. You had to go to Saint-Eustache to get a permit to shoot, which I did. I thought it would last a few days—78 days later, I was still there. It wasn't just difficult to document what was going on. The army, the police—even the Board—wanted me out. They said, "You can't stay there that long. It's expensive." But I have a hard head. There was no hotel. We stayed above a restaurant. And when I came out in the mornings, some guys waiting for the tavern to open would yell awful things at me—"Look, there's an Indian!"—yelling slurs.

But I didn't let that bother me. That was one side of it. I was there to document what was going on. So I stayed the whole time. Eventually, we were behind the barricade. It was scary. I'd be lying if I said I wasn't afraid. But there was an extra layer of difficulty because of who I was. I counted the days. For eight days, I was behind the wires. The press was allowed near, and I'd come forward. I remember hearing a soldier say in French, *"De la squaw"*—"Here comes the squaw."

Now, "squaw" is an Algonquin word. It means "woman." It's beautiful in our language. But the white men twisted it, used it to degrade us. When they say "squaw," it means, "I'm going to fuck you and kill you." Even there, even then—for eight days, the soldiers called me that. I was sleeping outside. I was scared. But I kept reminding myself: that's not why you're here. You're here to do your work. And I'm glad I did. "Happy" might not be the right word, but I'm glad I documented what really happened. Because what they showed on TV, what they said on the radio—it was awful.

VIC: Who sponsored the film? Who helped you financially?

ALANIS: The Film Board. It was difficult. They didn't want me there that long. But today, they're proud of the film. I ended up making four films, and they released them as a box set. This is history. It belongs to the people. We witnessed it. We were there. But don't let anyone say it was easy. It wasn't. And don't believe anyone who says I wasn't afraid. I was.

VIC: What else is important to you?

ALANIS: What's most important to me—and I tell a lot of young people this—the biggest damage in the world starts with the word "hate." I always say, don't let hate be part of you. Even the people you hate—whoever they are—they also have a good side. Everyone does. If you feel hate toward someone, you'd better look in the mirror and change that feeling. And you can. I really believe that.

VIC: Do your films reflect that message?

ALANIS: I think so. In a sense, I'm telling the truth about what's happening, but it's to show what hate can do. Hate lets you justify anything. You can do anything to anyone—and say it's okay, because you hate them. That's dangerous. It's terrible for children. If you tell your child to hate another child because of their skin colour or because they don't look like you, that child may grow up to do something terrible. For me, that's the root of it all. What I find difficult is when people justify bad things—when they normalize them. That's what's happening with Trump. Crime is being normalized. It's terrible.

VIC: Totally agree. Thank you. You have been a delight.

Chapter 9

GARY EVANS

Gary Evans is a historian, professor, and author whose work has helped define how Canadians understand their media institutions. With a deep knowledge of the National Film Board and its impact on national identity, Evans brings clarity and depth to the story of public broadcasting in Canada. A lifelong interpreter of culture and communication, he invites us to consider how stories—well told—become part of who we are.

VIC SARIN: Thank you for what you've accomplished on behalf of the industry. Absolutely brilliant. It's an honour to be with you. How did it all start?

GARY EVANS: It started when John Grierson turned up at McGill University. I was a student, just finishing my master's degree and wondering what's next—as an historian. Grierson was a natural contrarian.

I showed up at his door and the first thing he said to me was, "What do you know about Goebbels?" I said, "You mean Joseph Goebbels?" He said, "Yes," and I said, "but I came to talk to you about documentary." He replied, "Well, go read what you can about Goebbels," and he slammed the door in my face. That was it. And I thought, "Well, I'm fired." But no—I wasn't. I went and read everything I could about Goebbels over the next couple of weeks. Then I returned to see him and said, "Goebbels has taught me everything. You and he were in a chess match during the war, weren't you?" I asked. He said, "Very good. Come in. What are you drinking?" He then asked, "Do you know what documentary is?" I said, "Yes. The creative treatment of actuality." And that's what got me going—the idea of being an historian who could recapture, if I could, the essence of a moment, a time, a place.

VIC: The Film Board has a history alright. What was the basis of your capturing its place and time?

GARY: John Grierson had established the Film Board in 1939, just as the war was beginning. It was a response to the world crisis. One question was: What is Canada's position going to be? There had been an organization before the Film Board called the Canadian Government Motion Picture Bureau. Its function was to make semi-documentary films—mainly about tourism, the outdoors, naturalist subjects. But they were fundamentally films that were made but not often seen. When the Film Board came into existence, John Grierson was invited from Britain to come to Canada to see what he could do to enhance Canada's idea of film for the people, and about Canada for Canadians. He was given responsibility to create an organization that would, first, help with the fight in the Second World War, and second, create a school of filmmakers to succeed him. That, to him, was the most important part—making documentary film.

VIC: So it was John's idea to call them "documentaries"? As in, to document?

GARY: Yes, in fact he invented the word "documentary" in the early 1920s. He wrote an article about Robert Flaherty's film *Nanook of the North*. He explained that what Flaherty had done was, in essence, a documentary. He also clarified that a documentary doesn't have to mean capturing a moment in time, that is, a decisive moment. If you're lucky, yes, but documentary is also the creative interpretation of the actual. In other words, if you've missed the moment, is there a way to recapture it, in terms of its essence? That's what Grierson gave to the movement—the idea that documentary was an art form. He inspired young filmmakers to make films that would open the world. To make the world a window. One you could experience. One that could enrich you, and enrich the lives of those being filmed. Ultimately, he made peace as exciting as war.

VIC: That phrase—"making peace as exciting as war"—that was his, right? Something he often repeated. Have you researched, the very first film the Film Board produced?

GARY: The very first film was actually made to sell war bonds. A very simple film. The next film, though, was *Canada at War*. For that, they managed to convince the American filmmaker Louis de Rochemont—who produced *The March of Time*—to let Canada borrow a few feet of footage he'd already shot for the American audience. They blended that with material shot in Canada, and created a really fine short documentary.

Now, with the Film Board's original mandate, we have to think in terms of the war. It was essentially a newsreel war. What the young filmmakers were learning to do was take images of war and inspire people—to encourage them to fight against an awful scourge threatening the world: fascism.

What they were really doing was searching for what Grierson called "the quiet light of ordinary humanism." That's how he defined the goal—to find beauty in democracy, in everyday life. And how can you argue with that? Lorne Greene, of course, was the "voice of Canada" during the war. He narrated most of the theatrical films produced at the time.

VIC: Do you remember any one particular film where you saw that—where it really stood out?

GARY: Yes, actually. It was a film called *The Case of Charlie Gordon*. Charlie was a young man from Cape Breton, Nova Scotia. He was looking for something to do. The whole point of that brief documentary was that someone asks him, "What can you do? What do you want?" And Charlie says, "I think I want to be a detective." They tell him, "Well, there's not much detecting around here." So they put him into a training program. He learns a craft, and through that, he finds a way to contribute to the war effort. That was one of the early ways documentary film showed its power—taking an ordinary young man and showing how he could do something. Not necessarily become a hero, but build a meaningful life. These films showed how programs could help people learn skills and offer service to the community.

VIC: So the mandate really was about showcasing Canada?

GARY: No, actually. If you look at the original documentation, the National Film Board was established "to interpret Canada to Canadians." I'm quoting the legislation. That's a broad definition, but it gave creative freedom to directors, filmmakers, cinematographers. The real question was: "How do we bring Canada alive to its citizens?"

That spirit infused everyone at the Film Board. The underlying question was always, "What are we doing for Canadians?" After the war, when the National Film Act was rewritten in 1950, the language changed slightly. The mandate became not only to interpret Canada to Canadians, but to operate in the national interest. And that phrase, "in the national interest" is what guided the people at the Film Board. What you were doing was art, yes—but it had to serve a public purpose.

VIC: What about politics? There must have been some political implications, even back then. I mean, how much influence did they have over what got made?

GARY: Politics is always there. But one of the things people still find hard to believe is how much independence the filmmakers actually had. The government gave them money and said, "Do what you think should be done—responsibly." The Film Board commissioners ensured the money was handled responsibly, but the government didn't interfere with the films themselves. Of course, occasionally a filmmaker went too far—crossed a line—and caused trouble.

One example is that near the end of the war, there was a film called *Balkan Powder Keg*. It focused on the Balkans and the outbreak of civil war in Greece. It was an excellent film, but when Winston Churchill saw it, he blew his stack. He contacted the Canadian government and said the film didn't show Britain in the right light. They made few adjustments, the film was released, but it certainly didn't make Britain happy. There have always been moments when public reaction forced a rethink. People might say, "This has gone too far," or, "We should be doing something else." But the Film Board was largely left alone to channel its creative energy into serving the national interest.

VIC: Still, there must've been pressure from the public and political factions—trying to make sure the films didn't push things too far. Did they ever demand a film be pulled or recut?

GARY: There were a few times when questions were raised. A more contemporary example came in the 1980s with *Not a Love Story*, a film about the international trade in pornography. It interviewed women who found themselves in those situations—often driven there by socioeconomic conditions—and also interviewed the purveyors of pornography.

The film raised tough questions. Should the Film Board even be covering a subject like this? But it was ahead of its time. It asked: "What is the impact of pornography? Who is producing it? What are these women doing with their bodies? Why is this happening?" The film didn't offer simple answers. It wasn't about saying, "Here's the solution: one, two, three." It was about encouraging viewers to think—What should be done? It caused a huge public reaction. But most people responded with interest, even surprise. "I never knew," they said. That was the general feeling.

There are numerous other films where public response has played a role. But I want to stress that, for the most part, Film Board productions are artistic endeavours—films that present aspects of life not easily grasped by the general public. Yet through film and art, people are enlightened.

VIC: After the war, why was the Film Board moved from Ottawa to Montreal?

GARY: There had been a Royal Commission, initiated in 1949, which concluded in 1950. Its focus was on the future relationship between English and

French Canadians. The Commission recommended bringing the "two solitudes" closer together. Moving the NFB to Montreal was a symbolic and practical step toward that goal. Montreal was the best place to find both English and French communities—not just coexisting, but creatively energizing one another. Yes, there was tension, even competition. But it wasn't negative. It was a spark for creativity.

That's where the "Grierson torch" becomes significant again. Someone like Tom Daly, who was an executive producer at the Board, suggested, "Why don't we send some of our filmmakers back to places they knew when they were young—see if they can recapture the essence of those places?" One of the most famous results was the film *Corral*—a stunning short about a cowboy in southern Alberta who lassoes and breaks a wild horse. It follows him as he rides through the vast prairie landscape. It's a magnificent film and one of the most heartwarming depictions of Canada's immense, defining space. Alberta: the West. It becomes something spiritual.

VIC: Among English speakers at the time, was there a sense that the Film Board was mostly serving French Canada?

GARY: There was, yes. I remember my own experience with that. By the time we were in Montreal, many of the well-known filmmakers—Michel Brault and others—were French. There was a feeling among English Canadians, especially those not fluent in French, that they were a bit "out of it."

But overall, the Film Board reflected Canada. The decision to move to Montreal was mirrored by the creation of regional offices—another key step. These offices gave young, aspiring filmmakers in English-speaking areas opportunities to make short films. These works were distributed locally and nationally, nurturing the next generation of creators. The Film Board was known around the world long before Canada even had a flag, in 1965. Until then, we were still seen under the umbrella of the British Empire.

The Travelling Film Show program was a vital initiative. It began during the war. A mobile film van would arrive in a town on the same day each month, and people would gather at the town hall to see the latest NFB film. Access to moving images was rare then. So, the arrival of the van wasn't just a screening, it was an event that brought the community together. It helped unify the country. They were made for international distribution too, via the Department of External Affairs.

But often, the films that had the greatest impact were the ones no one expected. Take *Neighbours*, by Norman McLaren. A ten-minute film made using a technique McLaren invented—pixilation—which animates real people frame by frame. The plot was simple: two neighbours start fighting over a flower that sits on the property line. Eventually, they kill each other. The final frame reads *"Love Thy Neighbour"* in over a dozen languages. McLaren was a pacifist and a humanist. But he knew that simply saying "don't kill" wasn't enough. Neighbours is magical—it drops jaws to this day. It's a message about the futility of violence, delivered through radical visual storytelling. What's especially ironic is that Neighbours was funded by anti-communist money—part of a broader Cold War initiative to ensure Canada didn't "fall." But McLaren took the money, made the film he wanted, and ended up creating something profoundly human, and not political at all.

VIC: When the Film Board took films abroad—was it to inform the world about Canada? Or was it more about spreading a humanist message—love and peace?

GARY: Both. *The National Film Act* of 1950 made that explicit. It said the NFB should create films in the national interest, but that included "interpreting Canada to Canadians and to people abroad." That last part is just as important. As an artist making a film, you always have to think about your audience. First, who's going to see it? And second, what about people abroad? Will they even be interested in the subject? Can we find something that crosses cultures and languages? That's what inspires people to want to be part of the National Film Board. And again, it all goes back to Grierson. Everything goes back to his ideas, even in a vast country like Canada, with its time zones, small population, harsh winters. And its three distinct cultural threads: French, English, and Indigenous.

VIC: Do you think the Film Board played a role in informing those groups—or keeping harmony between them?

GARY: Absolutely. The federal government understood that this was precisely the task: How do you bring the different cultures together? You mentioned Indigenous as the third. We often speak of the English and French as the "founding peoples," but Indigenous Peoples were here long before. By 1980, the federal government acknowledged that Indigenous Peoples had been left behind—forgotten. So they began putting money into a range of initiatives to bring Indigenous communities into the contemporary world, while also helping them reclaim pride in the cultural heritage they'd been losing through neglect. One of the early developments was the Indian Film Unit, which actually dates back to the 1970s. A landmark piece from that period was *The Ballad of Crowfoot*—a powerful film that used music to recount the history of Indigenous Peoples. It resonated with both settler Canadians—English and French—and with Indigenous viewers. It served as a cultural bridge. The federal government supported it, saying, "We're giving you funding now—we want you to do something for and about the Native population."

Sounds simple, but let me give you an example of how complex it was. Take *The Cree Hunters of Mistassini*. It's an excellent documentary about a young Cree man who reclaims traditional ways of hunting and trapping in the winter. The Film Board followed his journey, documenting what that lifestyle looked like. It was shown in Indigenous communities across the country. The trouble? To live that way, you need about 50 square miles of land to yourself. Suddenly, everyone inspired by the film wanted to "become a hunter," but the reality was, there just wasn't enough room. So while it stirred pride and a longing to reconnect with cultural roots, it also created frustration. That's the paradox: You want to celebrate your culture, but can you live it in today's world?

VIC: It seems like the NFB gave filmmakers a lot of independence—to pursue what mattered to them.

GARY: They did. From the very beginning, filmmakers had a great deal of creative freedom. I mentioned Tom Daly earlier. He came out of the war years and became one of the most important producers at the Film Board in the 1950s. Meanwhile, technology was changing fast. Cameras were no longer just for the wealthy, anyone could access one. And with that came a shift in the whole concept of filmmaking. Video cameras changed how we made films and how audiences saw themselves in them. This was the spirit behind "Challenge for Change"—a program rooted in the belief that ordinary people could tell their own stories with the right tools. That power comes with responsibility. Because it's so easy to create images now, it's also easy to make mistakes. With *direct cinema*—or *cinéma vérité*—you can end up exposing people who didn't want to be exposed. Or who weren't ready. You have to be careful. Technology moves faster than our ethics sometimes.

If you're dealing with the problems of society—which many documentaries aim to do—you have to ask: "Does every film need to be about a victim?" Victimhood has become central to the genre, not just in Canada, but globally. But people don't want to see endless suffering. They want to see hope. Tom Daly always said, "Every film—no matter what—must end in hope." This is where technology sometimes got ahead of us. With all the tools available, we forgot the emotional responsibility of storytelling. And with *cinéma vérité*, that can be dangerous. You might be doing harm without even realizing it.

One example of a film that gained international acclaim featured a struggling family here in Montreal. The father was chronically unemployed. The film exposed the raggedness of human life—but Grierson hated it. He said, "Why are you showing that man's weakness? Why are you showing what's wrong with him?" Yes, they were in bad shape, but he felt the film lacked something. "I don't like films of that sort," he said.

He saw it just a year or so before he died. But then he pointed to another film, *Nell and Fred*—a documentary about two strangers, neighbours, who eventually come together as seniors. Love isn't just for the young, the film suggests, it's for everyone.

That, Grierson said, "That's the kind of film you need to make. One that gives people hope."

You see, too much freedom can be dangerous, but if the Film Board ever erred, it erred on the side of letting filmmakers follow their vision to see what came of it. Take *The Morgan Taylor Affair*, a film about abortion—an issue that's resurfaced in today's headlines. Dr. Morgan Taylor, a Jewish refugee who survived the Holocaust, ran a clinic providing abortion services to those in need. The film presents Taylor not as a killer, but as someone who believed a child should only be born to someone who wants and loves them. He made the haunting point: the people behind the Holocaust—they were unloved, neglected. He argued that someone capable of such monstrosity had likely never received the love a child needs. That's what the film was about—not the act of abortion itself, but the conditions of love and responsibility. And that nuance seems forgotten in today's debates. Even in American politics, the conversation is often reduced to: the poor thing being killed. But what if that child grows up unloved, becomes a criminal or a fascist—what then? Do we really want that? That's what *The Morgan Taylor Affair* dared to ask back in the early 1980s.

VIC: So, were these kinds of films driven by individual filmmakers—or by Grierson himself? I'm trying to understand how the independence and variety of films came to be.

GARY: It was both. There was a film committee that met every year. Filmmakers gathered to pitch and discuss their ideas. They thrashed things out together—passionately. Funding was limited. On the French side, they got one-third of the budget, with English Canada getting two-thirds—based on population. So the question became: Who's doing what? How is the money being spent? It was intense—tooth and nail fighting to make the film you wanted to make. Sometimes you succeeded. Sometimes you didn't. But it wasn't the federal government dictating what films to make. In fact, sometimes the government got into hot water because of a film that was made.

Take *If You Love This Planet*—an anti-nuclear film that won the Academy Award for Best Short Documentary. Directed by Terry Nash, it featured Helen Caldicott, an anti-nuclear advocate. Nash used clips from Hiroshima and Nagasaki to underline the horror. When I met her, she said, "I've read your book. Your book about John Grierson inspired me to make this film. Thank you." Imagine—an Academy Award winner thanking me. That was a highlight of my years of work—quietly, in the library, in the editing room, in the theatre.

VIC: Grierson comes across as quite the character.

GARY: Grierson was a character, alright. During the war years, they were trying to improve film distribution with mobile circuits. A young man he hired wrote a 90-page manual—everything you'd need to know to make it work. He gave it to Grierson, and Grierson walked over to the garbage can and threw it in. Just like that. The guy wanted to punch him. But Grierson's message was: "You've already figured it out. You don't need me to read it. Just do it." That's who he was. He didn't care if your feelings were hurt. His question was always: "What are you doing to serve the community?" That idealism, I think, came from his Calvinist upbringing, even though he didn't practice religion He once said—quoting a French duchess, I think—"Religion is like sex. I practice it often, but never talk about it." He loved lines like that. He was tough. Tough on people. Tough on me. Never said anything nice about what I was doing. But he let me sit, watch, and listen. And in that way, he was kind. He respected that I wasn't in it for myself, I cared about the work. He saw every film before it went out. His approval was essential. Without it, the film wouldn't be released—or it would be recut.

VIC: We hear a lot about the NFB Unit B. What can you tell us about that?

GARY: Let me tell you about the Unit B films. These films were intimate, universal, and remarkable for the atmosphere they created. They succeeded both domestically and internationally. One film that stands out is *Straight*

Railways, about an immigrant in Winnipeg who clears snow off the trolley switching tracks. A simple story—but deeply personal. You follow this man through his day. And what Grierson believed was: This is what you do. Focus on the individual. Turn the individual into poetry. Don't generalize about humanity—show it. Take a single life and make it luminous. That was the idea.

Another example: the Paul Anka documentary, *Lonely Boy*. It followed him when he was still a teenage sensation, just before he broke big in the U.S. The film captures those intimate, unglamorous moments of stardom—and acknowledges that the viewer is watching a film about someone being filmed. It's self-aware. And of course, it's edited in the studio afterward—carefully constructed so that it sings, not screeches.

VIC: In the 1950s, there were Oscars coming from Canada—mostly Film Board films, right?

GARY: Yes, especially in animation—and I haven't even mentioned that yet. If any NFB films are truly timeless, it's the animated ones. The animation department was formed by Norman McLaren, the genius behind *Neighbours*. He inspired so many artists to think: How do you say something new in film? Something artistic, something enduring. And NFB animation did just that—often avoiding direct conflict or confrontation, but still making bold, imaginative statements. These animated films tended to cultivate innocence. They're not overtly political. They promote a sense of wonder, of gentleness—sometimes, yes, even naivety. Is that good or bad? It depends. But it shaped how I saw the NFB's purpose in those early decades.

VIC: What role do you think the Film Board played in nurturing Canadian talent?

GARY: Absolutely essential. Without the NFB, you wouldn't have the creative heart of Canadian film. And we haven't even touched the French side—though I know your focus here is primarily English. But the entire French film industry in Canada was born through the NFB. Jacques Bobet nurtured French-language filmmakers. From that base, you got people like Denys Arcand, Michel Brault, Marcel Carrière—the whole generation. These filmmakers wouldn't have had careers—wouldn't have had livelihoods—without the Film Board. And crucially, they were given freedom. Risky, yes. But necessary. Take Carrière's film *On est au coton*, which criticized Canada's garment industry and its exploitation of workers. That stirred serious trouble in Ottawa. The clothing industry was an economic pillar, especially in Montreal. Even the Prime Minister got involved. When Film Board Commissioner Sydney Newman delayed the film's release, the PM said, "I'm glad you did what you did with *On est au coton*." The film was shelved for several years, only released after the hulabaloo passed.

So yes, Ottawa was there—but it kept its hands out of the pot. It didn't want to stir it. As politician Jack Pickersgill told me, "What we did with the Film Board...we said: 'Here is the cloth. It's up to you to cut it and make a piece of clothing.'"

VIC: Let's talk a bit more about Alanis Obomsawin. I've spoken with her, and you know—she did so many films with the Film Board. What can you say about her entry?

GARY: Well, I'm familiar with her work—of course. She's a perfect example of what happens when you give an extremely talented person the freedom to follow her own direction. Alanis could capture history in the making. And because she is Indigenous herself, she was able to access spaces and voices that white filmmakers simply couldn't reach. When the Oka Crisis occurred she went right into the heart of it. It was a highly volatile, dangerous situation. The government had sent in armed forces. It could've turned into another Wounded Knee. That's how close it was to disaster. Alanis went in to document the crisis from the Indigenous point of view. Through her film, *Kanehsatake: 270 Years of Resistance*, you understand both sides: the government's desire to avoid violence, and the deep pain and resistance from the Indigenous communities. That dual perspective—rare and powerful—could only come from someone with her insight and access.

There was also the Women's Film Unit at the Film Board. That unit was transformative. It brought women filmmakers into their own space, allowing for films about rape, abandonment, domestic life—subjects that were rarely addressed without that infrastructure. Those films simply wouldn't have been made without the Women's Unit. That's the kind of structural support the Film Board offered.

But then comes the perennial question: Who sees all these films? As technology expanded, and as filmmaking became more common in our daily lives, it became harder to secure audiences. A film like *Riel*, which you were involved in—great film—might once have drawn half a million viewers. Now, you're up against everything from game shows to new streaming content. Everyone's competing for attention.

So the Film Board made a wise decision. They shifted their emphasis: Let's get films into schools and educational institutions. The idea was to help kids learn about Canada. And if the Film Board ever failed at anything, it may have been this: building a national mythology. I've argued this for years. The CBC has done wonderful work with historical series, but what we really need is a constant reminder—a coherent cultural narrative.

A national mythology isn't just, "We climbed the mountain and reached the top." It's, "How did we climb? Who helped us? Who was excluded?" But by the 1980s, the Film Board was facing serious budget cuts—especially in salaries and staff. Why? Because if you were on a long-term contract with the Film Board, you became a government employee. And once you're unionized, you can't just make a film and move on. You're locked into the system. If I were a filmmaker, I'd want that security—sure. But too many people were drawing from the annual budget simply by being permanent. So they began cutting staff. But they tried not to slash people's livelihoods. It took years to wind that system down. Even now, budgets keep shrinking. There's often just enough money to pay employees—but not enough for actual film production. It's a bitter irony. The money that once went to the screen now goes elsewhere.

And what about the private sector? Canadian private production companies argue: We should be getting that money to make films for the public. Telefilm Canada is a perfect example. They've supported a lot of excellent films. But the problem remains: Who gets to see them? You send them to the U.S.—but guess what? The U.S. won't take your film. Why? Is there something wrong with it? No, it's just that they've got their own people. Then you try the CBC. And how does the CBC respond? "We've got people lined up here making films already—we don't need yours." That's the core problem: too much product, not enough places to show it.

Take one classic example: *Nobody Waved Goodbye*—I think that was from around 1980. A film about teenage angst, rebellion, conflict with parents. A solid film. But as one producer quipped to me, "Nobody waved goodbye because nobody said hello." No one saw it. And it's a reminder: you cannot make feature films in North America and expect to hit the jackpot. It's a brutal market. That said, some do persevere and produce extraordinary work. Denys Arcand is a great example—an incredible artist. And where did he start? With short documentaries at the Film Board.

VIC: What about the relationship between the Film Board and CBC? Was there much cooperation? Could they have joined forces more effectively?

GARY: It's always been an issue of personnel. Back in the 1950s, the Film Board did produce films for the CBC—shorts, half-hour programs. *On the Spot* was one. But eventually, the CBC said, "We've got our own young filmmakers now—we don't need yours." They wanted to develop internal talent. And they had aspiring producers who needed opportunities. So even though, legally, the NFB had a right to airtime on the CBC, the network would say, "We just don't have room for you this season—maybe next year." There were exceptions. Some NFB films did air on the CBC. But generally, it became a turf war. Two cats in a bag, clawing at each other. Eventually, the Film Board had to find other avenues for its creative output.

VIC: Let's talk about some iconic films that came out of the Film Board in the 1950s and beyond—ones that generated not only talent, but international inspiration.

GARY: Absolutely. One example: a film from the early 1950s—*Universe*. It inspired Stanley Kubrick while making *2001: A Space Odyssey*. He saw it and said,"That's it—I want to do what they did." He even hired the same narrator.

Another name: Donald Brittain. I worked with him several times, as a researcher. Don was a national treasure. He came from journalism and had an uncanny eye for what would capture public attention. His film *The Champions*, about Pierre Trudeau and René Lévesque, is iconic. But he also made *Bethune*, a phenomenal portrait of Norman Bethune, who gave his life in service to revolutionary China. The film ran into trouble—External Affairs said, "This glorifies communism." But it didn't. It glorified a man who saved lives. And eventually, it was recognized as an international masterpiece. But if I had to pick one film of Brittain's—it would be *Memorandum*. To me, it's one of the greatest films ever made about the Holocaust. It documents a postwar trial in Germany of Nazis who had been newly identified and charged. Sounds dry, maybe—but *Memorandum* makes the horror of the Holocaust immediate without showing a single dead body. Brittain understood: you don't need graphic images to communicate evil. He showed us what humanity had done to humanity—through restraint, not sensationalism.

There's a moment Donald Brittain captured in a film—he's interviewing a public servant in Ottawa. While she talks about her department, the camera slowly zooms in on a photo of her two dogs on her desk. And that's it. You learn everything you need to know about her. No husband, no kids.

Those dogs are her life. Brittain caught that moment. That essence. And that's what you get when you have time—and the ability to really see what's going on around you. It's a tremendous challenge.

VIC: You have such a strong memory of films—could you name a few more? Sequences or characters that still stay with you?

GARY: One that stands out comes from the French production side: *Les Raquetteurs*. It's about a snowshoe convention in Sherbrooke, Quebec—an actual race held in a local ring. It's wonderful. It shows human endeavour in all its awkwardness—people stumbling, falling, getting back up. And the film focuses not on the winner, but on the *losers*. And that's the beauty of it. For French Canada, *Les Raquetteurs* was very important. It helped people see themselves in cinema—and hear their language. "That's our language," they'd say.

Another film that stands out is *Flamenco at 5:15*—it won an Academy Award. It was about a flamenco workshop at the National Theatre School here in Montreal. The film follows young students learning flamenco under the guidance of a world-renowned flamenco artist and her husband, who accompanies on piano. It captures a real afternoon—a slice of raw, vibrant learning. It shows you what makes a young person want to live this life. It's directed by Cynthia Scott, with support from John Smith, Adam Symansky, and others. It makes you want to go out and buy a pair of flamenco shoes just to feel that rhythm. That's the kind of energy you get when filmmakers follow inspiration—to the National Theatre School, to young people, to the beating heart of the arts.

Another film—more critical—is Daniel O'Connor's *Voir Miami*. He goes to Miami to follow French Canadian retirees who spend their winters there, escaping the cold. But what he captures is their sense of displacement. These folks are just sitting on their houseboats, basking in the warmth—but also adrift. Culturally unmoored. It's a gentle but pointed look at identity: French Canadians in an American city, Canadians in a broader North American culture. It quietly asks, Who are we, anyway?

Nanook was another important film years later, but it's also about how you fake reality—well, that's the wrong word, maybe. In the famous walrus scene, they didn't have a walrus to film. So they used a dead one, attached a cable to it, stuck it under the ice, and staged the whole hunt. It looked like Nanook was spearing it. The audience believed it—that this was real life.

VIC: So it was staged, but it still told a truth?

GARY: Exactly. Grierson said it was a creative interpretation of reality. That fascinated me. It's magic. I love the magic of film.

One of the all-time greatest films at the Film Board is *Labyrinth*, done for Expo 67. They built a pavilion specially for this film that you would not do by sitting in a seat and looking at a screen, but by standing high up above it and looking straight down at a screen that was on the floor. And that's how you see the film—which is about the story of mankind trying to make its way through this life. It's such a brilliant film.

Yes, it cost $4.3 million in 1967. It blew the budget. It just destroyed everything. I worked at Expo 67 and I walked by that pavilion every day. I could walk in anytime I wanted because I carried a badge that made me into something. People would wait hours to get in to see *Labyrinth*. It's a story of human endeavour—just amazing. Maybe that's where the money should go—toward big, ambitious productions that millions of people can see. I think that's a real possibility. And maybe this business of constantly saying, "We've got to train the youngsters..." Well, the youngsters can go to university. All the universities have film schools. Some of the best filmmakers today dropped out right after they got in—because it wasn't what they needed. You need fire in the belly. I think Grierson was one of those who said it—you've got to have that passion. If you do, don't worry about money. Get the idea, and make it understood.

VIC: Any final words, Gary?

Gary: We need a return to a literate culture. Still, what you're doing with this project—I'm grateful for it. You're giving me a chance to speak to people who might not know about the Film Board.

Chapter 10
GEORGE STROUMBOULOPOULOS

George Stroumboulopoulos is a Canadian television and radio host known for his deep interviews with cultural icons, political leaders, and change-makers. He rose to prominence on MuchMusic and became a household name through his CBC program "The Hour." A lifelong advocate for social justice and mental health awareness, he has used his platform to elevate underrepresented voices. Today, he continues to connect with global audiences through Apple Music Hits and his work in independent media.

VIC: I want you to go back a little bit.

GEORGE: I was born in 1972, in Toronto on the west side, in these immigrant neighbourhoods. Most of the people in my life, my friends, we were the first ones in our families born in Canada.

VIC: And what was it like for you before getting into television?

GEORGE: I'm that prototypical Gen-X kid who grew up in poorer neighbourhoods. Weirdly, it felt so free. We were at the birthplace of hip hop, the second wave of punk rock, new wave was changing. British influence was there with music. Dance music had started, what would ultimately become house and big club music. So all of this was happening. From age 5 to 19, punk and hip hop and electronic music were forming. Some of it had existed before, but we were coming of age in these really creative times.

We were sneaking tapes of Scorsese films, watching bizarre Hollywood movies. It was just a weird time. My memories of my friends and I—we were free. Our parents were young, from other countries. They'd send us out in the morning and we wouldn't come back until late. A lot of autonomy.

Radio was bigger to me than television. We didn't have a TV. My mother found a television in the garbage. I was raised by a single mom. The TV she found had broken handles, so we had vice grip pliers permanently clamped on and that's how you changed channels. She'd keep it in her bedroom closet.

We could only watch TV on Friday nights, and maybe one period of the hockey game on Saturday. So radio was an instrumental force in my life. In Toronto in the '70s and '80s, there were two stations in particular that pushed the boundaries—not just musically, but with conversation. One was called Q107, the other CFNY. There was also a talk radio station but mostly, it was those rock stations. They were edgy. I think they imprinted on us and maybe made some of my friends and I more wild than we should've been.

I remember moving out, my roommate and I got cable. I'd never had cable in my life. I couldn't believe what was available. Growing up, I just didn't have television or cable. I watched CBC and CTV—that was it. There was also Channel 79, Citytv. It had a show called *The New Music*, with all these bands that would become so influential to me. I remember watching on that channel—coat hangers replacing the antennas to get a signal. And the people on the air? They were ethnic. They had long last names. They didn't look like the typical TV personalities we were used to seeing. I think that era of Citytv helped form a Toronto identity that wasn't represented elsewhere on TV.

VIC: You kind of got drawn to that?

GEORGE: Yeah. I remember my father left when I was 7, so I was raised by a single mom. No exaggeration, I don't remember a time before music in my life. I was around 5 or 6 years old, had young parents. My dad was maybe 19 or 20 when I was born, same for my mom.

So my early memories include Jimi Hendrix, The Doors, Cream records leaning against the couch. I don't remember a life before music. It became a huge part of who I was. But it was a challenging home, a challenging childhood. Things changed when my father split, and my mom, my sister and I moved to a neighbourhood called Malton, by the airport in Toronto. My best friend lived around the corner. My memories are tied to riding bikes, being free, being broke—and not having a lot of hope.

I know hope matters, but I placed no value on it. That's one of the things that made me so present in my adult life—I didn't have the luxury of hope. Or dreams, really. We weren't going to have that stuff. I've been so privileged in the second half of my life, and I'm grateful. But when I was young, it wasn't a thing. All my memories are music, fights, bikes, hanging with my mom, reading—so much reading. I was a voracious reader. Reading was a huge reason why my mind developed the way it did, why I'm curious about other worlds. I was introduced to them through all the books I was reading.

VIC: It sounds like you were so drawn to the world of music, yet you ended up really connecting with people.

GEORGE: I think the reason I care about the world is because of the lyrics I listened to. Bob Dylan singing "Masters of War" or "Shelter from the Storm"—to me, that was the same as watching a story about Ethiopia on the news when Brian Stewart was reporting on the famine. It was the same as watching my grandfather working on the Ford assembly line, and seeing what happened to the men when the plants closed or the lines shut down.

GEORGE: To me, it was all part of the same thing, which was the story of the disenfranchised, abandoned, the working class, the upstarts, the outsiders. So I've never had a separation between what I ended up doing for a living and my life in music, because, you know, a great film changes how you see the world, and a great song changes how you view the world. And I just tried to take all that—you know, when I had my talk show, and we built the set, I took a handful of records that I loved and built them into the platform of the set so that every time I took the stage to sit in those red chairs, I knew that I was standing on those records. And underneath me were these records that are the reason that we're here in the first place.

VIC: You said music was an emotional connection and you felt so strongly about it. Did you ever write anything? You used to play, didn't you?

GEORGE: Yeah. My mother forced me to become a classically trained piano player. She was trying to do anything she could to keep me off the street. My sister was taking lessons, and I used to just bring a hockey stick and a tennis ball and take shots against the wall while my sister was in her lesson. One day I was messing around on the piano before her lesson started, and the teacher said to my mother, "That boy should play because obviously music is a part of him." I'm a very extreme personality, so I listen to music very intensely. Obviously, I had picked up some of the stuff I had listened to.

I've written songs. I've written scores for the films that I've directed. I wasn't good enough to be a concert pianist, and I never really needed to be. I found my own way of expressing, which was in this career. But this career is by accident. For me, this was not the plan. I had no intention of doing this for a living. It just kind of happened.

VIC: I'm glad it did. You probably have a very strong power or talent or gift given to you—to communicate and to make people feel relaxed.

GEORGE: They said to me, it's a gift. And I really believe that everyone is given a gift—all of us. The question is how you use that.

GEORGE: My only real skill set in this life is that I am unbothered. I don't get overwhelmed. I look at the task at hand: What needs to be done? How can I be effective? How can I be either a tool for change or make the world a better place? I knew that I had to make a living, and I knew that if I did this for a living, I could have the things I wanted in my life. But I could also do the things I believed in. I have this desire to have truly authentic experiences and be very present. And once I realized that's something I could do, I tried to nurture that. I tried to remove all the artifice of television and radio and just be right there.

VIC: So how your broadcast career come about?

GEORGE: I was going to join the army. That was a bad fit. I'm not really good with authority or discipline, so it wasn't a good fit. But, you know, like things happen in life, there was an adult learning centre beside the movie theatre I worked at, and there was a woman who was working there who I was sweet on. She was way out of my league, but she obviously saw that I was a lost teenage boy, you know, just hanging around all the time. And she gave me a course calendar for the college. And I opened it up and I saw radio broadcasting, and I just went, oh, I'll do that.

I got into the school but I had terrible grades. I placed no value in education, I placed no value on school. And I really was the kid that's not supposed to make it. I just didn't care about many things. But six months or so into my schooling, something switched in my brain and I remember when I thought, "I'm paying for this." And I remember having a—not an epiphany, but maybe a mini one—which said it doesn't matter what comes from this. What matters is how you train your brain to do things you don't want to do.

I applied for lots of jobs, got rejected, got no notes back. And then I would work really hard and got the next one. I was told by some people who hired me that one of the reasons I got hired was because I was interested in a lot of things. I wanted to have a gigantic worldview. And so I explored worldviews, and that put me in a position, even when I was talking about records, to be able to connect it to history and things like that. I don't believe in destiny, it's not my thing. But when I look back, all of what I do in my life now, as surprising as it is, isn't really surprising because it's about feeding curiosity and honouring curiosity and working really hard

VIC: Talk of your work that was underway.

GEORGE: I was working at MuchMusic, and I was doing a lot of interviews with bands, and I built up some profile across the country as kind of the edgier punk rock metal kind of guy. You know, they build you—there's an archetype. I was kind of that version. And this guy who I worked with sent me an email saying, hey, we're working on "The Greatest Canadian." Is there somebody you would advocate for? And I remember writing him back in an email saying, "There are only two people I would represent. One is Tommy Douglas and the other is Neil Young. If Tommy Douglas or Neil Young are not part of it, I'm not interested." And then they wrote me back and they said, "Well, we can't tell you who's in there." And I said, "If Tommy Douglas isn't in there, what kind of list is this?" So they said, "You want Tommy Douglas? Then you do it."

So my friend and I—his name was Guy O'Sullivan, who is no longer with us—Guy and I had a meeting and we said, let's make a rock 'n' roll film and show people why the Canada they brag about is so closely connected to this Tommy Douglas guy from Saskatchewan. And we went and did it—and it won. But during the filming of it, I had somebody at CBC—I guess someone who had seen some tapes and liked what I was doing—offer me a job, but I turned him down. I didn't want to work at CBC. I had no interest in working at CBC at all. I had a particular kind of approach. CBC historically didn't have fellows with my kind of personality type on the air. They were a bit more conservative, a bit more steady. I just didn't want to work there. I liked my job at MuchMusic.

Around then, I had a moment where I thought... what if? My friend, Rain, who was the lead singer of a band called Our Lady Peace—Canadian legends—said, "Have you seen what's going on in Darfur?" I said, "I have, we need to go." And a month or so later, we were going to Darfur. But I'm sitting on a plane with him on the runway at Pearson in Toronto, and I look out the window and I see a guy on a forklift driving by, wearing the same vest that I used to wear when I drove a forklift at Pearson Airport.

I looked over at my friend Rain and I said, CBC's offering me this opportunity. And he said to me, "It'll never work." I said, "I know it'll never work. That's why I've turned them down." And then he said, "But... if it does work, you'll be pulling the sword from the stone. You'll be doing a thing that no one's been able to do quite like that yet. So it probably won't work because they won't let you. But if it does, how cool would that be?" And I sat there—I had already said no to the job—and I looked at him and I went, you're right. I pulled my BlackBerry out. I sent a message to my manager. I said, let's quit MuchMusic, let's take the CBC job. I'm going to Africa. Talk to you soon. Send. Turned my phone off.

And that's it. That's why I went. That's why I took that job at CBC. I'm so grateful. I am so grateful I ignored my instincts, and I listened to my friend Rain. Because most people in my life had told me not to do the job. They told me, CBC will never let you do what you do. And then I called Peter Mansbridge.

VIC: He was anchoring *The National* at the time?

GEORGE: Yeah. I was doing *MuchMusic News*, like music news, and Peter was doing *The National*. And every now and then, Peter would call me—he'd be travelling across Canada, get into his hotel room, and he would watch MuchMusic. Peter was always up on that stuff, so he would call me and we would just tell jokes about each other's job doing the news. And he was doing real news, and I was doing this. I said to Peter one day, hey man, let me run something by you. CBC's offering me this thing, blah blah blah, here's what it is. And Peter, who didn't really know me, gave me a lot of time. Walked me through the reality of it, told me what I should look out for, gave me insight on what it could be. I decided to take the gig.

I have to tell you, I wouldn't have taken the gig, and I wouldn't have re-signed—I only signed an 18-month deal—I wouldn't have re-signed with CBC if Peter hadn't really protected me and guided me through that place. It was Peter Mansbridge and Rick Mercer who were really warm and lovely to me, and I'm so grateful.

VIC: They were you mentors?

GEORGE: Yeah, in a sense. Peter had a certain kind of gravitas. When he would do his tour across the country and talk about CBC, he would very publicly support us. I'd go sit in his office and catch up with him regularly. We would just tell jokes. We wouldn't even really talk about the gig. He was so important to that show's existence for me. He helped me navigate a lot in the early days. Rick as well.

That's how I got into the CBC thing. The Tommy Douglas episode hadn't even aired yet. So I made the decision to do this—and I was advocating for Tommy on this whole series—knowing in my head that I had already signed the contract. Then Tommy Douglas won "The Greatest Canadian" thing, and right around that time we announced I was coming over. People thought, oh, they did it because of that. But that was never the plan. It all just kind of happened.

VIC: What was CBC like in those days when you first came in? I'm wondering how much creative freedom you had.

GEORGE: When I got to CBC, I was so lucky. I had enormous freedom. I know it was because my producers were insulating me from a lot of the network negativity. But there was a boss at CBC Newsworld—Heaton Dyer—and our very first show, we were live—8 p.m. on Newsworld. My first show, right after the news, I come on, no opener, just straight in. I quoted Howard Beale saying, "I'm here because I've run out of bullshit." I said that live on CBC Newsworld.

I saw Heaton's face go white. First commercial break, he said to me, "You've run out of bullshit?" I said, "Yeah." He said, "Do you mean that?" I said, "Yeah." He said, "Then just speak the truth." It was so empowering. Heaton Dyer and Jennifer Desmond, who was EP, protected me and let me learn. I hadn't done a show like that. I think we did a good job over time, but we had to learn. Small team. Nightly show. We were live. I still had my nose ring. I was wearing jeans and a studded belt. I was talking to prime ministers—and I was being me. CBC let me. I'm so grateful. I wouldn't have stayed if they hadn't.

But I knew I would walk from my desk past the CBC newsroom into the studio, and I could feel the derision from some of the people who worked there. And I don't blame them. They held CBC in high regard. They thought I was some kid showing up doing this thing, and I don't blame them at all. And I feel like we did a good job representing that place. And to this day, our interviews get played all over the world because I think we did a good job representing that network.

I was naive and I sort of viewed this whole thing the way a punk rock singer would view an audience. You go into a room. You're the opening band. No one's there to see you. They hate you just by your appearance. And you try to win them over by doing the good—by doing the good thing, telling the truth. I kind of looked at it like that. And it's interesting that it was a singer who put that seed of doubt into my brain that maybe I could do it. I spent ten years doing that show. Ten years—14 years at CBC in total.

VIC: Well, first you had the other show, right?

GEORGE: Yeah. And then we had *The Hour*. We would have three meetings and I'm a pretty open-minded person to ideas. I would sometimes say no to a story that I didn't think was fresh, compelling, but I was very open to it because the producers were really smart. But in terms of guests, yeah, I had an enormous amount of control. It wasn't just me—it's collaboration—but ultimately, if I didn't want to talk to somebody, I didn't have to.

GEORGE: When we were on Newsworld, we were live. And then when we went to CBC Late Night, we taped it at 5:30-ish, and then it went out that night, just because of time zones. So because of time zones, we had to be able to roll it out in different regions.

VIC: Most of the people you talked to were well-known Canadians?

GEORGE: Weirdly, not Canadians. A lot of it was news-based. So what we would do is, we'd take a story of the day. In the early days, I would talk to a reporter or talk to a newsmaker. So we started to build some momentum that way by talking to the person in the story of the day.

It was harder to book Canadian celebrities than you would think. I knew a lot of people in this world, so I spent a lot of time in the U.S. What I would do is, on the weekends, I would take a stack of DVDs and I would fly to LA. I would set up meeting after meeting.

I'd meet with publicists, go into boardrooms filled with them, play our highlight reel, and talk to them about why they should give their guests to us. And then I would say to them, "You have some celebrities we don't want. They're not good fits for us. Here's what we do want." And at that time, they were saying that no hosts really ever came into the meetings—especially talk show hosts. And I went into the rooms with all of them. But Canadian—bigger Canadian celebrities—we couldn't get them. We asked, but they would say no. Weirdly enough, some of my favourite Canadians—I remember interviewing one of them who had always said no to the show. He finally said yes. And then he said to me, "You know, I said yes because Tom Cruise told me I should do this interview." Then we started to get Canadians. But in the very early days, it was difficult.

VIC: Did any particular interview stand out for you?

GEORGE: June Callwood—you know Casey House? She had one of the first AIDS hospices in the Western world. She was this incredible activist in Toronto. I had never met her, but she was one of the greats and I got a call one day from somebody saying, "Hey, June Callwood has been diagnosed with terminal cancer, she doesn't have a lot longer to go. She wants to do one more interview in her life, and she wants it to be you. She knows that you're not going to be afraid to go dark in this country, to really, really get into it." And I said, "Well, I would love to." So June and I sat down in her home a week before she passed away, and we talked about life and what comes next.

That interview to me was the most intense one. And when her husband, Trent, walked in the door, she started to whisper a little bit because she said he still hasn't really come to terms with this, and it was just so human. I was aware that this had to work. I had to get this right because this woman deserved a really meaningful conversation. That interview kind of helped people see me and our show in a different light. It was very intense. Her son had passed away, and so there was a tree in his honour. The door was open and we could see his tree. And so there was this triangle of us. I remember feeling a lot of internal pressure to get that right.

VIC: Any other particular shows you can look back on now too?

GEORGE: I think about how brilliant so many Canadian minds were. In terms of specific shows, I remember interviewing Michael J. Fox for the first time and being really connected to how strong and open he was. Interviewing Rick Hansen for the first time was really impactful for me, but funny—the celebrity part wasn't nearly as interesting to me as the really truthful, open conversations. Interviewing David Cronenberg and Bruce McDonald, because those were two filmmakers who were influential to me as a kid. But I really think it was Mike Fox and June Callwood.

VIC: You've talked to so many people right across America, England, some Europeans probably. Is there any difference in some of these nationalities?

GEORGE: Yeah. Yeah, for sure. It's a good question because it's about the level in which they are protected by their team, the trust their team has in them, or they have in their team. When you deal with the bigger celebrities from the U.S.—way more closed, way more layers between them and their authentic self because of their team. You'd sit somebody down in a chair, and all of a sudden people would come in, move a piece of hair and make sure everything was so proper, and then that guest would be afraid to move. They would just sit there staring at the camera, dead, because everything was so controlled. I understand why they did it, but you get a couple of old-timer breeds, you don't worry about that at all. They were just ready to go. So you can really tell the difference between the U.S. Hollywood system—just how much more you had to get to it, which was not always, but often. But the British ones and some of the Canadian ones, according to me, were a dream. How I looked and dressed, I probably did myself no favours.

VIC: Most of the people, the guests who come in, they were nervous.

GEORGE: Definitely. I didn't know that until I got to CBC and I watched really famous people get nervous. I don't get nervous. Nerves are not part of my thing. I certainly don't get nervous on television. Why would I? But I watched people—really famous people—get freaked out. That's why we had an alcohol bar in our green room, because guests needed to take the edge off They're freaking out. Some of them just have a drink if they want, you know? Then they kind of settle. Sometimes they had too many drinks and they'd be hammered. So inside the green room, I don't know if we were allowed to, but we stashed some bottles of booze, just so people could take a shot if they needed to.

And many did. I remember one day Snoop Dogg came in, and the entire floor smelled like weed. Someone said, "Hey, there's no smoking in here." And I'm like, "Then you tell Snoop he can't smoke." I'm not telling Snoop he can't smoke. We were a strange bedfellow with CBC, for sure.

VIC: Do you remember Kristen Kreuk?

GEORGE: Did I! It's funny—why would you bring her up? That's interesting. I believe that, of all the people I've ever interviewed on that show, Kristen was the most compelling. For this very talented, very accomplished, very beautiful actor—she had all these things you value on the surface. And then there were all these other things inside her that people in her position never get to do. I think about Kristen Kreuk all the time. In that interview, I remember being so blown away by what a powder keg of intention she was—beyond the arts, just as a human. I loved talking to Kristen Kreuk.

VIC: During all that time with the Corporation, the media seemed to be that you had a lot of freedom.

GEORGE: Yeah, tons. It's a network television job, so it's never total freedom, but I had more than most U.S. late-night hosts. CBC was really good to us. Sure, there were internal pressures, things they wanted me to do—some I probably should have, others I'm glad I didn't. But the bosses trusted us. They saw my connection with the audience was real.

MuchMusic played a big part. If you started high school watching me there, you graduated with me at CBC. That continuity built something unique. At Much, the music mattered, but it was really about us. That's what I've always believed my job was: to help build the emotional and intellectual railroad of the country. You make a film—I put it on the tracks and get it across the nation. My job is to help people feel seen.

Growing up in immigrant neighbourhoods, I never saw our Canada on screen. Ever. So I made it a point to represent those of us who didn't fit the mainstream image. Even though I'm a white guy, I'm white-presenting in a way that didn't reflect the TV culture either. My name—seventeen letters—didn't look like a "TV name." But I had an audience that saw themselves in me. Whether it was music at Much or conversation at CBC, what mattered was truth-telling.

That freedom—to tell the truth—is everything. Same as with filmmaking. Cast right, then step back. Great shows come from that freedom. Overmanage them, and the audience knows. That's why people like me, Kimmel, Stewart—we all worshipped at the altar of Letterman. Because what you saw was him, not some polished head reading a script.

It's really about independence. That's what matters. Not just the host, but the whole crew coming to the audience without an agenda. That's rare. CBC's mandate was to let us do exactly that. You don't get that on networks run by algorithms. People say CBC was conservative—and to a point, sure. But if you want to see real fear, go to an American network. They're scared of the FCC, of complaints, of upsetting sponsors. They have Standards and Practices departments where scripts are vetted line by line. That never happened at CBC.

VIC: Did you ever have to get legal involved in a dispute at Much or CBC?

GEORGE: Sometimes I'd run a line by legal at CBC, just in case, but there was no top-down script review. At Much, it was even looser. I'd shoot a show, edit it myself, hand the tape to a VCR operator in the basement, and they'd hit play at 11 p.m. No one above ever saw it first. They trusted us. And that's how it should be. Sure, news shows need vetting, fact-checking, balance. But for everything else—let the artists do what they do. All those classic films we revere? They were made by mad people doing mad things while the studios were asleep. That's how you get brilliance.

I work for a big U.S. company now. I've been with them five years. No notes. They let me do what I do. Why? Because I learned how to be me at CBC and MuchMusic. And CBC let me really hone that. It wasn't about being the star—it was about connecting people, about making space for conversation. That wouldn't have worked if I'd been forced to fit a mold. They never tried to make me fit. Not once. In fact, when I first got there, they had this blue book in the news department with defined roles—commentator, journalist, anchor. They asked which one I was. I said, "A bit of all three." They said, "There's no page for that." I said, "Then make one." And they did.

Some folks inside didn't like that. Didn't understand why I could get away with what I did. But if you want new, different, fresh—you have to let the people who do that actually do it. I was lucky. I came in with a voice already established. People asked if I'd take out my nose ring. One of the

CBC execs told me, "Don't. If you do, people will think we changed you. And we don't want them to think that." That was Heaton Dyer—an incredible person to work for.

There's something different about Canadians in the U.S. You can always tell. It's not about style, it's about sensibility. Canadians are observers. And we don't carry that same burden of American exceptionalism. U.S. culture runs on that belief—red, white, and blue to the core. Even if you try to shake it, it's in your DNA. We're not built that way. That space from the myth of national perfection opens up a different kind of vulnerability. It makes us more receptive.

Canada innovated like crazy. In the '60s, *This Hour Has Seven Days* tackled pollution before *Time* magazine even ran their first cover on it. It was groundbreaking. *The New Music* on Citytv? That predated MTV. But we never really projected that outward. Walk down the street in Vancouver—ask someone to name a Canadian film. Maybe they'll say *Porky's*, if you're lucky. There's just no infrastructure to celebrate our own.

That was part of why we did our show—to give Canadian creators a platform. And early on, I wanted to bring on other CBC folks. But I was told we couldn't. "It'll look like favouritism," they said. And I said, "It is." Why wouldn't we promote our own? *The Fifth Estate* did an incredible story—shouldn't we talk about it?

VIC: What did you bring from the world of music to television?

GEORGE: On Much, our whole job was to elevate Canadian musicians and show they belonged on the world stage. That is what coming from music helped me understand. Even within CBC, there were producers who said "don't." But we did it anyway. Jen, my EP, said, "We do that now." Because that's how you build an ecosystem. That's why the U.S. dominates media narrative—they've got the infrastructure: late-night, entertainment mags, platforms saying, "Look what we did." We don't.

And Canadians in media? We haven't historically backed our own. You can't go on air every night and say, "Look at me." That makes you look arrogant. So you need something else—an industry that lifts everyone. Kirstine Stewart got that. When she took over, she pushed to build that platform and she created places to highlight Canadian artists. We didn't have that before. In fact, CBC often resisted it—out of a desire to protect journalistic integrity. But we had to show them celebrating success wasn't selling out.

We brought Adrienne Arsenault on. Lloyd Robertson from CTV. We brought people from every network. Because it was never about competition—it was about Canada. Their success was ours, and vice versa. Around 2005, we really leaned into that. A lot of the people we featured wouldn't have made it onto a U.S. talk show. But we brought them in. Because they mattered.

Having your own voice—it's everything. Because when culture gets flattened, nothing grows. Social media was supposed to connect us to more ideas. But it's done the opposite. Algorithms push sameness. You used to travel and see a distinct scene. Now? TikToks and Reels everywhere, all cut from the same cloth.

That's where public broadcasting matters. A commercial outlet chases what sells. A public one has a duty to represent. And corporate media? They've taken public funds too. They just don't admit it. They got grants, tax breaks—but didn't build Canadian culture. CBC, for all its flaws, had an all-Canadian primetime lineup when I was there. Even when *Jeopardy*! aired—Trebek was Canadian! We were proud of that. And that's the point—representing all Canadians. Urban, rural, Atlantic, Prairie, Northern, Indigenous—everyone. Because we don't need one voice. We need many.

VIC: True. If we all sound the same, what's the point?

GEORGE: Agreed. Canada is a mosaic. So every shard of glass deserves a chance to catch the light. Canada's weird. We're an experiment that mostly succeeded. And sure, some think if we're not perfect, scrap it all. Others want to ignore our history and wave the flag blindly. But I think both voices matter. A country is a promise. And it's our job to keep striving toward it.

We're so open to suggestion. That's why it's critical to present many voices—so people can find themselves in the conversation. That's not just about being Canadian—it's about being human. One of the best things about growing up here? You didn't have to think about being Canadian. You just are. I celebrated it at the Olympics, when the Habs played the Red Army. But mostly, I was just a kid with roots in Eastern Europe and Egypt, like everyone else from somewhere else. That you could be yourself—that's what mattered. Public broadcasters have the responsibility to reflect that.

VIC: Thank you George, that was terrific.

Chapter 11

BRIAN STEWART

Brian Stewart is one of Canada's most respected foreign correspondents, known for his fearless reporting from war zones and humanitarian crises. Over his decades-long career with CBC, he covered major global events from Ethiopia to the Middle East, earning a reputation for moral clarity and journalistic rigour. His reporting has won numerous national and international awards, including recognition for his early coverage of famine and conflict.

VIC SARIN: Where were you born?

BRIAN STEWART: I was born in Montreal in 1942, midway through the Second World War. My earliest memories probably begin around Victory Day, when I was about three and a half. I spent my first five years in Montreal, a kind of bridge between the war era and the postwar revival of the late '40s. That marked me deeply. My childhood was filled with war games and survival games with neighbourhood kids. From very early on, I felt history moving around me. It got into my system.

Around age seven, we moved to Halifax, Nova Scotia. I had an idyllic seven years there—those golden postwar years by the sea. Halifax felt like a small town, but it was also a port city connected to the world. You could bike across it, yet ships arrived from everywhere—naval ships, freighters, refugees from Europe. Even as a child, I had a strong sense of a wider world. I'd hear stories from my parents, and I was fascinated. I started reading about the Korean War, the French Indochina War, postwar Europe. The world beyond our shores captivated me.

We'd ride our bikes down to the harbour and see the ships come in—freighters, Navy vessels, even U.S. aircraft carriers. My dad had a prominent store in Halifax, and through that I got to visit old Canadian aircraft carriers—before *The Bonaventure*. I even started clipping news stories at a young age. The first one I remember hearing on the radio was about grenades thrown in a place called Gaza. I didn't know what a grenade was—I asked my mom if it was a fruit! That must've been 1948 or '49. And here we are in a whole new century, and Gaza's still in the news.

When I was 12, we moved to England. My dad had a commercial post there—head of a buying office for Simpson's department store. We lived in Surrey, near London, and he commuted into the city. So I went from a small-town port city to England, attending a very good school. At 14, I wrote a school essay on what I wanted to be. I'd been watching the Suez Crisis unfold—this was a big moment for me. In England we had TV, unlike Halifax. The Suez Crisis and the Hungarian Uprising both happened in a matter of weeks, and I'd come home from school and watch grainy footage of chaos and war. I was fascinated—these reporters, standing in the middle of Budapest, telling the story. I asked my mom, "Who are these people?" And she said, "They're war correspondents." From that moment on, at 14, I wanted to be a foreign correspondent. I was already a history buff, and I began reading voraciously—about the Second World War, about refugees, about global conflict. I became absorbed in those narratives.

VIC: You were always drawn to the human condition, weren't you?

BRIAN: Very much so. Even in sports. I was drawn to underdogs. I kept scrapbooks, and the Brooklyn Dodgers were my team because they always lost to the Yankees. I hated the Yankees and their authoritarian air—those blue-striped uniforms!

BRIAN: My father came from a fairly well-off Presbyterian background in southern Ontario. My mother, though, she came from abject poverty in southern Ireland. She was born out of wedlock and lived through the struggles of the 1920s. She didn't talk much about it, but once in a while, she'd tell us stories. One was about the isolated farm she grew up on near Mullinavat, near Waterford. The Black and Tans, the British mercenaries, would come through and burn hedgerows if they thought there were snipers. They'd barge in, demanding water, intimidating the locals. Her childhood was terrifying. And extremely poor. That basic sympathy for the underdog—it started there.

VIC: The foundation of your desire to tell stories, and especially stories of the underdog, really began with those two influences?

BRIAN: Yes, and I'll say this, God help me—but part of it, too, was the thrill of war. As a very young teenager, war just seemed... thrilling. Big events, history being made, a front-row seat to transformation. I imagined being right there, witnessing the creation of a new Europe or a new Middle East. Of course, at that age, you don't think about death or trauma—just the adrenaline of it all. The excitement of a press scrum, of reporters swarming a crisis.

BRIAN: But also, there were the deeper things—the horror stories of Hungarian refugees, Russian tanks in Budapest, Suez unfolding. So much suffering and so much upheaval. All those bad things got into me too. And later, I learned that the terror could be more thrilling than the glamour. The real thrill was breaking news, getting the story out.

I went to a school called Baden College. There were 110 boys, but only five of us were day boys. I was one of them, so I'd go home at night and didn't have many friends around—most of the kids boarded. I'd listen to the radio—Voice of America, Radio Moscow, Radio Luxembourg, BBC. And I'd catch the evening newscasts, short as they were. Next day at school, I'd become "Radio Free Brian." The others didn't have access to TV or late-night radio, so I'd fill them in. Even some of the masters would come up and ask, "What happened in Suez today?" And I'd say, "Well, they've landed at Port Said. The French moved across the Channel. I think they're heading for the Red Sea now—maybe Cairo." It gave me this thrill—communicating news, telling stories others didn't know. I think most journalists have that in them.

I was reading the *Daily Telegraph* when I was 14 or 15—mostly for war news, world events, and UN updates. My ambition back then was to be a print foreign correspondent. It never even occurred to me that I'd work in television. I liked writing essays in school. I thought if I could become one of those print guys with a little press badge, I might get into baseball games for free—and then maybe go off and cover the odd war, witness history first-hand. That was my dream. All print. Television was so far outside my realm of ambition, I never even considered it.

As a kid, I saw the odd Hollywood movie—*The Jackie Robinson Story*, *Angels in the Outfield*, silly baseball films like that. There were always guys in the press box with press badges. My dad explained who they were: "Those are the newspaper guys," he said, "they get in free to the games." And I thought, imagine being paid to sit in Yankee Stadium, watch the Yankees play the Dodgers. That would be heaven. That was my first ambition.

But the more I got into international news, the more I was drawn in. And let's not forget—back then, newsreels were a big deal. You'd go to the movies, and before or between the films, you'd get ten minutes of action-packed updates—Suez, East Germany, riots, tanks. I was enthralled. I'd ask my dad if we could sit through the movie a second time just to watch the newsreel again. You couldn't record anything back then, so that was it. Newsreels, newspapers, and TV. That's the world I wanted to be in.

VIC: You need emotional connection to write something meaningful.

BRIAN: Exactly. You can't write about something you don't feel. And some of the events I covered... they were very hard. Devastating, actually. I paid a price for that later on. I'd realized early that journalism wasn't just about victory marches or celebrations. It was about burned houses, families walking the roads burdened with their lives, people dying in the streets. Refugees. Dead bodies. I learned very young that the world could be a cruel place for many. And I believed—naively perhaps—that we had to stop that. That villainous regimes like Nazi Germany had to be defeated, that unjust wars had to end. I had a simple-minded but passionate view. And emotionally, I couldn't help but be touched by what my mum had endured. Seeing a refugee mother on the road, I could picture her as my own mother—leaving Ireland at 14 with just two dollars to her name.

So, that was always on my mind, yeah. The seeds were planted early, I think. I was drawn to dramas that dealt with hardship and displacement. If there was a historical drama on the BBC—or any channel—that focused on refugees or suffering, I was immediately drawn to it. There was always this quiet voice in me asking, "How do we help those people?"

VIC: But did you ever struggle with the role of journalist versus witness?

BRIAN: Absolutely. I mean, I've done a few things that felt helpful, but there was always guilt. I'd be standing there with my camera, then going back to my hotel. What am I really doing? Am I just a voyeur? I remember Bangladesh during the famine. I didn't go on assignment, I went on my own. I wanted to understand what starvation felt like. I found a family I could shadow, try to grasp what they were living through. But by the end of the first day, I couldn't do it. The guilt was overwhelming. I could go back to my Hilton. Was I just exploiting this? The emotional weight became stronger as the years went on.

Eventually, that helplessness evolved into what I now know as moral injury. It stayed with me. I'd think back to families we passed by the side of the road—people who had to walk for two days to reach help. And I'd wonder: couldn't we have put a few people in our van? We always had a few U.S. bills in our pockets. Couldn't we have done more? But then the questions haunt you: Am I playing God, choosing one family over another? That line of thinking sticks with you. Sometimes it hits harder years later than in the moment. I still think about what we could have done for those people.

VIC: Any particular story you'd want to share from that time?

BRIAN: Well, maybe I'll come back to that, but just to cover how I got into television—originally, I was in print. My first love. I worked for the *Montreal Gazette* in the '60s—an incredible time for journalism. The Expo year, Centennial, 1967. I'd just come back from two years working in London in print. Joined the *Gazette*, and it was fantastic—nightlife, politics, culture. I wasn't married, life was fabulous. I was the first reporter, I believe, to use the term "Trudeaumania" in a news story. Then came the FLQ, the October Crisis—all of it unfolding around us.

Near the end of the '60s, I was offered a chance to work in local TV. It was never in my plan. I figured I'd try it for a year—see what it was like—and I stayed. That was around '69. I joined a show in Montreal called *Hourglass* as a studio host. Then, in '73, I became the CBC's first investigative reporter on television, based in Ottawa. I spent about six or seven years doing investigations and foreign affairs reporting, and that led to my first overseas assignments. Eventually, I was posted to London.

But through it all, I still felt like a newspaper man working in TV, not the other way around. And I think that newspaper discipline—structuring stories, writing clearly—served me well. Even so, I knew nothing about television at first. I was terrible. But later, based in London with my producer, Tony Berman, we caught wind of a famine in Ethiopia.

This was 1984. We'd already come through Beirut and other war zones that had left their mark. But in '84, we were one of the first crews, along with the BBC, to get into northern Ethiopia, into Tigray—ground zero of the famine. On November 1st, 1984, we aired our story. And I think it shook Canada. The response was unprecedented—an outpouring of compassion, support, donations. But for me, it was just the beginning of a series of devastating assignments. I returned to Ethiopia several times, also to Sudan, where we covered child slavery, refugee crises—it just kept getting darker.

I don't want to sound dramatic, but at times it felt like descending into a vortex of horrors. Each story pulled us deeper—across barren, drought-stricken lands, into camps filled with tens of thousands of people slowly dying. It felt like the aftermath of a nuclear war. And we were just trying to make sense of it, document it—witness it.

I remember a couple of times people said to me, "We know you Canadians are just Americans in disguise. You come in here trying to act all special, like the Swiss or something. But we know what you are." That really got my heart pounding, because I knew what that kind of suspicion could lead to. It became something I worried about. But aside from a few tense moments, I didn't encounter much suspicion. During the Cold War, when I went to East Germany or Poland for CBC, we were just seen as another NATO member. We got the same level of scrutiny as the rest—watched carefully, but nothing out of the ordinary.

VIC: And didn't North Korea at one point use maple leaf insignias to confuse the enemy?

BRIAN: Yes, exactly! They'd put maple leaves on their equipment—trying to pass as Canadian peacekeepers. There was so much confusion about who was who, and so we always tried to be very clear: "We're not Americans." We leaned into Canada's reputation for neutrality. It helped us feel more human, less politically threatening.

Looking back, that was one of our strengths. Being from Canada gave us confidence. We knew that most places we went, we'd be met with goodwill. People were usually helpful. Rarely did we find real animosity toward Canada. There were exceptions, of course—like South Africa. During the Mulroney years, with his vocal opposition to apartheid and support for Mandela, there was definitely suspicion from some white South Africans. They saw Canada as playing a mischief-making role. But that was rare.

Most of the time, I felt this strong sense of: "We're the good guys in the story." We're Canadian television. We're not exactly peacekeepers, but we're close. CBC News had this reputation—calm, neutral, peace-loving. That gave us a moral footing. And then there was the freedom we had. The CBC gave us extraordinary independence. Other journalists would say to us over drinks, "You guys are so lucky." Their networks needed to know their exact location every hour of the day. We could vanish for two or three days to chase a story.

VIC: You could write what you wanted?

BRIAN: Exactly. We'd decide what the real story was. We'd talk it through with head office, but they trusted us. They believed we were capable. And that kind of trust fuels you. It makes you want to do your very best. We'd say to ourselves, "We can't let them down." The last thing we wanted was to send home something weak—something subpar. The standards back home were high. You felt them behind you. And I think that's why we worked so hard. You didn't want to disappoint the team that believed in you.

BRIAN: I remember being on a trip with Bill Cunningham. We'd be sitting in a bar and I'd feel this guilt—like, "They brought me here. They're backing me. I'd better find something worthwhile." So I'd go back out and chase more leads, even when I was dead tired. It's a kind of reverse psychology. They didn't pressure us directly. They didn't micromanage. But precisely because they didn't, we pushed ourselves harder.

VIC: Because they believed in you.

BRIAN: Exactly. That belief made you anxious—not in a bad way, but in a way that kept you striving. The worst feeling would be to return with nothing. Nothing strong. Nothing original. You wanted to prove that CBC had made the right choice in sending you.

There was something else: a real pride of nationality. We didn't talk about it often, but we felt it. In the '80s, we felt like Canadian television news was entering a golden age. We were competing with the BBC, with the Americans—and they noticed us. At feed points, they'd see our material, and they'd compliment us. They knew we were doing excellent work.

To me, it felt like: Good. Canada's on the podium now. Not just in sports, but in journalism too. By that period, CBC had really become a top contender. It was known for its strong work. We took genuine national pride in doing stories with more context and nuance than what the Americans—or even sometimes the BBC—were feeding that night. That pushed us forward too. There was always this expectation that we'd perform well, and a real desire to show that Canadians were as good as anyone at this game. We were motivated—not just to do the job, but to excel. To not let our energy drop, to never go slack. We all bring our own background, values, and upbringing to the work. So the question becomes—how important is honesty when you're reporting a story?

Because you're inevitably looking through your own lens. And what's reality for you may be completely different for someone else. But how you feel—how you deliver it—goes into people's homes and can shape how they see the world.

VIC: There's that famous image—the photo of the colonel shooting the prisoner in Vietnam. It changed public perception instantly.

BRIAN: Absolutely. One picture can change everything. And that's a huge part of the responsibility. Sometimes, the visuals are so powerful, they overwhelm the story, and maybe that's okay. Take Ethiopia, for instance. Video was still relatively new, especially satellite video. So Canadian audiences saw the footage almost the same day. And we were showing them brutal, horrifying, gut-wrenching images of famine—images they hadn't seen before.

And I knew: yes, the visuals will carry this story. But I still had a job to do. Because it wasn't just about food and emergency relief. The deeper story was about systemic failure. That famine wasn't a one-off—it kept returning every ten years. So the real message was: we need long-term development solutions, not just aid. In those cases, we had to fight the visuals—to insist there was more to say. At CBC, we took that balance seriously. I would do tons of prep before a story—going beyond news feeds. I reached out to activist groups, think tanks, academic studies—what some might call the dry stuff. But that's what gave the story depth. That's what let me say, "Yes, here's what's happening—but here's 'why.'"

I was lucky, being based in London and Ottawa, to have access to those resources. That's how I avoided letting visuals dominate. I wanted nuance and substance to come through too. It's not easy. Covering a refugee crisis or famine, it's impossible not to be biased. When people are starving behind you, of course you're biased. You're standing there thinking: are we going to help, or are we just going to watch this get worse? But then, if you're covering political stories—South Africa, for example—you have to be more cautious. You can't be a mouthpiece for either side.

VIC: You did a lot of work in Africa.

BRIAN: Yes, I did. Partly because I was genuinely interested, and partly because the London bureau was responsible for much of Africa. We didn't have a CBC bureau in Johannesburg at the time—that fell to us in London. So I was in and out of the continent regularly. I liked working there. I found the people and the stories incredibly compelling. One story that's stayed with me for years was from Sudan. Around 1985, during the civil war in the south, we covered child slavery. It was horrifying. I remember going to see the International Anti-Slavery Society in London. I couldn't believe it still existed—but it does. Started in 1809, and they told me: there's more slavery today than in the Victorian era. That story haunted us. We wanted to raise global awareness. I think we did break some ground there.

And then, of course, there was meeting Mandela. Covering the anti-apartheid movement. That was a rare story with a hopeful ending. When we arrived, apartheid was crumbling, and we got to see the change happen. Mandela walked out of prison. Apartheid, this monstrous system, effectively dissolved before our eyes. Canada played a strong international role, and it felt like—for once—we were part of a genuinely good story. And that doesn't happen often in journalism.

I was also there when the Berlin Wall fell. I stood in Berlin that night. I watched the Cold War dissolve across Eastern Europe. For a kid who grew up thinking that divide was permanent, it was staggering to see it fall. That night, the joy was palpable—people celebrating freedom and imagining better futures for their families. It was unforgettable. As a journalist, you don't often get to witness that kind of light. But every once in a while, you do—and it reminds you why the work matters.

VIC: Exactly. We know from the moment of conception that we're headed toward the end. So the journey we take—this life—it's important to give people something for tomorrow. Hope.

BRIAN: Yes, absolutely. Hope is essential. It's not just about saying, "This is wrong." It's about asking, "How do we fix it? How can we help each other?" Finding that balance is crucial. I remember during the first Great Famine in Ethiopia in 1984, I was interviewing an aid worker on the ground. We were preparing to leave when he said something that's stuck with me ever since. He said, "You news people are very good at coming in and covering disasters and calamities. But you're not very good at sticking around, are you?" And I thought, he's right. We're not the first ones there—aid workers are. We arrive somewhere in the middle or near the end. We stay a short time and then leave. And the impression we leave behind is often one of hopeless ruin. We unintentionally suggest: this is the end. This place is lost.

That hit me hard. So I went back to Toronto and spoke with management. I said, "We have to do a better job covering reconstruction—the recovery." We need to show viewers that when people fall into catastrophe, into civil wars and unimaginable suffering, that's not permanent. That doesn't have to define their future. So they sent me back to Ethiopia six or seven times. I was able to report on Ethiopia emerging from famine, on the recovery, on resilience. We returned to South Africa and other regions where we'd previously witnessed terrible events—this time to document the rebuilding. These were stories of life after death.

We were showing that the people viewers had seen in the depths of tragedy were now educating their children, piecing their lives back together, moving toward a brighter future. Because things *do* often get better. Of course, there's a kind of guilt. You walk into disaster zones, you get your footage, and you leave. There's a question that lingers: what am I doing? Should I be in the trenches helping, feeding children, fetching water? Instead, I'm standing there with a camera.

Lebanon in the 1980s was another example. We'd go in for weeks—covering militias, truck bombs, unspeakable carnage. Then, just four hours after leaving Beirut, I'd be back in London, meeting friends at a pub, going to a dinner party. The contrast was surreal. After a while, I started asking: is this it? Year after year, are we just documenting pain? What's the point, if nothing improves? It gets to you—this idea that all we're doing is showing people more carnage. That's not sustainable.

So I tried something different. I learned that a renowned architect was still living in Beirut. This was during the shelling—missiles were falling nightly. And he was working on plans for the future of the city. We visited him up in the hills. On his patio, overlooking the smoke rising from the ruins, he laid out maps and drawings. He told us, "Beirut is going to be the most beautiful city again. Better than Paris on the Mediterranean." It might've felt like a stretch—but it mattered. We were trying to show that even amidst devastation, there was a vision for something better.

I liked that story. And about fifteen years later, people began returning to Beirut and saying, "Wow. It's beautiful again." It wasn't a fantasy after all. But the biggest problem I see, looking back, is this: how do you convey the true complexity of governance? Governing in this world is exhausting—physically, emotionally, intellectually. Especially in an age of 24/7 news cycles, social media outrage, and vanishing civility.

The issues are increasingly tangled. Populations are growing. Demands are multiplying. NGOs, factions, insurgencies—it's overwhelming. And television struggles with that. We often oversimplify. I was fortunate that CBC gave me the scope to dig into those complexities. But the average viewer sees a news clip and thinks, "Why don't they just fix it?" They don't see that what looks like chaos is often the result of twenty competing factions and centuries of unresolved tension. TV hasn't yet figured out how to explain that.

VIC: And now, with the digital world, we're connected in real time. We can see what's happening anywhere instantly.

BRIAN: Exactly. The reporting has definitely changed. This new technology—instant updates, social media—has shifted everything. I'm sure it's changed even more than I realize, since I've been out of the newsroom for a few years. If I were still there, I'd be pushing for value-added journalism. Reporting that gives people more than just the surface. Something that makes them come back to TV news—not for sensation, but for insight.

That's what we have to emphasize—areas where we're genuinely strong. We could be leaders in local reporting, in explaining big geopolitical stories, in dealing with nuance and complexity. It's about educating the audience, helping people feel that if they come to us, they'll get a well-thought-out story. Not something that just echoes the loudest advocacy group—but something grounded and fair. We should give them the full picture—not only the demands being made, but why governments are having trouble addressing them, and what complexities lie underneath. That's the direction I'd push for. No misinformation or disinformation. Because let's be honest—ten people might tell you ten different versions of the same story. How do you know which is true?

VIC: What you want is honesty.

BRIAN: Exactly. Honesty—no matter what you're doing—is fundamental. But there's always subjectivity. And it's so important for people, especially the broader public, to feel that there's a place they can go for the honest story. A trusted source. I've never seen myself as some media guru. I'm not someone like Mark Starowicz, who designed some of the best courses and formats for journalism in this country. But one thing I do believe in strongly is this: mainstream media has to fight back—differently. When you had brilliant minds like Mark Starowicz, Stéphan McQueen, Tony Burman, and of course, Peter d'Entremont—people who brought ambition, originality, and drive—they didn't want to be third-rate. They wanted to lead.

Why shouldn't CBC open itself up to collaboration—with newspapers, with local broadcasters, with radio? Imagine a centre for communications where CBC shares its facilities, its journalism, and welcomes in some of the best and most respected minds. That kind of collaboration could give public media a rebirth. There's got to be a sense that we can turn to the big battalions, the reliable brigades, so to speak. I honestly think we're approaching a point where all these separate networks—especially smaller ones—won't be viable. It would be smart to start sharing news and current affairs content more strategically. Print media, too, is in terrible shape. So why not share? Work together. Create a unified mainstream media that can be respected again—not just at the top, but at the local level too.

VIC: You were influential at the start of *The Fifth Estate*, weren't you?

BRIAN: I was actually the first person to work on *The Fifth Estate*. Yes, the very beginning. I did the first two seasons. There was so much vision and boldness in that team. I remember asking myself—reporting, to me, is about going to find the truth and then reporting it. Honesty—that's always been crucial for me. Whether you're a reporter in the field or a parliamentary correspondent, it comes down to honesty. Yet I started to notice how much preconditioning was happening—how many people were coming in with a pre-written narrative.

VIC: So, do you think honesty has shifted in journalism? And how does that relate to the commercial model—where ratings are everything?

BRIAN: Exactly. When you're working in a commercial station, it's about audience share. What segment of society are you trying to attract? And then you tailor the story to meet their expectations. But that's where public broadcasting plays a critical role—it's one of the few places left where true independence can exist.

VIC: So independence—an unfiltered voice—that's what matters?

BRIAN: Yes, absolutely. The ability to describe a situation honestly and without preconceptions is vital. That's one of public broadcasting's greatest strengths. It shouldn't aim to please advertisers—or political parties. Its job is to serve the people of Canada, the taxpayers. And presumably, what they want is the truth—not a biased or slanted version of events.

Now, one thing that worries me—and I've talked to people like Chris Waddell about this, who taught journalism at the University of Ottawa—is that since around 2010, many journalism students have been entering the field as activists. Their goals are set from the outset: they want to campaign for environmental issues or racial justice, for example. All noble causes, but they come in with a mission. And the danger is, if your entire journalistic career is built around promoting one message, I have to wonder, how independent is your mind, really? How much are you questioning your own sources, your own assumptions? That's where public broadcasting must be especially cautious. It's not meant to serve causes. It's meant to serve truth. And it's not a soapbox for leading movements. Deciding what to cover, what not to cover—it's a big responsibility.

VIC: So how do those editorial decisions get made?

BRIAN: Usually in story meetings, where you've got fifteen people around a table debating what's worth covering. That's the ideal approach—it's how we did it on *The Journal*, under people like Mark Starowicz. You bring in competing interests: foreign affairs, domestic issues, everything gets a hearing. It's democratic, but you still need strong leadership. Someone has to say, "We are a marketplace of ideas—but we cannot become an incoherent shouting match." We have to deliver news that's as close to reality as we can get. That takes discipline. If leadership caves to internal factions pushing particular agendas, that's where things fall apart.

People at the top of journalism spend a lot of time thinking about new directions, new approaches. It's a fine balance—if you fall behind, you're in trouble. But if you get too far ahead, that's dangerous too. If you look like you're out there every night trying to lead society in a particular direction, that's trouble. But if you're constantly playing catch-up, that's another kind of problem.

VIC: Let me go back to something more personal. As a journalist, are there stories that have stayed with you, sustained you—or haunted you—all these years?

BRIAN: Absolutely. The one story that still haunts me is the famine in Ethiopia in 1984–85. Nothing has ever affected me like that. I thought I'd seen the worst the world had to offer—in places like El Salvador and war-torn Beirut. But Ethiopia was something else entirely. When I heard I'd be going into northern Ethiopia, into what was expected to be the worst famine since the Second World War—or perhaps the worst in peacetime—I prepared myself physically and emotionally. I trained, expecting it would be tough. But nothing could have prepared me.

What I saw was almost otherworldly. The famine was at the gates of every city, at the doors of every town. The dead lay along the streets. Children were completely emaciated. It was like concentration camp footage—people just lying in the streets, wasting away. The wind howled, dust filled the air. At one point, the Red Cross estimated that six million people could die. It felt like witnessing a slow-motion Holocaust.

In one village, we encountered a little girl who was starving. She seemed to die on camera. We stopped recording to give her dignity in death. Hours later, we returned for the funeral—and there she was, alive in a nurse's arms. She'd been given one last injection and survived. That moment never left me. I grew close to her family—they'd endured every imaginable horror. Years later, I kept thinking about them. Around 1987 or 1988, Tony and I decided to return. We wanted to find that family again—to show that survival is possible, that there can be life after death. We did find them, and we made a documentary called *Life After Death*.

By chance, footage of that girl's face was used during Live Aid, and she became an unintentional symbol of the famine. Even now, I remain in touch with her family. I've supported them through education. They've become friends—dear friends. And of course, as many people know, northern Ethiopia has again faced war and near-famine in recent years. The family's situation remains precarious, so we stay in contact. I'll never stop following Ethiopian news. I'll never truly be free of that story. Even after I retired, I went back on my own, just to see how things were. It saddens me, in some ways. But I'm also deeply grateful for the connection. That story lives in me. Always will.

VIC: You've lived a rich, meaningful life. Are there people outside of family—mentors, colleagues—who helped shape that journey?

BRIAN: Oh yes. Besides my family, I owe so much to people like Trina McQueen. She had an enormous influence on me. I was terrible when I started in TV—just awful. But she saw something in me. Some potential. And Tony Berman—one of the best news producers I've ever worked with. He could get us into countries others couldn't dream of accessing. He was amazing in the field. It was a privilege to work with him. We shared a vision, and he helped me do some of the best work of my career.

Tony and I were very different in some ways, but he had a huge influence on me. He was incredibly organized—the kind of person who could handle any problem that came up on a shoot. I was hopeless at that. And then, of course, there was Mark Starowicz. What can you even say? He brought us to a level in current affairs television we didn't know was possible. He put us on a world stage. Honestly, we haven't really seen anything like it since. I was so lucky to have worked with that generation of professionals.

And the producers—I had extraordinary producers over the years, with very few exceptions. Carmen Merrifield, for example, taught me a great deal about visual storytelling. She helped sharpen my eye, helped me grow in that area enormously. And then the camera crews—someone like Mike Sweeney—he was brilliant. You'd come back from the field and want to rewatch everything, not just to edit, but to marvel at how he captured the perfect image for every moment. He had such precision, such intuition. Working with people who had pride in their craft, who'd fought their way through a very narrow door to be where they were—that's inspiring. It creates an atmosphere where everyone is determined to do the best job possible. And you rise to meet that.

VIC: Do you have any regrets?

BRIAN: Sure, probably quite a few. I can think of stories I should've done better—five or six that still bug me. I've kicked myself over them. And then there are the emotional costs. Some stories wounded me, and I carried that grief for years, even decades. But that's part of the deal. You don't go into war zones or humanitarian crises without knowing you'll pay a price. I knew, going in—not fully, but I had a sense. Those wounds, though, they remind me I was alive. That I wasn't just in it for the thrill of the story. They're proof that I was human in the middle of it all.

VIC: Let's talk about something I think about a lot—the chemistry of the person on camera. I work with actors, and I see it all the time. You can have all the technique, but sometimes it's just about presence. It's intangible, but real. I feel like you had that kind of chemistry—very human, very personal. Do you think that had something to do with your success?

BRIAN: I was mostly unaware of it. But I do think there were stories where I felt things very deeply, and that shaped what I wrote. When I was on camera, people sometimes said they remembered a line I'd used, or a phrase with a bit of poetry that stayed with them. I'd say, "Well, it got through to you because it got through to me first." I was putting my emotion into the story, and maybe that's why it resonated. I wasn't trying to be more emotional than anyone else, but I had a connection with the audience. People would say they felt it. And the truth is, sometimes when I was writing, I was close to tears myself.

VIC: That's the part that moves me most—how you carried that pain, and yet still had to deliver the facts. Especially in Ethiopia. Was that hard?

BRIAN: Very. We had constant discussions—especially during the El Salvador war—about what horrors could or should be shown on TV. I was quite conservative. I saw footage in El Salvador and Beirut that I thought shouldn't be broadcast. Body parts, mutilation—I didn't think that served the story. But Ethiopia was different. The images were worse, because people weren't just dead—they were dying, right in front of us. I struggled, but ultimately we decided: we had to show the worst. We feared the world wouldn't respond otherwise. And if the world didn't respond, millions would die. We felt a responsibility to make the audience see what we were seeing—not just sanitized suffering. If they felt even a portion of what we felt, they might act. And many did.

VIC: And the responsibility didn't end with the footage…

BRIAN: No. Even a few months later, I began to worry. I thought—what happens the next time? What if there's another famine, but the images aren't as shocking? Maybe aid delivery is more efficient, maybe the streets aren't lined with bodies—but the need is still there. Did we set the bar so high for horror that people will wait and wait until it's "as bad as Ethiopia" before they care again? That thought has troubled me ever since.

I always loved the interview shows. I loved sitting where you are now—beside a camera, across from someone, just talking. That was a real love of mine. But being in the field was great too. I also loved playing with the new technology. Being able to tell foreign affairs stories with real tools—maps that move, graphics that explain—it was revolutionary. The tools we have today are remarkable. Forty or 50 years ago, it was basically the chalkboard. Now, we can walk people through incredibly complex stories.

VIC: What brings you happiness?

BRIAN: What gives me happiness? A story well told. Then coming home, opening a good book, putting my feet up, and reading—having nothing pressing for a couple of days. That's happiness for me. And I'm a hopeless nostalgic—my wife says so. I love revisiting the better parts of life, reliving key moments. The whole arc of time—from the Second World War right up to today—fascinates me. I get real pleasure going back and reading about it.

As for what's next? I think I've done it. I don't really have a desire to report anymore. Certainly not to be a foreign correspondent again. I'm too old. I don't have the nerves. I probably never did, to be honest. These days, I'd rather hide under the bed than go abroad. And I don't want to be an analyst either. That feels like a younger person's game now. The old, moth-eaten lion has had his time. I'm content. I do wish I'd written more on the side—maybe even tried fiction like a lot of reporters do. Espionage, maybe. But aside from that, I've got no real regrets.

VIC: You've made peace with your journey?

BRIAN: Yes. I'm not sitting in the press box anymore. I don't need the ringside seat to history. I'm perfectly happy in the upper bleachers now, coffee and hot dog in hand, watching it unfold from a distance.

VIC: What would you say is the greatest richness of your life?

BRIAN: People. That may sound corny, but it's the truth. Meeting people from every walk of life—hearing their stories, finding common ground—that was the greatest privilege. It was always about people. Not just the "interesting" ones by some standard, but the so-called ordinary lives. Those were often the most fascinating of all. Extraordinary lives are impressive, sure. But people raising families, holding things together, showing up—that's genius in its own way. That's the richness. I thought, when I started out, it would be about dramatic events. Riots in the streets, mountain bombardments, thunderous history. But in the end, it was about the people.

One day in Beirut, I interviewed a man I called "the guy with the worst job in the world"—he was the bomb disposal expert. He disarmed 18 bombs a day. And he was raising his 12-year-old son to take over the job. He said the boy was looking forward to it. I wasn't so sure. The next day, I met a Quebec wrestler making a name for himself in Beirut. East Beirut loved him. That's how it went. One day bombs, the next day wrestling. And on and on. The celebrities, oddly enough, were often less interesting. Their lives were so managed—so scheduled, so curated. But the so-called ordinary people? That's where the real fascination lay.

VIC: Empathy really comes through in everything you say.

BRIAN: Well, I sometimes think of myself as the last of the cowardly correspondents. People assume foreign correspondents are brave, that they love the bang-bang, the danger. I hated the danger. When I was young, I studied bullfighting for a while. At 16, in Spain, I thought maybe I could do it. I ran in front of the bulls in Pamplona, nearly got killed, and turned against it forever. I realized my nerves had limits. In El Salvador and other war zones, I was never brave. That gave me empathy for the rest of the world—for people who don't want danger, war, or trauma. It's good for a reporter to have a little coward in them. It helps you understand fear's impact on the world. I think that traces back to my mother's childhood trauma—growing up in Ireland during the Civil War in deep poverty. That left a mark.

VIC: Do you miss anything?

BRIAN: Not really. I used to think I'd miss the great meals in Paris or that 1969 six-week shoot on the future of Europe where we stayed in the best hotels. But now I just remember how overfed we were. The glamour doesn't appeal to me anymore. I like the simple life. Maybe 30 years ago I'd have wanted to be back in Spain covering some crisis—but now, I'm very happy in the sedate sanctuary of old age. As Shakespeare said, age makes cowards of us all. In my 40s and 50s I was still a foreign correspondent. I even covered Afghanistan in my 60s.

VIC: So you don't miss the money or the spotlight?

BRIAN: You know, I never gave much thought to money in television. I was well paid, yes, but I wasn't ambitious for more. I was just grateful for the life—the opportunity. Even when exhausted, it saw me through.

VIC: You were wonderful, Brian. Thank you. You gave so much—and not just stories, but heart. That connection will stay with me.

Chapter 12

TRINA MCQUEEN

Trina McQueen is a pioneering journalist and broadcasting executive who helped shape Canadian media through her leadership at CBC and CTV. She began as a reporter and news anchor before rising to executive roles that influenced programming and public policy. Throughout her career, McQueen championed Canadian content, journalistic independence, and the advancement of women in media leadership.

VIC: Let me take you back in time a bit. Where were you born?

TRINA: A little Ontario small town on the Bay of Quinte. I had a very ordinary upbringing. My mother was home all the time and my father was an engineer. So, I started out very well. But one thing that happened to me when I was in school was my English teacher, Mr. Read. I was in grade 12 and Mr. Read went to the *Belleville Intelligencer*, the newspaper, and said, "I've got somebody who could do some writing about high school for you. Will you take her?" My last name was Janitch then, so it was by Trina Janitch. The other thing that happened was Mr. Read had another good writer in his class. So, he went again to the *Belleville Intelligencer* and said, "I have another wonderful student." At the time she was called Stephanie Dahl. Her name now is Stephanie Cameron and she became a co-host of *The Fifth Estate*. So, Belleville gave something to the CBC. Besides that, I was a cheerleader and I was on the student council. I was the kind of person that got involved.

VIC: So, very early in your life, you were drawn toward journalism?

TRINA: Oh, of course. My mother would listen to CBC radio all the time.

VIC: Do you remember any of the shows or events you were drawn toward?

TRINA: I remember as a teenager going upstairs at night to get ready for bed, and my father would have the 11 o'clock *National* on every single night. I remember saying to him at the top of the stairs, "Can you turn that stuff down?" So that's how I got introduced to national news—by having to listen to it. I eventually went to Carleton and took journalism there. My first job after that was a summer job for the *Toronto Telegram*, which was the big newspaper in Toronto. They always hired six interns for the summer. This was a big step for them because they were going to hire one female out of the six—and I was the one who was hired. And, by the way, the union said the *Telegram* was being unfair to men. They said you couldn't have a woman unless there was no better man. So, it was ruled an unfair labour practice. They didn't want me to have the job. However, the *Telegram* editors were pretty tough, and I did get the job.

VIC: Do you remember your first assignment?

TRINA: Yes. I went to the CNE—Canadian National Exhibition—and they put me on stage as a clown. I was made up as a clown, and I wrote my story. I think the first line was, "All beginning reporters feel like clowns. I was one." And the story continued about being up on the stage as a clown.

VIC: Did you ever feel like you were a clown?

TRINA: There were lots of times when I felt like a clown.

VIC: Do you remember when you joined the CBC?

TRINA: How did I join the CBC? Oh yeah—I was about to be fired. My first job in television wasn't at CBC, but at a CTV show. It lasted 50 years. It was *W5*. They were just starting *W5*, and the guy who produced it made a deal with the news guy that I would work on *W5* over the winter, and when it was off for the summer, I would work in the CTV newsroom and do journalistic things. They shook hands on it. That was great—but they didn't tell the guy who was in charge of CFTO *(Ed's note: Toronto's CTV channel)* that this was happening. He didn't want to deal with the CTV network and added, "Besides, a woman doesn't have the authority to do the news." He said I had to go. So, I hopped over to the CBC and tried to get in there. They gave me a summer job, and I stayed there for a very long time.

VIC: I remember you so well. My own recollection, the real job you had—you were very gentle, very soft spoken and that helped people open up. That was your strength. But inside, you were still—which I discovered later—very strong in exactly what you wanted. Did you ever feel that, being a woman, you were receiving a bad time from male reporters?

TRINA: I didn't feel uneasy about men as a group, but there were plenty of men I felt very uneasy with individually. Not because of anything sexual, just because they had their own way of behaving. They weren't really interested in having a young woman with them.

While I was new at CBC, I got married to my husband who was a producer there. When I got pregnant, I wanted six months off, and I was told by the CBC that I couldn't have leave—paid or unpaid. This was long before maternity leave. They said I would lose my job if I took the time off. But my boss at the time—a guy—took on the CBC. He kept writing little notes to them: "What if she only works two days a week?" And then they'd put it in the mail, and the HR person would be away on something else, and the answer wouldn't come back for weeks. When it finally came, it would be a "No." So, then he'd wait a while and think up another good reason why I should be allowed to stay. The same thing would happen again. That guy saved my job. Because by the time I was ready to come back, the whole matter was still floating among memos. It was really wonderful—he used all the politics and internal workings of the CBC to save my job.

VIC: You were in the news as a reporter?

TRINA: I decided at one point that I didn't want to be a reporter. The thing about a reporter is you don't always get the best story. Sometimes the best story is in Vancouver, but you're in Toronto—you don't get to do it. So, I wanted to be on the assignment desk. Then I'd know whatever the big story was, I'd be covering it. I wouldn't be on air, but I'd have my fingers in it and make decisions. I loved that. I became the assignment editor.

VIC: So, it wasn't about being a star on camera.

TRINA: No. It was about what you're doing and how important that piece is.

VIC: Can you talk a bit about management? Because you've done both sides—you've been in the trenches, and also a boss. I'd love to know, when you were in control, what kind of stories drove you, what made you say, "This is important?"

TRINA: How can I say this? I liked stories that were changing things. If something in a legislature was making a big change, or in business we were getting something new—or a disaster had happened. I liked stories that pushed forward or fell off. Both of those were interesting to me. It was just as interesting to investigate why something bad had happened as it was to put something amazing on air.

We were very proud of our foreign correspondents. One of the things about those correspondents is they looked at the world from a Canadian viewpoint. Yes, they were in a foreign country—but they were thinking,

"What do I have to tell Canadians about this story so they can appreciate it?" That's what I liked to look for.

VIC: Can you recall a story that still stands out as absolutely brilliant?

TRINA: I have a couple of stories. This one is funny, and it's about Joan Donaldson. I don't know if you ever worked with her. Anyway, I was Head of News, and she reported to me as Head of the very brand-new news channel, then called CBC Newsworld. To launch it, we were going to do it in a way that newsrooms all across the country would be part of, all throughout the day. Halifax was the morning show and Calgary was the evening show. On the day it began, we decided that she and I would go to Halifax and say, "Good morning, we're on the air." Then we would rush to the airport, and be in Calgary in time for the evening show to wrap up the whole thing.

Well, Joan enjoyed a good time. And the night before we got on the plane, she had enjoyed a good time. She was sort of, you know, out of it, the whole thing. On the plane, I watched a movie—*Beaches* with Bette Midler. It was a really sad movie, and I cried the whole way through. So, when we got off, she was still sort of half asleep, and I was stained with tears. And that's the way we started the news channel.

But while we were in the air, there was more going on. You could tell as soon as we landed—people were looking at us like something serious had happened. Turns out there'd been a major technical problem. Every time the hosts would introduce someone—like, "And now here's Wendy Mesley"—instead of the right tape rolling, Knowlton Nash would appear. Over and over again. The control room couldn't figure it out. Total chaos.

And that's how CBC Newsworld went on the air: two of us a mess on arrival, and everyone else scrambling. Somehow, we got through it.

VIC: Brilliant. Do you have another?

TRINA: Here is another one I remember. Michael Maclear was in India and I had booked him an interview with the President of India—can't remember who it was at the time. Anyway, he arrived at the President's office and sat there for ages. Finally, the President came out and said, "I'm sorry, Mr. Maclear, but we have just gone to war" and then explained about the war. Mike was able to get on the phone right away, flew back to Canada, and we had that story straight from the President's mouth—minutes before he officially declared war. That was exciting.

VIC: Did you ever feel pressure as Head of CBC News—like from directors or politicians?

TRINA: Oh yes. During the referendum, Brian Mulroney was Prime Minister and the Meech Lake Accord was going on. We had just launched Newsworld—live news. He was absolutely convinced that CBC and Radio-Canada should be on his side—talking about how the Quebec referendum must pass and Canada must stay united. He felt the French network was giving too much time to the separatist side.

They even came after some of our coverage—especially on *The Journal*. I never really understood it, but Barbara Frum did an interview with Mordecai Richler and Mulroney went bananas. He thought Mordecai was saying, "Let them go, let them separate." The fallout landed on my head. I never told anyone involved, but they just wanted me gone.

VIC: So, you felt the pressure? What did you do?

TRINA: I never told *The Journal* team or any reporters. They just carried on doing what they were doing. Mulroney had a French news staffer fired, and he tried to have me fired too. That one was fuzzier. They didn't fire me, they just transferred me to another job. I'm not sure how to talk about it because in the middle of it, Barbara Frum died. In some ways… I don't know what to say about that.

VIC: Canada was sad when Barbara died.

TRINA: Yes, you are right. She was brilliant.

Overall, Meech Lake was about how news stories come alive, or die. The Meech Lake Accord started to be debated in 1994. The idea was that if all the provinces signed a document, then we would be a country that was not going to be separated. At the time, there was a strong belief in separatism in Quebec, and the provinces went at it—conference after conference—and it wasn't settled.

What started the death of Meech Lake was a feather. Elijah Harper, a member of the Indigenous community and an MP, held up a feather and said, "No." That brought down Manitoba. Around the same time, Clyde Wells in Newfoundland was still deciding whether to support it or not. A few hours later, he announced that Newfoundland would not. And that's how it died—on television. There was no time to write about it, no time to hold meetings. Elijah stood up on CBC Newsworld. Clyde Wells stood up on CBC Newsworld. And just like that, the constitutional initiative was gone. We were suddenly back in that place of fear that Canada might come apart.

So what saved it? Well, people just went home. They slept on it, maybe for a year or so. And eventually, they started again. That time, they managed some kind of settlement. But to me, the point was this: television—live journalism, moving from province to province—was part of Meech Lake. It marked the beginning of something new: television becoming more than just an observer.

Look, the big picture is that we almost lost the country. I'm not saying television caused it. But without live TV, maybe things would have slowed down. Maybe they could've talked Elijah out of raising that feather, or talked Clyde around. But because it happened live, it happened. Period. Television became the rule. And before that moment, it didn't have that kind of power. Canadian journalism changed that day.

VIC: What role, then, did CBC or media in general play in keeping Canada together—or pulling it apart?

TRINA: It is not one or the other. The point is, we had this instrument of live television that people could watch and react to instantly—and we used it. At that moment, we used it in a way that nearly made the country come apart. But it could have gone the other way. The possibility with live television is that things happen instantly, without any way to control it—except to go back and do it again. That had never happened before. That leaders of the country could, in a few minutes, change the direction of the country. The responsibility of media—particularly news media—is huge. You have to expect that if people are on live television, they're going to do something either wonderful or something that starts a terrible occasion.

Live television can make good things happen too. I'm just saying this is a technology. Like going from daguerreotypes to actual pictures. It changes everything when you can hear something the moment it's said. Elijah Harper and his feather—that was the beginning of that for Canada. Not good, not bad—just powerful.

VIC: You just mentioned the truth—how fast perception can shift.

TRINA: I've always believed the destiny of Canada was tied to technology. We're still here, but we could have fallen apart that day.

VIC: All right. That's fantastic. You really got to the core of it. As head of CBC News, how was your relationship with the correspondents and reporters? How much control did you have, and how much did you listen to them?

TRINA: I tried to listen. Ottawa was always the big place for stories. The Ottawa bureau had brilliant reporters, run by a guy named Elly Alboim. He really knew his stuff. If he came to me and said, "We've got to do this story," I'd say, "Fine, but keep it under 2.5 minutes." I was pretty easy on people I trusted. And I was lucky to have him and those reporters. The news was hot.

VIC: You seem to have had a strong feeling for that relationship.

TRINA: Of course. They'd bring me stories, I'd relay them. But yes, I also had my own mandates—stories I thought were important.

VIC: Can you give an example?

TRINA: I do remember one story that upset me. An artist had drawn a portrait of Mulroney that made him look like an obscene object. It went on the air without my knowledge. I hit the roof. I remember writing and saying, "What are you? A bunch of frat boys in Grade 12?" I was furious.

VIC: How much control did you have over reporter assignments and hiring?

TRINA: I was usually consulted about hiring, sometimes did the hiring myself.

VIC: Didn't you hire Brian Stewart? What did you see in him?

TRINA: He was in love with the news. As a reporter and anchor, that showed. His heart was in it. A good reporter gets the facts, but when they have heart—that's the best. Brian was one of the smartest reporters ever. His stories showed that. He could find out a lot, diagnose it, and decide how to approach it. We had a very funny lunch recently—him, Tony Berman, and Don Newman. It was very good. We vowed to do it more often.

VIC: How much freedom does a journalist need to tell a story without bias?

TRINA: You can't always control the story the way you'd like. You have to take the story as it is. Be truthful. Let the viewers decide, let the reporter decide, let the people in the story be part of that. You have your lens, but others do too.

Technically, journalism has changed since I started. It's easier to do stories, get them on the air. We can use pictures in new ways. Cameras and film have improved. But the essence of journalism—if you read the *New York Times* in the early 1900s—you'll still see the same persuasion, instinct, and desire to do the story properly and help people understand why it matters.

VIC: Sometimes I'm there when something happens, but the way it's reported in media—TV, radio, print—it's like three different stories. How do you know what to trust?

TRINA: There are two things: the journalist and the audience. They may have completely different ideas about the story. That's true even more now with social media. Journalists get criticized, blamed, and hung out to dry by people who aren't trained, who have different objectives. There's so much untruth in the viewer now. People used to be willing to think and consider. Now they turn to TikTok or X. They're not getting the facts or real examination of what's going on. It's harder for people to really understand the facts of what's happening now—in this country, Canada, or in other countries. The people who run the countries... there are so many strange stories out there because people feel something, rather than examine something and learn something, like a journalist would.

VIC: What do you think of public broadcasting as you sit here?

TRINA: Well, public broadcasting varies from country to country. For instance, PBS in the United States is entirely different in every way from the BBC, and CBC fits in a different way. Some public broadcasting, in countries that are controlled at the top, is made to fit whoever is running the particular country. It's hard to decide which opinion you'll go with as a viewer, more so than it used to be.

VIC: Do you still follow the news?

TRINA: Well, I don't write anything now, but I teach. I'm a teacher in an MBA program *(Ed's note: Schulich School of Business at York University).* And I do that to encourage this program we have now, which is arts and media. We're trying to keep that as part of the MBA, and it's been pretty successful so far. But not everybody wants to be a journalist, so we have to be very good recruiters. We make sure that students with brains and management ability and leadership—and understanding of all the technology we have now in journalism—get into the MBA course. It's not easy, but the ones who are in it are absolutely brilliant. I'm thrilled to be in class and hear the opinions of the students. It gives me as much pleasure as breaking a big story did in the old days.

VIC: Anything you'd like to add?

TRINA: What makes me thrilled, happy, excited is when I see a journalist who has figured out something I've never figured out—someone doing something remarkable. It's not what I did, it's what others in my environment did. And there's nothing better than being part of a group that's intelligent, thoughtful, concerned about the issues they report on. That's what excites me. It doesn't exist any longer, but I was the first person at the CBC to start a program called *Witness.* It was only open to journalists, photographers, camera people who were freelance. In other words, it was their place for an independently made documentary on the CBC. Then, of course, I went to Discovery Channel after that, and it was all *Witness*-type programs because we had independent producers doing our work. And I've always felt that was really important in Canada. I'm very sorry that the rules, regulations, and investment in independent production aren't as good as they should be. It's really hard to get something made in Canada.

After Discovery Channel, I was hired by Ivan Fecan. He bought that channel, and other media companies, and asked me to run CTV. I liked that he was always pushing new ideas, sometimes risky. One of those was buying *The Sopranos* for CTV. It was wonderful—a deep and beautifully produced series, but with its high levels of violence and sex, it definitely was a risk. In the United States, it was turned down by all the major networks. At CTV, we decided to buy it. We did advance showings to opinion leaders, including Italians, religious leaders and some CRTC people. We put 'warning' signs throughout the program. The U.S. lawyer who did the sale contract to us insisted on paragraphs releasing the seller from responsibility for a list of every naughty word in the series. But, it was a huge success. There was controversy, but there were also rave reviews and a huge audience. I am proud we did that.

I was also at CTV when 9/11 happened. Of course we went to air live, I think for two or three days. We got CRTC approval to run it on all our networks, I think we programmed ten. We put crews on the road, they crossed the border about three hours after the attack. It was a dark time, but a time that journalists were the most committed and determined I have ever seen.

VIC: How important do you think journalism is to society?

TRINA: Essential. It is essential. But what worries me is the kind of unfettered, unregulated, unthoughtful journalism. There's so much stuff on social media that people don't research or understand. They may be completely lying, but it's read just like news. I get on TikTok and see all kinds of stories that I know aren't accurate—but I enjoy reading them! So, I imagine that's a big problem. The other thing is AI. Stories done by AI and published—that's a concern. What we've lost is the importance of traditional journalism. Newspapers are dying. Fewer audiences watch networks. People are communicating through all kinds of media that cater only to what they want to read.

VIC: Thank you Trina, you've been fantastic.

Chapter 13

MARK STAROWICZ

Mark Starowicz is a legendary journalist and producer whose innovations transformed Canadian current affairs television. He was the driving force behind As It Happens, Sunday Morning, *and* The Journal, *and later created the landmark CBC documentary series* Canada: A People's History. *His work laid the foundation for generations of Canadian storytellers and continues to inspire long-form journalism today.*

Vic: Tell me about your early years.

MARK: I came to Canada when I was seven and a half years old. I was born in England to parents who were Polish refugees. My father had been a Polish pilot who fled to England and joined the Royal Air Force. My mother was in the Polish resistance, and they met in a POW camp at the end of the war. When we arrived in Canada, I was the only one with a passport. I still have their travel documents, which state: "This is not a passport. The carrier of this document is under the care of the International Committee of Refugees." I had a British passport.

We arrived in March of 1954, and I didn't speak English or French. Unlike others who might have found snow magical, I had no desire to see it—I had been raised in the wonderful climate of Argentina. Suddenly, I found myself walking to school in Montreal during winter. The streets were icy, the sewers were slushy and backed up, and I was going to a Catholic school where I couldn't understand anyone. My parents were out all day looking for work, which took them a couple of months to find. We hadn't had television in Argentina, so I watched the French network—*Peppino and Capucine* and shows like that. Eventually, I learned English and French.

I decided I wasn't going to be a lawyer, a doctor, or work for the United Nations. I was going to be a newspaperman. My parents were disappointed. They said, "Marek, a newspaperman is like a gypsy or an actor. Get a real job." But I got a job at the *Montreal Gazette* as a copy clerk. I didn't want to work at the CBC—I didn't even listen to it. I wanted to be in newspapers. At the *Gazette*, I covered the FLQ bombings, riots, de Gaulle's "*Vive le Québec libre*." It was wonderful. We worked nights in a car with a scanner radio. The whole Shakespearean drama of a city was unfolding in front of us—murders, heroics, triumphs. I once arrived at the scene before the police where an FLQ kid had blown himself up trying to plant a bomb. I had to break the news to the boy's mother.

Later, I worked at the *Toronto Star*, the largest newspaper in the country. I did well there too. One important moment was an exposé I wrote about the Greek embassy during the junta—the generals were intimidating democratic Greeks in Toronto. Papandreou was based there, and people were being beaten on the streets. I did a commentary about it on CBC Television, a short viewpoint segment at the end of the news. After that aired, a woman I had never heard of, Margaret Lyons from CBC Radio, called me and asked if I'd like to work there. I said thanks, but no thanks. I didn't listen to CBC Radio and I wanted to be a foreign correspondent

About six months later, I was fired from the *Star* for helping to set up a journalistic magazine, inspired by *Ramparts*, something like *Mother Jones*. The *Star* didn't like that I'd written an exposé about Canada selling arms to both sides of the Middle East war. They had refused to publish it, so I gave it to the magazine. I was out of work, and union proceedings take time. I was running out of money.

I remembered Margaret Lyons' phone number. I called her and explained the situation—told her I'd been fired, needed work, and would return to the *Star* if they rehired me. She said, "We'll take you on those terms." The next morning, I was in the CBC Radio building. What a place. The equipment was all WWII-era Northern Electric. I was put in charge of commentary and a program called *Five Nights*, a daily, 15-minute documentary that aired after the 10:00 news. The place was a madhouse. People would come in off the street and pitch documentaries. My job was to assess if they were crazy or credible.

It's important to say that for the first six months, I wasn't very good. I found the commentaries boring. I had my own little office, but the environment was bizarre. Glenn Gould didn't smoke, but there he'd be in the summer wearing gloves, chatting with Peter Gzowski, who smoked Buckinghams by the pack. The building housed some of Canada's most iconic figures. Lorne Greene had already moved on to *Bonanza*, but the atmosphere lingered.

One day, out of the blue, Margaret Lyons handed me *As It Happens* with just 36 hours' notice. At the time, it was a struggling two-hour show, a phone-out rather than a phone-in format. Four producers, Barbara Frum as host, and Alan Maitland. I saw its potential. The show would no longer revolve around playing Joan Baez records between long interviews. I told the team, "We're going to be the news of the world." We boosted the number of stories per night from six to sixteen, and we weren't pre-taping anything.

Each morning began with a blank slate, *tabula rasa*, and we would decide what stories to chase. We started calling world leaders. During riots in Belfast, we leaned on our good relationship with the Bell Telephone ladies in Montreal, who handled international calls in those pre-direct-dial days. Every Christmas we sent them wine. During riots in Belgium, the operators told us about a directory of public phone booths. We asked them to call one in the riot zone. Human nature being what it is, someone answered the ringing booth. Barbara asked, "What side are you on?" We interviewed that person and then asked if they'd cross the street and hand the phone to someone on the other side. They did. That's how we got both sides of a riot.

Within six months, *As It Happens* had gone from the lowest-rated program to the highest among 12 to 24-year-olds, beating even CHUM, the big rock station. We always made time for one quirky item each night: the woman who grew the largest carrot in Manchester, the man who played "Beethoven's Ninth" on his metal teeth, the world's oldest turtle owner. These stories had character and humour. People told us they would sit in their driveways listening, not wanting to miss the end.

One day we saw a small item: a man in Hamilton, originally from Newfoundland, had been arrested for stealing two trout from a hatchery. The case was remanded. I thought: What happens to the fish? We called around and eventually reached a corporal with the Ontario Provincial Police. "Do you still have the fish?" we asked. "Yes," he said. "They're in the freezer." Well, it turned out he had them in the freezer... at home. We asked, "What does your wife think of that?" He replied, "She's not very pleased." So, we kept following this story. The case was remanded again. We'd call back: "Are the fish back in your freezer?" And, "Could we speak with your wife?" It became a multi-day saga. People loved it—these ordinary human dramas with strange hooks. Meanwhile, we were still covering coups and revolutions, giving listeners both the news and the nuances.

And we didn't take ourselves too seriously. We once found someone claiming to have a UN document granting them an acre of the moon. We broke it into one-inch plots and started mailing out deeds to schools and kindergartens. Mailbags arrived. Everyone wanted a piece of the moon. Along the way, they learned about lunar law and exploration. So yes, we were tabloid. But we had some of the best frontline journalists in the world, and that format is still alive today.

It was classic tabloid storytelling, something I learned at the *Gazette*—every story is a human drama. By then, I understood the depth of the CBC's roots—its origins in the war, the pressure of national storytelling. I began listening to old broadcasts from the *Battle of the Atlantic* and became captivated by the CBC's history. I felt like I wasn't just a journalist; I was part of a national force.

Margaret Lyons: she deserves a moment. Barely five feet tall, a Japanese-Canadian and first-generation born here, she was nicknamed the Dragon Lady, though in truth she was one of the kindest people I've ever met. Her firm tone came from her training at the BBC.

VIC: Fantastic. Margaret Lyons. How did she end up on CBC in the first place? Do you know?

MARK: Turns out she had been under the War Measures Act during World War II. Her family had their berry farm in British Columbia seized. They never got it back, her parents went into a camp. This is the tragic story of what we did to the Japanese-Canadians during the war. But she was a young woman, so she was just ordered East. She could not be in British Columbia—nowhere near the Canadian coast. She ended up working as a maid in Hamilton, Ontario.

VIC: Wow.

MARK: Margaret Lyons, the woman who hired me, ends up working as a maid because she's been displaced by the Canadian government. She completes studies at McMaster University, while she's working as a maid. Decides she wants to be a journalist. Doesn't do it in Canada. Goes to England. I think she had a bit of a chip on her shoulder—who could blame her? She ends up working her way from typist to producer at the BBC, at Bush House in the international section. She works on a program that broadcasts Shakespeare for the Caribbean Service with V.S. Naipaul. Can you imagine? Taking *King Lear* and chopping it into 15-minute episodes in Jamaican patois? Then Lester Pearson is on his way back from getting the Nobel Prize for helping achieve peace in the Middle East. They need a Canadian to record a message to the Commonwealth. Margaret ends up recording Pearson. He says, "What are you doing here?" She explains, and he says, "Get the heck back to Canada and knock on the door of the CBC and tell them I sent you."

So she goes to CBC Television—can't get past the front door. Goes to CBC Radio—they make her a junior producer. She rose to become the deputy head of current affairs. She made a point of collecting misfits. I was one of them. I didn't apply to the CBC, she came after me because I had been editor of the *McGill Daily* and had written edgy stories. As a young man, I found that intoxicating—to be part of something larger, something vast, something with a purpose. I wasn't even that much of a Canadian nationalist. I was a Quebec boy. I identified more with Quebec nationalism. I'm still a Montreal boy. Still don't like Toronto. So I wasn't predisposed to being a Canadian. I became one, largely because of the CBC. That's the sense of the institution I'm trying to paint.

MARK: For one thing, we've had five Ministers of Heritage and Communications in seven years. Five in seven. There is no cultural imperative, no cultural policy. There's no debate. There's no battle for the soul of the CBC. You can like it, or think it's too woke, or not right-wing enough, or that it's too highbrow—or whatever. But the *Broadcasting Act*, which says its role is to "inform, enlighten, and entertain the people of Canada, regardless of race, colour, creed, or region"—well, that's a magnificent constitution. And it is not mitigated in any way by current technology. It's very fashionable to say, "Well, that's an old-fashioned idea. In the age of Netflix, we don't need that. You can find anything on the internet."

Listen. When the CBC started—the reason we have the *Broadcasting Act* is because Canada nationalized the airwaves. The reason Canada nationalized the airwaves was because of American border-busting stations in New York, Buffalo, and Salt Lake City. Utah sits on the salt flats, and their 50,000-watt stations just obliterated the airwaves. We couldn't get on the air in our own country. There were four competing radio stations on the same spot on the dial. They had to divide the day. Competing companies had to share the same frequency. Same thing here. So there was no way there was going to be any Canadian broadcasting unless we declared that the airwaves are sovereign to Canada. And that became the *Broadcasting Act*.

Subsequently, we set up the Canadian Radio Broadcasting Commission. So from the very beginning, broadcasting has been a declaration of national sovereignty. "We will tell our own stories. We will tell the world's stories through our eyes. We will communicate with each other, and we will settle disputes and debate them. We will become a parliament of the air. We will become a national theatre."

I mean, there used to be seven CBC regional orchestras. But I worry that nobody even remembers that there ever was a high watermark—or a bathtub ring, whatever you want to call it. That there was a drama department. That there were institutions called *The Journal* or *As It Happens* or *Sunday Morning* or *Newsmagazine* or *This Hour Has Seven Days.*

I live across the street from the CBC building. In the day, 140 of us worked on *The Journal.* If we stopped the first 200 people walking by the front door now, I don't think anybody would recognize the name Barbara Frum. Certainly not *The Journal.* Or even remember who Knowlton Nash was. So our capacity to even remember what the purpose of the institution was, or that it actually endured, is fading. It has faded so much that I fear for its future.

VIC: But how do we change this.

MARK:The downward spiral—what can we do to change it? In the end, it's a national issue. A national political issue. We have lost the political will to affirm our cultural sovereignty. We do spend a fair bit of money on it—$1.7 billion. But I think the first failure is political. We've had a series of governments that don't particularly think in terms of national culture and national sovereignty.

They've been seduced by the idea that technology means it's time to lay aside the things of childhood. The world is different now. There's the internet. But what they forget is: we began as a response to technology. We were created to beat off the 50,000-watt American stations in the 1930s. And then when television started, we created the CBC television network so that everybody wasn't just watching Boston, or Seattle, or Plattsburgh, New York. Along the border, the point was not the ratings. It was the menu.

What do I mean? We've become a restaurant where, when you walk in, it's a Canadian restaurant, but you can get Chinese food, Indian food—anything but something local. The point isn't the ratings. The point is: you should have a choice on the menu. Do you want your story? No? That's fine. You can have all the American channels you want. All the Netflix you want. But there should be a Canadian choice. A Canadian story. That's how we affirm ourselves as a people.

VIC: Do you think maybe—demographically—that the birthrate in Canada being so low has something to do with it? That the only population growth now is through immigration? And because immigration is going quite high... maybe there's a disconnection? People who've recently arrived haven't had enough time to feel for this land the way some of us do. Maybe they feel more international than national? Less of that cultural attachment?

MARK: Yes. Immigration is a factor. But listen, I'm an immigrant. You're an immigrant. Margaret Lyons was born in Canada, but her family were immigrants. The whole country's immigrants. We all came from somewhere and became eight million overnight.

We did *Canada: A People's History*, which was the scariest thing I've ever done in my life—16 episodes, 32 hours of the history of Canada. It cost $25 million, in French and in English. It was multi-platform: books, television, everything. The first episode is entirely Indigenous. The next three are entirely French—before the English even arrive. The English don't show up until 1759. And it dawned on me: the CBC couldn't get any sponsors for it, because everyone assumed nobody was going to watch it. And I began to believe nobody was going to watch it.

So I'm sitting there watching this—watching Donnacona, the Iroquois Confederacy, the Wendat assembly—and the first rule of television hits me: people only watch what speaks to them personally. Their own story. I was thinking these episodes were really good, but they didn't speak to anybody named Singh or Wong or Rabinovitch. Nobody except the English would watch the French part. And nobody except the five percent of the population that's Indigenous would watch the Indigenous part.

I was starting to panic. And then it turned out to be the highest-rated documentary series in Canadian history. Because if your name is Wong, or Singh, or Rabinovitch—or Starowicz—you want to be part of an epic story. You're not diminished by seeing 20 minutes of Donnacona or a Huron war party. You're enlarged by it. You belong on the same shelf. If you can show people the epic—the sometimes tragic, sometimes majestic—they want to be part of that drama. It doesn't matter if it's about them directly. People watch *Romeo and Juliet.* It's not about Italy. It's about love. The series was translated into eight languages. It was a hit with all of them. Immigrants are often more eager than anyone to learn about their new country, to adapt, to embrace its history and mythology.

VIC: I'm in the film business. I mostly do fiction, though I've done a lot of documentaries too. And when I walk down to the street here in downtown Vancouver, and I ask people, "Name one Canadian film you love," I bet you half of them can't name a single one. Or they don't know it's Canadian.

MARK: I wouldn't take that bet. I agree with you.

VIC: Thank God for Telefilm, because without them we wouldn't have a film industry at all. They've supported it since the days of Michael Spencer. But for almost 40 years now, Telefilm has shelled out so much money, produced so many films… and yet, there's nothing people really remember. So my question to you is—what's wrong with our storytelling here? We make all these films, and no one talks about them.

MARK: I can't even get *Canada: A People's History* rebroadcast. Eleven million people have come to Canada since it was first aired. But CBC won't rebroadcast it because they'd have to pay step-up rates for musicians and actors and things like that.

VIC: Yes, that's expensive.

MARK: We had very popular programs. We had excellent dramas. We had *The Beachcombers* and our own quiz shows. We had *Quentin Durgens, M.P.* We've done better than the English in a lot of ways. And Quebec has done even better in cinema. But that's because Quebec is protected, linguistically, like an island. Here's where we went wrong: we succumbed to a lack of ambition, a lack of faith in our own country. Not among the people—but among the governments.

VIC: Let's get back to radio for a minute.

MARK: In 1968, CBC was seriously thinking about getting out of the radio business. The evidence was there. We were at the bottom of the market. But fast forward to 2024—except for two markets—we're number one in the country in the morning show. Instead of dying, radio became dominant.

I remember when the board of directors actually commissioned a study on how to get out of radio. They thought it was a dying medium. That's why they gave it to the kids. That's why you could find somebody like me, 22 years old, given the keys to the network. Not just a show—the network. All the decisions for a hundred low-power relay transmission towers, two satellite channels… given to a 22- or 24-year-old.

There were four of us. Nobody supervising the scripts. No rehearsals. Live. God knows what anybody could've said on air. And yet Margaret Lyons gave us the key to the kingdom. Peter Herrndorf didn't even ask to see a rehearsal. He was the VP of the CBC. He was the one behind *The Journal.* We just went on the air. I wouldn't have the guts to do that today—to trust people the way they trusted us.

People talk about podcasts. Well, this week there was a report: there are over one million podcasts now. What's a podcast? It's a radio program. I don't care if it's transmitted on amplitude modulation, frequency modulation, or over the internet. It's still a radio program. That thing behind you—that's a TV set. I don't care what wires lead to it. The point is: are you putting anything on it? Are you telling your story? Are you helping your children tell their stories? Are you building institutions that bring in your children, train them, support them?

You need to produce. And the bigger the world stage gets, the louder you have to speak, the more you need to produce. If you want to exist, you have to affirm yourself. Tell your stories.

Yes, technology is a challenge. But so were satellites. So were thousand-channel universes. So was cable. So was AM versus FM. And remember, everyone said the day of the documentary was over, right? Everything's supposed to be five minutes long. Excuse me, ten seconds now—because it's TikTok. People won't watch anything over an hour. Twitter—140 characters. Okay, it's 280 now. This is the golden age of the documentary. There are more documentaries available on screen than have ever been available in the history of civilization. From countries all over the world. Just... not as many from Canada as there should be.

VIC: Tell me—how do you see the future now for institutions like the CBC and the film world? I'm still coming back to that idea of storytelling and connection. Where are these two institutions headed? What's your vision?

MARK: The future of the CBC... well, I've done my last five films with the CBC and I'm grateful to them for financing those for *The Nature of Things.* But I think the CBC has been misdirected in its policies over the past five years. The radio budgets have been cut. The news departments have been cut—by $40-million or maybe even $80-million, I forget which. And all that money has been ploughed into building alternate platforms. I think we've got something like 30 different platforms now. The BBC has 17. There are podcasts going into the ether, hoping to attract more advertisers, more young people, and so on.

But let's distinguish here. The question is: do we have the wrong administration? Or is the theory behind how the CBC is being run flawed? Among the things that have gone wrong—again, I'm talking CBC, not the NFB—first, there came this wave of silo-busting. Everything had to be homogenized. Remember? *The Fifth Estate* became *CBC News: Fifth Estate. Marketplace* became *CBC News: Marketplace.*

The idea that you could have regimental pride in your program or your department—that you could build a family around your team—became totally unacceptable. In the CBC's management thinking, everything had to be interchangeable. Assignable to an E-unit. And to a certain point, I'm okay with that. *The Journal* was one big room with 140 people in it.

But we've destroyed unit culture. And I am for silos, if the silo means you're building a theatrical company, or a sports team like the Blue Jays. You need to develop a sense of family. You can't just put it all in a blender and standardize everything. CBC News keeps making the mistake of offering a one-hour newscast regardless of whether there's news or not.

A year into *The Journal*, I realized: there are maybe two news days a week where you really have a story. The other three days? You're filling time. So we cut in different patterns. We did the history of the French Resistance on an anniversary. We did *The Third Angel*—the story of a woman who lived her whole life with orangutans in Borneo. She was one of the three great primatologist friends of Jane Goodall.

We did the history of pizza. We did two full editions on menopause—on the theory that either you're going to go through it yourself, or you're part of the 48 percent who's going to be married to someone who goes through it. Every one of those episodes was a huge hit. So maybe the issue isn't the audience—it's the structure. Maybe we need to reform the news.

Maybe we need to reinvent the current affairs department. Maybe we need a documentary unit that focuses on health and social documentaries. Why? Because have you ever tried to finance a war documentary on the free market? The reason you didn't see any Canadian documentaries out of Syria during the rebellion is that there was only one—and we did it in-house. If you go out to get financing from the CMF, Telefilm, Ontario Creates, Rogers, or Bell, it takes you a year and a half to pull the money together. By that time, the war is already won—or lost.

Then there's insurance. You can't get war insurance. You could be on the hook for $20,000 a day in the free market. Plus, a war doc doesn't have a long shelf life. If you're making a documentary, you have to pick a subject with a long shelf life—because you need time to pay it back. That's five years, minimum. And if you sign a deal with a distributor, they want seven to 10 years of exclusivity. The only people who can pack up a crew and go to a war zone—or some urgent equivalent—without setting up a separate corporation and chasing five different funding bodies is the CBC.

We failed in Syria. We're failing in other places, too—not because we had to finance troops, but because we failed to finance coverage. And for that, you need in-house documentary. Now, I think 90 percent of documentaries should be made by independents. But there are stories—urgent stories—that simply won't get financed, won't earn their money back, won't have that shelf life. So, either you create a self-insuring organization, or you don't do the story. And that's a problem.

We've got to pass this problem down and ask: how are we failing, exactly? How are we failing in Canadian documentary? In Canadian drama? But instead of asking that, we throw the whole baby out with the bathwater. We say, "Well, technology is the new world." That's nonsense. The BBC still sends out crews. It's one of the biggest commissioners in the world.

There's been a loss of vision. This started around 2012 or 2013, with a housecleaning. We had two presidents in a row who believed in eliminating silos, flattening the organization, removing impediments. And in the process, I think they threw out the mandate. I was part of an administration—though not a happy one—where a vice-president once said, "If I ever hear the word 'mandate' again, I'll reach for my gun." That was the attitude.

We used to say, "We have a mandate." But mandates don't necessarily translate into commercial value. Some things you do because you're working for the taxpayer, for the people. Now, even the CBC won't give you money unless you bring in matching funds from other broadcasters. That's rational—to a point. We shouldn't create an elite club. We should be open. We should compete internationally. We should co-produce. But we've gone too far. We've lost the idea of affirming ourselves. In the process, we're losing our cultural sovereignty. We're not telling each other our stories.

It's not. Technology is a factor—we have to adapt to it—but it's not the cause. The real cause is the erosion of political will. The failure to remember the foundational principles of why we got into the game in the first place. That's the issue. And it's political.

VIC: Just keep that thought. I'd like to talk now about your personal life. I think your ideology, your philosophy, are very clearly defined. But I want to get to know you as a person, not just your mind and your ideals.

MARK: Yes. What matters, what's so important to me now, is that time is limited for all of us. The climate crisis—that's what my last three films have been about. The disappearance of nature and the environment. I want to work closely with David Suzuki. And in the last few years, this mosquito film I'm working on with my daughter, we jointly have a company. It's about how mosquitoes are going to transform the world due to global warming—how they might bring about the next epidemic. So yes, it's a climate crisis film, in a sense. That's what I think the most existential crises are.

VIC: What makes you very happy?

MARK: Telling stories. I saw an afternoon movie on CFCF in Montreal called *Deadline U.S.A.*, with Humphrey Bogart about a courageous newspaper editing trying to fight the mafia. I wanted to be a newspaper man. I realized that what I enjoy most is telling other people's stories. There's a word for it in almost every culture. In Canadian Indigenous culture, it's "keeper of stories." I'm a chronicler. I see things through—this will sound arrogant—a Shakespearean lens. I see dramas in every window.

There's a unity to being in a car at night with a photographer, listening to the police scanner, filming lions or gorillas in Uganda, Kenya, Tanzania—or going through the jungles of Borneo. There's an epic human drama happening somewhere, and I want to capture it.

I love meeting people. I'm not comfortable at parties, but I love meeting people. The worst thing you can do is leave me alone in a room for three hours. And I think I know why. I'm an immigrant. I had a happy childhood in Argentina. My father went broke trying to start a trucking business. The remnants of our refugee family sent us the money to come to Canada. It was a wonderful two-month voyage on a tramp steamer. But I've always been an outsider. I didn't speak English. I didn't speak French. I was always treated well—but still, once you're in the room but not part of it, you observe things differently. You're always the outsider, and that changes how you see. You're fascinated by the contents, by the people, because you're not fully part of it.

So, as a journalist, I look for unity. I'm the outsider chronicling all sides of the story. I observe—but I don't see the point of observing without sharing. That's what I do. That's what makes me happy.

VIC: So when you look back on your life, how do you feel?

MARK: About the arc of my life? I feel happy that I've drunk as richly from the well as I have. I regret I haven't drunk more. I regret I've spent too much time in offices, in politics, in maneuvering.

MARK: I could have drunk so much more. I mean, it's harder going into the field now. I'm not going to be much help carrying 14 cases in Borneo or climbing a volcano—but I can still do it. So yes, do I have regrets? I have regrets every day. But retroactively... thank God I became a reporter, a chronicler, a storyteller. I am at peace with that. I'm proud that I did that. I told the stories of my people. I shared them. I was a citizen of the world. I shared the stories of other peoples. I've sounded the warnings of what threats are coming to us if we don't pull together. So, I feel I've contributed—not as much as I should have—but I have contributed to the welfare of those neighbours and citizens I was raised to care for.

VIC: And how much of that fulfillment did the CBC help shape?

MARK: The CBC shaped my life. As much as I wanted to be a newspaper man, those were private companies, private institutions, for-profit. The CBC, as an institution, was a cathedral. It was a university. It shaped me. It not only allowed me to do things I didn't think I could do, it pushed me to do them. It had more faith in me than I did in myself. But I want to pass that legacy down to people. Yes, I met a lot of idiots at the CBC with stars on their doors, sure, but I also met some extraordinary people. When it came time to leave the CBC, this new regime had a universal policy. You get to take one box, and they walk you out. I wasn't fired. I retired. And yet, I had to be escorted out. But I asked to be escorted out by two former vice presidents—Peter and Margaret—on the principle that you leave with the ones who brung you.

VIC: Did you have any experience with John Grierson and the National Film Board?

MARK: Not directly. I became a good friend of Sandra MacDonald when she was at the Film Board. *The History of Canada* was originally meant to be a co-production with them. But as you know, they have a "director culture." At CBC had more of an "institutional culture." At the Film Board, you'd have ten directors, each going their own way. But we needed a Bible—a series style, a framing and narrative structure. That doesn't sit well in the same room as the NFB's director-driven model. But I did work with Adam Symansky, who was good.

VIC: Let me ask you something, from someone who's really close to the lens. I'm not an intellectual. I'm more emotional. So when I look at this country—such a large country, with four and a half time zones, a small population, and two official languages—how does the country stay together?

MARK: You're right. I remember when people in Quebec always felt like, "People in the West don't know about us." And people in the West would say, "The East is basically another country—and we don't care." So how do we keep this country together? The Film Board was vital. It was essential during World War II—that's where it originated. It was also vital through the '50s and '60s. Technically, I remember NFB films in the church basement, the pull-down screen—those screenings shaped generations. Multiply that by ten thousand and it had a real impact. It shaped views during the Vietnam War, too.

The studio nurtured women's voices, the voice of dissent, and Quebec nationalism. Remember, I started out as a Quebecer. I was disdainful of the rest of Canada, ignorant of it—just like how B.C. might feel about the rest of Canada. But over time, I came to realize I have a deep attraction to particularity. I love Quebecers who live in Toronto. I have friends in Saskatchewan who are more nationalist about Saskatchewan than anything else. That pride—those regional loyalties—made Canada. We are a collection of particularities. You have to respect each one. So, when people ask, "When will we finally settle this eternal cacophony of debate?" my answer is: never. That's not the problem, that's the point. It's an eternal dialogue. Sometimes rude, sometimes uplifting—but always a dialogue between our constituent parts.

That's the definition of this country—to maintain the civility of the dialogue, but also its vibrancy, its interconnection. That electrical circuitry between particularities, that's what binds us. And we're all just as Canadian as anyone else. But we need a unifying platform for dialogue. "Stage" is too limp a word—but we need that platform. That's why we can't afford to lose it. Because we are so diverse, so scattered, and so isolated in our neighbourhoods—neighbourhoods that are, by necessity, protective and nurturing.

If we threaten that interconnectivity, we risk becoming the United States. And the U.S., frankly, is on the verge of splitting into its parts. Three years ago, I said we'd see a civil war in our lifetime—or the emergence of fascism on that stage. That sounded extreme. But I observe the United States now with great trepidation.

We all know about Trump—everyone does. It's a civil war. A cultural civil war. It could explode at any moment. We do not want that happening here. But... imagine if the United States had been founded differently. Imagine if it had been a bilingual union, with Mexico, and they had to construct a polity around that. It would be a totally different country today—just as an exercise, imagine it. But you know what? That's what we did right from the beginning. We created a duality. And duality isn't enough. There's more than two peoples in this thing.

VIC: Are you at peace with your life?

MARK: Yes… and no. I wish I could work more. I wish my body were growing stronger instead of weaker. I wish I hadn't lost so many friends—three good ones just in the past year. I feel a real urgency now. Urgency to set things down.

VIC: A bit of a cliché question, but—how would you like people close to you to think of you?

MARK: That's a fair question. I hope they'll say I was loyal. Loyal to my friends, loyal to my team. If you write anything on my grave, write: "He was loyal. And honest." To me, honesty is the most important thing. In your work, in your films, in whatever you do—that's the foundation. So my reply is: To the best of my knowledge, I tried to be honest in everything I did.

VIC: Thank you for the honour of doing this.

Chapter 14

BOB McDONALD

Bob McDonald is the longtime host of CBC Radio's Quirks & Quarks, *where he has brought the wonders of science to Canadian audiences for over four decades. He is a respected science communicator, author, and Officer of the Order of Canada. McDonald's work bridges curiosity and clarity, making complex scientific ideas accessible and engaging. His passion for knowledge and storytelling is rooted in a deep love for public broadcasting.*

BOB McDONALD: I was born in a small town called Wingham, Ontario, which is between London and Sarnia, I think. But that's not what I call my hometown, because as soon as I was born, my family left. I actually grew up in Orillia, just north of Toronto. Gordon Lightfoot came from there—my sister dated him! I'm the youngest of four, and there's a big gap between me and the other three. I'm a latecomer to the family. Our house was pretty close to a big park by the lake, so I spent summers running in and out of the water, collecting pop bottles from tourists for penny candy. In the winter, it was all about playing in the snow.

I also spent a lot of time alone, just wandering. When I got a bicycle, I started exploring streets I hadn't been down before. That evolved into a motorcycle, which I still ride. I'm still riding bikes all over the country. I like exploring, going places I haven't been before.

Our home—well, it's not really a great story. My father was an alcoholic. A serious alcoholic. And an abusive one. That's another reason why I wasn't home much. I never knew if I was going to get Dr. Jekyll or Mr. Hyde. And when it was Mr. Hyde, it was loud, angry, and not very nice.

In my last book *Just Say Yes*, I came out with something I'd never talked about publicly: I was sexually abused by my father when I was eight, and then again later—though not in Orillia—by a stranger. That affects you. We were also low income—the poor people on the block. We couldn't do what the other kids did—no holidays, no Disneyland. It leaves you with this feeling of not being good enough. Subpar. That's how I felt growing up. But I still had a good time in Orillia. It was a beautiful town. Home life could have been a lot better, but the place itself was wonderful.

VIC: What about your friends? More about school—what about other kids around?

BOB: Well, we were the only Catholics on the block. The other kids didn't understand what went on in the Catholic Church. They'd ask why I had to go so often, not just Sundays but holy days too. Some even thought we really drank blood—that the wine turned to blood. They thought we were druids or something! So we were seen as a little weird. But we all played together, outside, in the streets. The town was quiet enough for that. No parents around, just us. It was the classic, "Go out, come back when the streetlights come on" kind of thing. I really enjoyed that.

The other thing that happened while I was in Orillia—this affected my entire life—was in 1957. The *Orillia Packet and Times* had a front-page headline and an image: a drawing of the Earth with a little ball and antennas going around it. The headline was something like, "Russians Launch First Artificial Moon." It was Sputnik. And I was enthralled. A satellite in space!

From then on, I followed the space program religiously. I knew all the names—John Glenn, Alan Shepard, all of them. I watched all the moon landings. The whole space program has happened during my lifetime. It captivated me—the idea that we were leaving the Earth. That one day, I'd be having holidays on the Moon. That hasn't quite happened yet, but I really thought about it back then.

Space was an escape for me, yes. My mother also gave me a book—I still have it—called *The Planets*. It's an illustrated guide to the solar system from the 1950s, and it was quite accurate. It showed me how different all the planets are from Earth. I found that fascinating. I dreamed of exploring them.

But my home life also made me a terrible student. I barely passed. My report cards would always say, "Bobby can do better." I'd get marks in the 50s or 60s, just scraping by. Memorizing stuff just wasn't for me. So by the time I got to university, I failed second year and dropped out. Became a construction worker.

VIC: When you were young—was that your radio time? Or was television around?

BOB: We had television. It was CBC, of course, and black and white. I remember when we first got it—wow. That was really something. You had to adjust the volume, the channels, and there was a vertical control knob. I remember watching *Howdy Doody*, and all of a sudden the screen went sideways, but the show kept playing on this weird slant. My dad came in and said, "You idiot, you've got to turn this and put it back up again."

Sunday nights were *The Ed Sullivan Show*. We all gathered to watch the Beatles, Elvis, and all those folks. There were also a number of kids programs I loved—*Lassie*, and one in particular called *Fury*. It was set on a ranch with this black stallion that only the boy could ride. The boy was adopted, and he and Fury had this bond. I really identified with that, the idea of escape on the horse. As for radio, the only thing I really remember is the farm reports that came on at noon. They'd give hog prices and weather updates, right down to the millimeter. That's what stuck with me.

VIC: If you look back again at that early time—anything you still remember vividly? Something that left a strong impression? An event? A discovery?

BOB: Yeah, like I said, the launch of Sputnik. That was a big one. Why was it so big? Because I was just old enough to understand what it meant. Sputnik marked the beginning of our exploration of space. And they were talking on the news about the fear that if the Russians could launch something around the Earth, they could drop a nuclear bomb at any time. That terrified me. There was fear at first. But then the excitement of the space race took over.

Later, after the family split up, my mother took my sister and me to Saint John, New Brunswick—her hometown. That was around 1960 or '61. And during that time, the Cuban Missile Crisis happened. And talk about radio—we were glued to it as the Russian ships approached Cuba, with Americans firing warning shots across their bows. There was real fear of nuclear war. In school, we were doing duck-and-cover drills, getting under our desks. Air raid sirens went off as practice. It was terrifying, thinking the world could be destroyed.

VIC: It's interesting that you remember the fear more than the wonder—more than the idea that it might open a new world for you.

BOB: Well, it was both. The fear of nuclear war didn't last long—it got separated from space in my mind. Space became too exciting. It was about adventure. These astronauts were heroes. They were taking incredible risks. And I've been lucky, as a journalist, to meet some of them as an adult. I took Buzz Aldrin sailing once in Toronto. He was visiting, and I said, "Hey Buzz, want to go for a sail tomorrow? No cameras, off the record." He said, "Sure." So I took him out on my sailboat—it was great.

He told me that when they landed on the Moon and had to open the hatch, even though they'd evacuated all the air, there was still suction. They didn't want to bend the door, because if it bent, they wouldn't be able to close it—and they'd be stuck. At one point, he broke a switch and had to use his ballpoint pen to fix it. That pen saved their lives. That kind of risk just doesn't happen today. We're far more cautious.

Something else Buzz Aldrin told me too: "The Moon's an interesting place, but it's not a very nice place." That stuck with me. It's not like science fiction. Every world we've found—whether in our solar system or among the five thousand exoplanets we now know about—none of them are like Earth. They're fascinating, but they're deadly.

VIC: Let's talk about after you left Orillia. Where did you go from there? How did you get into what came later on?

BOB: After I dropped out of university and worked in construction, I made billboards—the outdoor signs you see on top of buildings or out in open fields. That was my job. I also drove a ten-ton truck, which comes in handy even now on moving day! I rent trucks now, but I can still back one down a narrow alley without scraping the mirrors.

I have a lot of respect for people who work in the trades. You're out there in the winter, in the elements, your hands freezing, trying to use tools while you're wearing gloves. I've been a janitor, too—working nights. Those jobs taught me a lot. They grounded me.

The big break that changed my life actually came through my girlfriend at the time. I was in my early 20s. She had stayed in university and got hired at the Ontario Science Centre in Toronto as a student host. They took on students in the summer to work with the public, doing demonstrations with static electricity, that kind of thing. She told me, "When we go back to school, the Science Centre is hiring full-time. You'd be good at it." I liked science, and I had theatre experience. So I went to visit. I saw the place and thought, "This is amazing."

She made me an appointment. I took some company time—drove my truck down to the Science Centre—and met the guy who was hiring. I said, "Hi, I'd love to work here. I love science, I love theatre..." I don't even remember what I said exactly. I was just excited. I guess my enthusiasm bubbled over, because he stopped me mid-sentence and said, "You're the kind of person we'd like to have here." And he hired me on the spot.

It changed everything. That was in 1973. I was 22 years old. I had to learn all the science behind the demos—like why static electricity makes your hair stand up. We had this giant laser that could burn holes through firebrick. I had to learn what a laser even was. You know what the word means? "Light Amplification by Stimulated Emission of Radiation." I couldn't even say that when I was a kid, but they taught me. They took me under their wing and taught me about lasers, physics, cryogenics—supercold liquids that could freeze a flower in seconds. I had to understand it and learn to make it fun and entertaining. All my media connections started at the Science Centre.

VIC: That element of curiosity... it was already there, wasn't it?

BOB: Yes, definitely. Science is curiosity. That's what it is—it's how we explore the world. It's our best tool to figure out how things work. And it all starts with questions: Why is the sky blue? Why is grass green? How does reproduction work? How big is the universe? How did we get here? Science is all of that. To me, it's wonderful. I love it. I'm not good at doing it, but I love understanding it—and trying to convey that excitement to the public. I feel very privileged to be able to do that.

VIC: So what came after that?

BOB: I was at the Science Centre from 1973 to 1979—six years. And while I was there, in 1976, NASA landed a robot on Mars: the *Viking* lander. It was the first really big machine to land there—about the size of an office desk. First with colour cameras. First to run experiments to search for life. I had developed a public program about Mars exploration at the Centre, and CBC called and said, "Can someone come on the news tonight to talk about this thing that landed on Mars?" I said, "I can do that."

I had never been on television. I brought a globe of Mars with me and went down to the CBC building on Jarvis Street. I went on air and said, "Here's Mars, here's where we landed, here's what the lander is doing." I was excited. I said, "These cameras are at eye level—what we're seeing is what you'd see if you were standing on Mars." I went on and on—just bubbling with enthusiasm. When the interview ended, I was unhooking my microphone, getting off the set, and the director came down from the control room. She stood in front of me with her hands on her hips and said, "You are very good on camera. If you want to come back and do stuff for us—we'll have you."

Then she turned and walked away. I was like, "Okay..." And I'm still doing it. They still call me. I became, as Peter Mansbridge once said, "a lump of organic matter who talks about science." He and I had a great relationship. I'd go on with him and do these pieces—no script, just live.

Then, the following year, while I was still at the Science Centre, I was approached by the *Ideas* program on CBC Radio. A friend of mine was developing a five-hour series—get this—on climate change. In 1977! At the time, I was also doing a program at the Science Centre on weather and storms. He came to see it as part of his research and said, "How would you like to do one of the hour-long documentaries?" I said, "I've never done radio before." He said, "You know the science—I'll show you how to turn it into radio." So, he taught me: how to do interviews, how to cut tape with razor blades and grease pencils, how to edit it all together. I took it on. The documentary I did was a history of the Earth's climate—from when it became a planet until now—because the atmosphere has changed dramatically over time.

But how to make that interesting? At that time, *Ideas* was incredibly creative. There was a whole sound effects department that could create any kind of atmosphere you needed, and there was budget to support it. So I decided to do fictional weather reports from different geological eras. I got Jan Tennant, one of CBC's newsreaders, to go into the studio and read them straight—like actual forecasts. We even used the CBC news jingle. She'd say things like: "This is the first weather report for planet Earth. Well, there's no weather to report yet because we don't have an atmosphere. The ground is still molten—but cooling. Volcanic activity is expected to begin shortly." And then: "Next report: It's been raining for a million years. Oceans are filling up nicely." We went through all the major epochs. The producers loved it.

And that's when I realized something big: Radio makes better pictures than television. Because it works through your imagination. The images form in your mind. After that, the producer, Bernie Lucht, asked, "How would you like to do your own series next year—on geology? Earthquakes, volcanoes?" I said, "Sure!"

So I did five hours on that. I went right through the centre of the Earth and out the other side. In the final hour, I destroyed the planet—had the Sun turn into a red giant and consume the Earth. We had atmospheres, music, layered sound effects. It was amazing. Then they asked, "Want to do five hours on the oceans?" "Sure!"

So I started doing more and more freelance work outside the Science Centre. By 1979, I was loving that side of the work. So I gathered my bosses at the Centre and said, "I'm thinking of leaving to become a freelance science journalist—unless you can entice me to stay." They told me: "Because you don't have a science degree or a teaching certificate, we can't promote you." I said, "Okay. Thank you very much." I wrote my letter of resignation and left.

The Science Centre gave me a great foundation, but I'd plateaued. So I threw everything to the wind. I loaded my motorcycle with a typewriter, a few books, and drove to Nova Scotia. I set up by the ocean to write my five-hour series on the oceans. That was the beginning of my freelance career.

VIC: That's great. It's extraordinary—for someone like me, from the outside—to see how you had no formal training in science or physics or chemistry, and yet you were able to share it honestly.

BOB: Yeah, I sometimes wonder how that happened. I think it's partly my personality, but mostly—it's curiosity. If you're curious, that comes across. I think my lack of formal education actually brings me closer to the audience. I don't get tangled up in jargon or inside conversations. I can translate. And I've been doing this long enough now that I understand the scientific language. I can turn it into plain English—and excitement.

When I was asked to do five hours on geology, I had to learn it. But I had incentive: I wanted to do good radio. I studied, read, interviewed the scientists who were doing the work. And their enthusiasm rubbed off.

One of them was Robert Ballard—the guy who discovered *The Titanic*. I interviewed him before *The Titanic*, when he was diving to the deepest parts of the ocean and discovering hydrothermal vents—those underwater oases where life thrives. He said some poetic things. He told me: "I've been to the bottom of the ocean more than anyone else. It's dark down there. Totally dark. Cold. Immense pressure. That's what most of the Earth is like." Then he said: "Take away the polar ice caps and the deserts—there's not much left of Earth that you can live on. That's why I really like my little piece of land on Cape Cod." That stuck with me. That's the kind of insight I love from scientists.

I don't learn a lot from books. I learn from people. That's how I've gotten my education—by talking to the people who actually do the science. That's the privilege of working on *Quirks & Quarks*. Every week, scientists from around the world tell me about their latest discoveries—and it's all new. Just today, I was in the studio. I interviewed a cosmologist who thinks our entire universe might be inside a black hole. Isn't that amazing? Right after that, I did another interview with someone who studies krill, those tiny shrimp in the Antarctic seas that whales eat. That's what I love about it. These scientists—they're telling me their stories. I guess I've become a science storyteller. That's really what I am.

VIC: Were you ever challenged by anyone in the so-called scientific world? You know, the PhDs, the doctors—did anyone ever question your credentials?

BOB: You know, not really. Actually, I've had scientists tell me I've set a bar. I remember one Canadian scientist say—this was during a visit to a university—"When we're on your show, we try to get through the interview without you saying, 'Let me see if I got this right.'" Because every time I say that, it means they just got a bit too deep or technical, and I'm thinking on the spot, trying to turn it into something digestible. So, I'll say, "Let me see if I got this right…" and spin it back in a sentence or two, usually with an analogy. And they'll say, "Yeah, that's it." So I actually take that as a compliment.

I was once invited here in Victoria to be the keynote speaker at a national astronomy conference. I said, "What can I possibly tell you that you don't already know about space?" And they said, "Nothing. It's the way you tell it. We admire the way you communicate science. We need to learn that." I was stunned by that.

So no, no one's questioned my academic background. If anything, they compliment my enthusiasm. And I work closely with my producers to make sure what I say is right. They do the heavy lifting—we don't want to make mistakes.

VIC: I think you've made everything so accessible. For people like me, science is something for PhDs. But I listen to you—and I understand.

BOB: Common sense does the trick. And the truth is, you understand it because I have to understand it. That's the whole thing. If I don't get it, I can't explain it. My producers educate me. They're the ones who find the scientists, choose the stories, and do the pre-interviews. Then they brief me—tell me what it's about—so by the time I talk to the scientist, I already know the answers to most of the questions I'm going to ask.

But when it comes to subjects I'm less familiar with, like medicine, I struggle. The terminology is brutal. Words like *bovine spongiform encephalopathy*. I'm like, "What the heck is that?" Oh, mad cow disease. Okay, now I get it. It's a constant learning process for me. I just try to give the best interpretation I can.

VIC: What role has the CBC played in your career?

BOB: The CBC changed my life. Totally. When I first came in with ideas, they didn't question who I was. No one asked where I went to school or what my grades were. No one asked who my teachers were. They just listened to the ideas.

I'd say, "How about weather reports for planet Earth?" And they'd say, "Great idea. Let's do it." Or, "Let's follow the flight path of a neutrino through the Earth." "Let's explore the geology of the Atlantic Ocean floor from Africa to Florida." They said, "Great idea. Let's go." They encouraged creativity and gave me the resources to make it happen.

When I got into television—the *Wonderstruck* series for kids—Liz Fox was the producer. She was amazing. She said, "Be crazy! This is kids' television." We used to call ourselves "*The Nature of Things* with a sense of humour." We were encouraged to have fun—but still get the science across. It was wonderful. To be given that creative freedom—to communicate in whatever way worked best—and to never be questioned about who I was? That meant everything.

So I have the CBC to thank for that. And all the producers I've worked with—I feel like I'm standing on the tip of an iceberg that is the intellectual capital of the CBC. It's enormous. These producers are smart. They have impeccable journalistic standards. We have a manual this thick, guiding how to stay accurate, fair, balanced, and objective—not swayed by politics or pressure. It's a real privilege to be part of that family. I never thought I'd be with them this long, but I'll keep going as long as they'll have me.

VIC: You've seen the CBC change over time. From your perspective, how has it changed?

BOB: The technology has definitely changed. Everything's digital now—so editing and shooting are much easier. Cameras last longer. You don't have to change film or batteries all the time. Everything's smaller, more mobile—drones, compact rigs, all of that. But what I've also noticed—and maybe this is me getting old—some of the younger people coming in don't know the fundamentals. They don't know the weather, or the basics of science. They don't have a sense of history.

The CBC is still reaching out in new ways—social media, online content. That's important. But one of the things that really concerns me, as a science journalist, is the rise of "pseudoscience." There's so much out there now—conspiracy theories, flat-Earth believers, anti-vaxxers, climate deniers, UFO obsessives. And they're very good at confusing the public. It's getting harder to tell the difference between pseudoscience and real science.

That's why the CBC has such a vital role to play: we need to make sure we're delivering credible information. Coming from trusted sources. Not just someone with an opinion. Because someone saying, "I don't believe in climate change"—well, I don't care what you believe. It's not about belief. It's about evidence. They can't show me evidence that climate change isn't happening. They just can't. But they'll put out all kinds of claims to suggest it's not real. That's the challenge we face in journalism today.

When I started, there were only three networks in Canada—CBC, CTV, and Global. All the stories were vetted by producers. They made sure everything was right—tight and true. We were doing the best we could. Now? Anybody with a camera and a YouTube channel can put stuff out. And to me, that's dangerous. There's no filter. It's a real challenge to get it right.

VIC: You must've interviewed so many people in your life. Could you name a couple that still haunt you—or stay with you?

BOB: Yeah. We did a calculation at *Quirks & Quarks*, and just during my 32 years hosting, I've done over 7,000 interviews. That's just for *Quirks & Quarks*. Before that, I had a whole other career. So, it's probably closer to 10,000. Every time the Nobel Prizes are awarded, I get to interview someone who's just won. That's a thrill—especially when it's a Canadian.

Like Dr. Art McDonald, from the Sudbury Neutrino Observatory. I've known Art for many years. When he won the Nobel, it was fantastic. That always stands out. Then there's Carl Sagan. Big name. Famous astronomer. He was an inspiration to me back when I was at the Science Centre. I not only got to interview him—I got to attend space events with him. One of them was the launch of *Voyager*—this model behind me, here. *Voyager* was launched in 1977. It was designed to fly by Jupiter, Saturn, Uranus, and Neptune, which were all in a line at the time. The gravity of those big planets flung *Voyager* right out of the solar system. It's still out there, and it'll keep going for more than a billion years—crossing the galaxy.

Sagan convinced NASA to put a message on board: a golden record with music and digital images—a small cultural time capsule, in case some intelligent life ever finds it. A clue that humanity existed, and that we valued music. I was there at Cape Canaveral with Carl when it launched. The rocket took off in this thunder and pillar of smoke—it clawed its way into the sky until it vanished.

Carl turned around. He had tears in his eyes. He said: "We just sent a spaceship to the stars." And he was right. Until then, everything we'd launched stayed within the solar system. But *Voyager* was different—it was going out. On the ride back in the van, everyone was quiet. We were all thinking about what we'd just done—launched a human-made artifact that might last longer than anything else we've ever built.

The pyramids are only about 5,000 years old. I've been to Africa, held a 2-million-year-old stone tool from *Homo habilis* in my hand. That felt like time travel—like shaking hands with someone from the past. But *Voyager*? That could last a billion years. And I thought: all the things we argue about here on Earth—all the lines in the sand we draw, all the division—it's so trivial. The continents will shift. Ice ages will come and go. Humanity may vanish… and *Voyager* will still be out there. So yes—meeting Carl Sagan, and sharing those experiences—that had a huge impact on me.

VIC: Your curiosity—it's obviously taken you so far. But is there still a challenge left? Something you still feel drawn to explore?

BOB: Personally, I want to see as much of this planet as I can—while I still can. That's my own challenge. And I want to stay creative. I've written seven books. I'm working on another one now. I want to keep challenging my brain.

From a scientific point of view? The biggest challenge is understanding dark matter and dark energy. They make up 95 percent of the universe—and we have no idea what they are. We think we're smart, but we still don't know what most of the universe is made of.

I find that exciting. There's still so much to learn. And I've always believed that our ignorance exceeds our knowledge. Always. That's still true. So yes—what is this dark stuff? Why is the universe expanding faster and faster? What's out there? Those are the frontiers I care about.

VIC: You know, in this digital world—and this is just from my experience—it's getting hard to know what's real anymore. Does that concern you?

BOB: Yes, absolutely. I'm concerned about artificial intelligence. On one hand, it's an incredible tool—especially for science. It can process massive datasets, detect patterns that people can't see, and do it all quickly. That saves time and opens doors. But when AI starts imitating people, or when students use it to write essays without thinking—that worries me. It could impact our education system, and society itself.

Facts and pseudo-facts… or "alternative facts," as they say—it's hard to tell the difference now. So yes, it's powerful. But it needs boundaries. We put boundaries around nuclear weapons. After Hiroshima and Nagasaki, we said: "We'll have them—but we won't use them." We need something similar for AI. Guidelines. Guardrails. We need to use it for good—not in nefarious ways. But I'm not afraid of it taking over the world. There's an old joke: Someone asked a computer, "Is there a God?" The computer replied, "There is now." I don't think that's going to happen.

VIC: Are you a religious person?

BOB: Well, I was brought up Catholic. I went through all the rituals. As a teenager, I was up on the altar doing Bible readings. I was even in a folk group—we sang at folk Masses. I was really into it. But as I left the Church—and as I got more and more immersed in science, and in the wonders of the universe, God just stopped being part of the equation for me.

We're figuring out how the universe came to be—how it was created—and divine intervention isn't part of that explanation. I don't need to invoke God to understand how the universe works. In a way, I guess science has become my new religion. I don't pray. I don't ask God for favours. To me, that's what prayers are—"Give us this day our daily bread." I'll get my own bread, thank you very much. I want to survive on my own. I respect people who have faith. I have no problem with that. Just don't try to convert me. I've got my own view of the universe. I see science as a way of understanding how things work.

Faith can answer the question why—"Why are we here?"—but I'm not as interested in the why. I'm more interested in the how. And there's so much we still don't know about that. And it's wondrous. The universe is beautiful. I'm humbled by it. It's so vast, and we're so small. And to me, it's a kind of miracle that we know that. We know our cosmic address: we live on a ball that's orbiting a star, which is moving through a galaxy, which is part of an expanding universe. There are more stars than grains of sand on a beach—and we've figured that out. We know what DNA is. We know why a child looks like their parent. That, to me, is miraculous. I don't need a mystery deity to explain it. Science does that for me.

VIC: So, in a sense, you've replaced the spiritual with the scope of science?

BOB: Yes. And I also believe we're already living in the Garden of Eden. This is it. Right here. If there's an afterlife—when I get there, if it exists—I'll say, "Wow, this is great. Thanks." But I'm not living for that. I'm living now. I'm trying to make the most of this life. Because this is it. And when you die, you die. That's death. I'm not counting on more. I want to make the most of this amazing place we live in.

When William Shatner went up into space—on that tourist rocket—he came back in tears. He saw how thin Earth's atmosphere really is, and how fragile. That's the overview effect—seeing our frail little planet from above. That's a kind of religious experience. I get that same feeling—by looking at the world through the lens of science. It's like putting on special glasses.

You look at the same things as everyone else—but you see them in exquisite detail. You look at a plant leaf—and realize it's turning sunlight into food. You look into the sky—and notice the black between the stars, because that is what the universe is mostly made of. There are eight billion people in the world. We all look different. We all sound different. That's amazing.

VIC: To someone who's not a scientist, that might feel like magic. So who—or what—creates all that magic?

BOB: An evolutionary biologist would say, "That's natural selection." And if you rewound the tape of life—went back to the beginning and let evolution play out again—you and I wouldn't be here. Something else entirely would. Because it's all random. Some things worked, others didn't. That's still going on. And here we are. What worries me is that the dominant species on the planet right now—us—is consuming and burning everything in sight. We're not destroying the Earth. The Earth has been through ice ages and heat waves before. The planet will be fine. It's us I worry about. We've become narrow-minded. We think in the short term—what we can take and use now. We don't think long term. Our energy philosophy is still "drill, baby, drill" instead of "let's find new ways to move and heat and live without destroying our atmosphere."

VIC: And yet, people like me—we're living longer. We have more than ever before. Travel, food, health…

BOB: Believe it or not, I'm an optimist about the future. I discovered something hopeful: We already have the technology we need to go green. We can generate electricity, drive cars, heat homes—without wrecking the planet. Solar, wind, geothermal—we know how to do it. I just hope we don't wait for a full-blown crisis before we act. Some countries are doing it. Canada could do more. We started… but we've pulled back a bit. Still, I'm optimistic. I think common sense, good science, and strong engineering will help us find our way through this bottleneck. We've done it before. We got to the Moon. We revolutionized medicine. We extended lifespans and cured diseases. We can solve these problems if we focus on solutions, not just problems.

VIC: I'm overwhelmed by the human brain and heart. Absolutely overwhelmed. And you are at the head of that, because you've been curious all your life. So how can you translate that—this curiosity—to others? What can we do to make people feel the magic of the human race?

BOB: Well, one thing you can do is go outside. Get off your devices. Get out into nature. Take a really close look at a tree. Turn over some rocks and see what's crawling underneath. Stick your hand in a creek and see what comes up. Just look at this incredible planet we live on—and appreciate where we are, and how privileged we are to be here. And look at good people. Your neighbours. Most people aren't trying to shoot at you—most people are generally good. So, get out. Stop looking at the world through the lens of the media. Go look at it with your own eyes. You'll be amazed.

VIC: Excellent advice. So, how do you feel about your life at this point?

BOB: I feel great. I just turned 74. I feel healthy. My brain is active. And—I'm engaged to be married. Go figure. So yeah, I'm very happy. I'm looking forward to getting out there and looking around as long as I can. I've got a great job. I work with fabulous people. I'm part of the CBC family. I feel really privileged to do what I do.

VIC: Can you talk about what public broadcasting means to you?

BOB: Well, the CBC reflects Canada. It's an archive of Canadian history. It's been around long enough to have significant events on record—bringing the Constitution home, the referendums, elections, the *Avro Arrow*—you name it. But more than that, it reaches people. It reaches remote communities. It reaches all of Canada. I've been to the far north. People in small villages have told me, "Thank you for getting me out of my town. You bring me into the cosmos. You take me away from here." Because their world can be very restricted. That's what the CBC does. It introduces Canada to itself. It introduces Canada to the world. And through international broadcasting, it introduces the world to Canada. It's a vital part of our national conversation. Especially radio. We don't run commercials yet on radio. And I hope we never do. You can take it with you wherever you go. There's a saying: "You can't force people to watch, but you can't help but listen." And with radio, we can create wonderful pictures in your mind.

VIC: Is there anything else you'd like to share that we haven't covered?

BOB: Yes, I do have a message—especially for young people: Don't be afraid of the world. If there's something you want to do—really want to do—just say yes. Go for it. Don't make excuses. That's been my life. Someone asks, "Want to host a television show?" I'd never done it before. But I said yes. And yes—you get scared when you say yes. But when you're scared, you learn really fast. And then, the third thing: finish what you start. Just get it done. Don't worry about being the best—there's always someone better. But if you finish the job, people will appreciate it. Also: ideas are everything. Don't just walk into a room and say, "I want to work for you." Walk in and say, "I have an idea and you need me." That's what I did with *The National* in 1995. I walked into the documentary office and said, "There's a new Canadian astronaut named Chris Hadfield. He's training in Moscow. He's going to launch on an American shuttle to a Russian space station. We need to do a documentary on him—and I need to do it." They said, "Never heard of the guy." Next thing I knew, I was on a plane to Moscow. I followed Chris through the Russian space program. And that's how I met him. I wasn't a seasoned producer. I just had a good idea. So again, ideas are everything. Keep your ideas flowing. Go for what you dream up.

VIC: You have a very strong foundation. And that foundation is Canada.

BOB: Exactly. We are so fortunate to live in this country. Canada is the gem of the planet. We have choices. That's what sets us apart—choices. I've been to third-world countries. I've seen people who have no choices. What we can do—what we must do—is share what we have. We can share our science and technology. We can share our medicines, our knowledge, our talent. I know that in Africa, solar energy is growing because there's so much sunlight. That's fantastic. Science and technology can help them progress too. I met a Canadian doctor—also a pilot—who took a year off. He flew his own plane to Africa and went around setting up medical clinics. Showed people how to do it. All on his own. He got the Order of Canada. And that's what we can do. We can share the incredible intellectual capital we have here—with the world.

VIC: Yeah, let's do that. Well, I'm so grateful to you for your time.

Chapter 15

KRISTIN KREUK

Kristin Kreuk is a Canadian actress best known for her roles in Edgemont *and* Burden of Truth, *both airing on CBC. Her performances combine quiet intensity with emotional depth, earning her a devoted fan base across genres. A producer as well as performer, Kreuk has been a strong advocate for women's voices in media. She remains a prominent figure in Canadian television.*

KRISTIN: Well, you know, let's face it, when I was born, the world had about 2.5 billion people, right? Oh my God, a lifetime of it. That's crazy. That's true. Yeah, that's huge.

VIC: Exactly. Where were you born? What was it like growing up?

KRISTIN: Vancouver. I was born and raised in Vancouver. It was lovely—I have nothing to compare it to, because it's all I knew. But you could go out to the beach, look at tide pools, hike through the trees. It was beautiful. You didn't need a real winter coat; the winters were mild. I loved walking in the rain and getting soaked. And as a moody kid, the fog, the mist, the grey—all of that really suited me.

VIC: Were you close to your parents growing up?

KRISTIN: Close enough. I was especially close to my grandmother. My family did things together—we had dinner every night, and my parents worked regular 9-to-5 jobs. I was involved in lots of extracurriculars: gymnastics, piano, swimming, karate—you name it.

VIC: So there was encouragement from your parents?

KRISTIN: Oh God, yes. My mom is Chinese, and not to lean into stereotypes, but in my experience, Asian parents often have strong expectations. You're expected to meet them.

VIC: And your dad?

KRISTIN: He's European, but born in St. Catharines, Ontario. A real hard worker—he values consistency and effort. He started his own business as a landscape architect. He really pushed us to our limits and encouraged play and exploration. I wasn't allowed to just stay inside, it was always, "Go out! Play in traffic!" So we did—ran around the alleyways in Vancouver, which has lots of alleys unlike places like Toronto.

VIC: Were you the type of kid who confided in your parents?

KRISTIN: Not really. I wasn't the kind who poured my heart out to my parents, but we were around each other a lot.

VIC: Did you have siblings?

KRISTIN: Yes, I have a younger sister, five years younger. No one else in my family is an actor—that would be crazy talk! I'm the weird one.

VIC: So you didn't set out to become an actress?

KRISTIN: No, but I always loved acting. I used to gather neighbourhood kids to put on plays, choreograph dances, write stories. I took acting classes from a young age, and loved it, but it wasn't a career path I imagined for myself. I wasn't one of those kids getting agents or headshots. I wasn't precocious that way. I wasn't one of those six-year-olds saying, "I am this." I thought I'd be a marine biologist. Or a forensic scientist. I applied to SFU for psychology, and then suddenly I was asked to audition for a role. I got the part, and that sharp turn changed everything—I entered a world I never expected.

VIC: What did you do for fun or recreation?

KRISTIN: So many things! I was a competitive gymnast, which took up a lot of time—straight from school to training, bus rides to the gym, evenings full. Not every day—I wasn't Olympic level—but I loved it. And, like I said, I enjoyed performing. I'd rope my sister into shows, write things, put on little productions. I loved reading and writing, and I really lived in this imaginary, make-believe space. I had a few close friends, and we'd talk a lot—especially during our early teens when you start thinking globally. Many of my friends weren't from Canada originally, so we had deep conversations about identity and the world.

VIC: So you were social?

KRISTIN: In some ways, yes—and in other ways, I was a bit of a loner. I wasn't a partygoer or the popular kid. I had two or three really close friends, and then the girls from my gym team, which felt like a separate universe. I've always thought of myself as an introvert. But when I was with people I trusted, I wanted to go deep. I wasn't into drinking or drugs. That stuff never interested me. I wanted to sit on the beach, go for long walks, share writing, and talk—really talk.

And that friendship, those same friendships, are still there. But once I started working, my life changed dramatically. One of my close friends from high school just texted me the other night. She said, "What are we going to do? America is… this is going to be so difficult with these terrorists. We need to watch more Canadian programming. Kristin, how do we change this industry?" I told her, "Listen, man, we've been trying—harder than you think. You can't just snap your fingers and say, 'Let's make amazing stuff.' We're trying, but there just isn't a large demographic here. We don't have the same market—fewer people purchasing content."

VIC: Since you mentioned it, how do you feel about this whole surge of nationalism that's taking place?

KRISTIN: Nationalism is complicated. There are upsides to it, and I think, in the case of Canada right now, we need that unity. But I'm no expert, this is just my opinion. I do feel, though, that when you're building Canadian TV shows, it's challenging. America has a unified mythology. They have a clear sense of who they are and what they value.

When I was in school, we were taught that America is a melting pot, while we're a patchwork quilt. There's some truth to that—well, not truth exactly, but mythology. And myth matters. People believe in it. In Canada, our mythology isn't as strong. And in a way, I like that. I like that we're made up of diverse individuals, and we understand this nation in a more nuanced way. We can see the problems in how the country was formed. We can acknowledge that we aren't unified, that most of us are immigrants—apart from Indigenous Peoples, of course. There's a kind of complexity in that. So yes, nationalism can be important, and I think right now, it is—but I always feel a bit conflicted about it.

VIC: You've done so much work in both Canada and the U.S. You've never stopped. You're in a good position to give insight into both industries.

KRISTIN: That's a dangerous area to tread into! But yes, broadly speaking, Canada tends to be more risk-averse. We don't take big swings, especially in TV. That's just not what we do. America is different. Sure, they play it safe too—we've all seen the endless stream of Marvel movies—but there's also a willingness to take risks. And big swings are rewarded there. There's a mentality that supports risk-taking, which we don't really have here.

That said, when I worked on *Burden of Truth*—a Canadian production I loved, and where I was also an executive producer—it was such a joy. It felt collaborative and warm. Everyone on set was part of a team. American sets don't always feel that way. There's often a bit more tension. Of course, I'm generalizing, but the vibe is different.

VIC: As an artist, what do you want?

KRISTIN: God, what do I want? I don't know. But I do know that I want creative freedom. My path, as both actor and producer, has led me to seek out that freedom—to find ways to create my own work. I've been working on projects while also producing, so I can have a voice and a say in how things are done. Earlier in my career, I didn't have that freedom—and that's okay. When you're starting out, you're there to learn. You can't walk in and throw your weight around with no experience. There's value in apprenticeship.

But now, at this point in my life, I start to feel stifled if I don't have some creative input. If I'm just acting, I need other spaces where I can be fully creative and free. Whether or not people ever see it doesn't matter. A few years ago, I went back to school to get my bachelor's degree—partly to stimulate my mind. I studied history, not the arts, but I found so much creative freedom in that. I loved diving into research, building arguments—it was freeing and beautiful.

VIC: That makes sense. Because on one side, this is a business—you can't avoid that. But the real thing that drives you is your own inner voice. That desire to do the work. So let me ask—how important is that inner drive, especially in an industry like America's, which is so ratings-driven?

KRISTIN: Yes, 100%. They are driven by ratings. But is that necessarily the only thing that matters? I guess you could argue both sides, but for me, as an artist—sometimes, yes. And sometimes… no.

Sometimes I think relying on ratings is actually a hindrance to creative freedom. Relying on them means you're constantly checking in with an audience—which isn't inherently bad. There's value in audience feedback. But to really explore a story or an idea the way you want to as an artist, sometimes you have to isolate yourself from that external feedback. Not always—but sometimes. When everything becomes about appealing to the broadest audience—often a demographic with more buying power—it becomes about sales and capitalism more than art. I mean, television is a business, and I'm mostly talking about TV because that's my world. There are ways to make art within that system. We've seen incredibly artistic and free shows, especially recently. But if you're constantly shaping what you make around how people respond, it can limit the work.

That said, total isolation can muddle things too. You get lost in your own feedback loop. So I guess what I'm saying is, there has to be a relationship between the two—artistic integrity and commercial awareness. But when ratings become the only metric, I think the creative project suffers. Streamers, for example, operate more on a membership model. People pay for the whole platform, not individual shows, so there's more freedom in what gets made. On the other hand, traditional broadcasters are more tied to audience response, so their shows don't tend to be as bold. They occupy a different space, which has value, but isn't always liberating.

VIC: Exactly. Because at the end of the day, someone has to pay for it. And to me, the hardest part of life. If you lean too far one way or the other, there's always a price. So I ask you, as an artist who's worked on both sides—what works better for you? Which country gives you the environment you need?

KRISTIN: That's a really good question. If I think about it in terms of my own experience, the most creatively satisfying TV show I've worked on was *Burden of Truth* for the CBC. It was deeply fulfilling because we had the space to explore ideas and find our rhythm. You can see, season by season, how the show evolves and gains confidence. Would we have been able to make the same show with an American partner? I don't know. Maybe not—not us, at least, not at that time. But maybe if I were more famous, or had more clout, it could have happened in the U.S. I think there are avenues there for bold, creative television. The problem in Canada is more about lacking the resources to do it consistently.

VIC: I agree. And I think Canadian sensibilities are different. How important is it to you that we don't lose our sense of identity?

KRISTIN: That's hugely important to me. I worry sometimes that Canadians will lose ourselves in the wave of American media. It's everywhere—so much money and power behind it. And because it's in the same language and looks the same, it feels like ours. But it's not. It's fundamentally different. There's a distinct Canadian sensibility that I don't see reflected in American art. And it does exist in Canadian art. It's subtle, and it's complex, and it needs to be nurtured. The problem is, we just don't have the same population or funding to push our stories as far as they deserve to go.

VIC: Exactly. The Americans dominate through soft power. Their art spreads effortlessly. But Canadians have produced some of the best comedians.

KRISTIN: Absolutely. People say Canadians don't have a sense of humour—and I have no idea where that comes from! Some of the greatest comedians came out of Canada—John Candy, just to name one. And yet, somehow we still get labelled as the dull ones.

VIC: And then they went on to become... you know, that Canadian sensibility, that sense of character—it's strong. Canadians are among the funniest people. Just look how big they become elsewhere! But why don't we make them big here? Why do they have to go away first? Is it the market?

KRISTIN: You're asking huge questions—ones that have so many layers. I do think we have a bit of a tall poppy syndrome in Canada. We tend not to celebrate our own until they've already been embraced stateside. Maybe it's part of our self-deprecating nature. Part of the problem is that we don't have a functioning star system in English-speaking Canada. Quebec is totally different. Quebec celebrates its artists. It nurtures their work and takes pride in their stars.

In English Canada, we struggle more. And even though outlets like APTN are doing creative, compelling work with Indigenous content, there's still a gap. We don't do enough to raise each other up. I don't know exactly why—it might be something deeply ingrained in how we see ourselves. We just don't seem interested in lifting each other until someone else gives that stamp of approval. Maybe that's where nationalism could help—not jingoism, but a kind of cultural pride, enough to celebrate our own before America tells us they're worthy.

VIC: Exactly. I could name four or five internationally acclaimed films from Australia. Even from New Zealand—one or two easily. But if I walked down Georgia Street in Vancouver and asked people to name just one memorable Canadian film, chances are slim. People will likely name American films.

KRISTIN: Right. And the issue isn't that we don't have great Canadian films or talent—we absolutely do. We have brilliant technicians and artists. But do people know about them? Do we push our own stories far enough? Maybe it's about comfort levels. Maybe we're not used to boldly putting ourselves forward.

VIC: Yes, that boldness. It's about main character energy, right?

KRISTIN: Exactly. The youth today talk about that—"main character energy." In Canada, we're not taught to embrace that. Instead, we're taught to think collectively, to be kind, to look out for one another—and that's a beautiful value. But it doesn't create stars. Sometimes, in order to celebrate, we need a bit of that main character energy. Even as I say that, I'm questioning myself. Scandinavian film, for example—those communities are tight-knit but they've managed to build strong, cohesive identities. In Canada, we've always struggled with that. We don't really have a strong, shared sense of who we are. And maybe that's why we lean toward American content. Even when we do watch Canadian work, sometimes we don't even realize it's Canadian.

VIC: I feel like we're caught in between. We have that original British, Scottish, Irish sensibility. But we live next door to America, and we consume American content constantly.

KRISTIN: Yes, exactly. We're somewhere in between. And now we're more diverse than ever. My own family doesn't come from the original settler populations—there are constantly new Canadians arriving. But that's something I love about Canada. And I love that Indigenous film and television are rising. That gives me hope—that there's a creative path forward that's truly Canadian.

VIC: Do you think developing our own voice is essential?

KRISTIN: Absolutely. Every country needs its own voice. And for us, it's vital. We're huge geographically. We can't all just hang out in one café and talk about who we are. We need media to be that connective tissue—a way to share, to communicate across distance, to show one another what matters to us. What defines us. What we value—and what we reject. Of course, all of that evolves. But we still need a way to have that conversation as a country. And if a big outside force overwhelms that conversation, we risk losing this very fragile, very abstract idea of what it means to be Canadian.

VIC: Yes. Because "Canada" is just an idea in the end.

KRISTIN: Right. There are borders and laws, sure. But Canada lives in our minds. We create it every day. And if we want that to continue, we have to want it. We need to engage. We need to care about Canadian-made content. Maybe that means building a real star system—celebrating our own filmmakers, actors, and artists more openly. We do a better job with writers, I think. The literary scene in Canada is vibrant, and it gives me faith.

VIC: But how do we make that happen? How crucial are national broadcasters?

KRISTIN: They're essential. National broadcasters are the engine behind all of it. They allow us to create Canadian content without worrying about profit as the primary motive. That's their purpose—to tell our stories, deliver our news, and reflect our reality without being steered entirely by advertising dollars. Without institutions like the CBC or the NFB—publicly funded institutions—we simply can't compete. They make it possible to create and distribute content that belongs to us, that speaks to us, and that sustains us as a cultural community.

VIC: So it's the taxpayer's voice that makes it all possible?

KRISTIN: Exactly. And for that, I'm deeply grateful.

KRISTIN: As a taxpayer, I want some of my money going toward a broadcaster that speaks to the interests of the public—not to the interests of corporate entities. Sometimes that means not everyone will watch what's made, and that's okay. There are people in remote areas who only have access to the CBC. In those cases, it becomes the thread that ties them to the rest of us—and that's deeply important. The moment things become entirely about corporate interest, so much of the texture and edges of the art get shaved off. They die out. And we're left with content that looks a lot like what's already coming out of the United States.

VIC: You started with the CBC, didn't you?

KRISTIN: Yes, I did. I was in drama class in Grade 12 when a casting director reached out. They were doing a wide search for a character on a CBC show. On a whim, I auditioned—and I got the part. Suddenly, I found myself walking across the Cambie Street Bridge to the CBC building in Vancouver. I had my backpack, my Discman, and a chai latte—headed to work in what we affectionately called the dungeon of the CBC. I loved it. That time was such a transition in my life. Personally, the CBC has been a gift, and I think that's true for many artists in this country. It made it possible for us to build careers, take creative risks, and tell Canadian stories.

VIC: And you returned to work there again years later?

KRISTIN: Yes, I did. I was brought on to a project by a wonderful writer named Bradley Simpson. He won support for it, and we pitched it to the CBC. That show became *Burden of Truth*, which I worked on for four seasons. We filmed in Winnipeg, which was a joy. That's something I really appreciate about the CBC—it lets you illuminate different parts of the country. And there are so many underrepresented places in Canada. Getting to tell a story based in Winnipeg was an honour. Working with the CBC again was really wonderful.

VIC: Did you ever do anything with the Film Board?

KRISTIN: No, I've never worked with the National Film Board. I'd love to work with a Canadian broadcaster again, though. What we've been talking about—the space to take creative risks—is so important. Not everything has to be obviously consumable or marketable. It would be wonderful to collaborate with the CBC again, and I'm sure I will.

VIC: Let me ask—were there any difficult scenes you didn't want to do or didn't understand? What kind of help did you get to get there?

KRISTIN: Well, I was 17 years old when I started that show. I had no idea what I was doing. I had never acted in front of a camera before. I barely knew what a mark was. And yet, I was number two on the call sheet. I had no clue, and it was hard. I really struggled through the first season or two. I questioned everything—whether I had made a mistake, whether I should've just pursued a psychology degree instead. But Ian Weir, the head writer and show creator, was lovely, and the scripts were strong. I had to learn how to emote on camera. You can feel something deeply, but if the camera can't capture it, the emotion gets lost. Bridging that gap is technique—and a lot of actors learn that in school. I learned it on set. I was so young. So green. It's always horrifying to look back on that early work.

VIC: Was there a particular scene that really challenged you?

KRISTIN: It was so long ago—I'm 42 now. That was 25 years ago. I was scared, and honestly, my memories from that time are a bit blurry.

VIC: How about more recent work—anything challenging?

KRISTIN: Definitely. On *Burden of Truth*, there were constant challenges in shaping the story, figuring out where to take it next. A lot of it was strategic—big-picture stuff. Right before we shot the pilot, we had to change head writers with just days to go. The CBC was incredibly supportive during that scramble. When we needed reshoots to finesse things, they made it possible. They gave us room to get it right.

VIC: And from an actress's perspective, can you talk about the difference between working for a public broadcaster like the CBC versus the commercial side?

KRISTIN: As an actor, you don't always feel that difference directly, because of the layers of hierarchy—showrunners, producers, and so on. But there's definitely a contrast. On a big-budget American network show, you've got studio and network executives on both sides. Notes come from everywhere. As an actor, you're impacted by everyone's vision of what the character should be. The character becomes less yours and more a product of committee. It's a business construct more than a personal expression. Sometimes that's okay—but it's hard.

Over time, audiences stop paying attention—that's okay—but it's really about that initial grab. That happens on every American show, and it usually centres on surface things: hair, makeup, wardrobe. There's so much concern over whether a female character is smiling enough or likeable enough. These become the main considerations, especially for women on screen. Crunchy, more complex edges? Not so appealing. Though I do think that's beginning to change. The market is shifting—but it's still the market driving that change, not the art itself.

VIC: How important to you is the honesty of the character?

KRISTIN: That's everything. Honesty is the most important thing in acting. That's what the job is—creating something that feels true. All the other stuff—how something looks or how it's perceived—shouldn't be my concern as an actor. From a producer's perspective, maybe. But as an actor, it's all about the character. That's why people tune in—because something feels real. It resonates. Acting is creating the illusion of truth, and sometimes that illusion becomes real. But focusing too much on the external—on appearances or perception—can pull you out of that. It turns into this meta thing, where you're always aware of yourself, and that undermines the work. That same dynamic plays out in life too, but it's especially disruptive in performance.

VIC: You've worked on shows where you felt that tension?

KRISTIN: Oh yeah. All the time. I mean, I was on smart TV—that was the dream, right? And sure, acting is fun. Pretending is fun. It's silly, and it's joyful, and it helps me understand myself and others better. There's something enriching in that. But the business side? That's always the challenge. You're constantly negotiating with producers about wardrobe, or a scene that feels gratuitous or inauthentic. That kind of thing can make it all feel like a dream—disconnected from the craft. It becomes less about acting and storytelling, and more about meeting external expectations. Of course, the money matters. It has to. That's the world we live in. But it complicates things when you're trying to find something real. That's why freedom matters—creative freedom. But for an actor, that kind of freedom is rare. It's what keeps you going, though. Those brief tastes of something true, something alive—that's the spark. Those are the moments that feed me.

Most of the time, this is a practical job. You're on a show, you do your work, you hope people watch. And that's fine. But the artistic moments—the ones where something genuine happens—those are the ones that stay with me. Honestly, the most rewarding acting experience I've had recently was on a strange little film for a Japanese director called *Vampire*. He barely spoke English. We improvised a scene—I didn't have to be pretty, which was refreshing. I had weird makeup on, and he just said, "Go." So I went. I ended up dancing on a freezer, doing wild things. I was terrified. I didn't know if it would make any sense. But it was fun. It felt alive. It wasn't commercial—it was about truth.

VIC: I understand. I started as a cinematographer, and back in the day, I was the first one watching the film take shape through a lens. Especially when shooting in places like Africa or China, we'd go days without dailies. So after a scene, everyone would look at me—"What do you think?" I'd be the one deciding, "Should we do one more day?" It felt collaborative. We were all making the film together. But now, it's like every Tom, Dick, and Harry has an opinion. It becomes a committee. That's the least satisfying way to make a movie. I believe everyone on set is there for a reason, and they should be allowed to do their job. I'm not there to micromanage the camera—I trust the team. That's how freedom works.

KRISTIN: I get that. And you're right. Freedom on a set is rare—and asking an actor about freedom is tricky. Because we don't really have it. Even though we're the face of the show, we're in service of the script, the director, the story. We don't exist in a vacuum. Even in the most creative, generous environments, the actor's freedom is limited. We have freedom in the choices we make, in how we interpret the material. But the more voices weigh in, the more diluted the vision becomes.

I think it's helpful if someone has a vision—if there's someone carrying the vision, with a strong point of view you can follow. For me, as an actor, that gives me the freedom to explore within the bounds of that vision. That feels like real creative freedom. Ultimate freedom? That doesn't really exist on a set. But when a production becomes super corporate, you start losing that creative vision. It becomes a numbers game. "We want this because audiences like it," or "We need that to reach this demographic." That's no longer art. It's something else entirely. My job, for it to feel satisfying, is to be in scenes that hold together, with a character who holds together. And there has to be space to play. That's much more likely to happen if there's a strong, unified vision behind the project. But the more voices trying to control that vision, the more it disintegrates.

VIC: Could you share any personal stories—maybe one of your most difficult scenes or moments?

KRISTIN: Honestly, my first few seasons of *Smallville* were the hardest. I was suddenly famous, which was overwhelming. I didn't know how to express what I needed or how to give constructive notes. I thought I just had to shut up and do the job. I felt boxed in, expected to be a certain kind of person, and that freedom I keep talking about—I lost it.

Smallville was all about close-ups. We were young and pretty, and everything lived in the frame. When you're constantly in tight shots, there's very little room to move or express. Your vocal range shrinks, your movement is restricted—it's hard to breathe as a performer. I came from doing theatre in high school, where I felt much more free. Balancing all of that, at that time in my life, was tough. I wasn't very happy. It took a long time to find my footing.

VIC: Is there anything you'd still like to do as an actor?

KRISTIN: I don't have a specific role in mind, but yes—there's so much I'd love to do. I want to expand creatively, to explore more avenues for storytelling. That might be through writing, producing, podcasting, graphic storytelling—there are so many exciting mediums now. I just want to keep creating.

VIC: Can you share one of your favourite films or characters?

KRISTIN: Whenever I get asked that, I fall back on my tried and true from childhood: *The Princess Bride*. It's still my favourite film. It's not a sophisticated choice, I know—but it brings me joy. The performances are lovely, the story is charming. Even though it's dated now, I love it. It's a beautiful, lovable film.

VIC: Do you feel happy on set?

KRISTIN: Yes, I do. On set, I know my place. I feel confident and capable. I understand what everyone's role is, how we work together. There's a symbiosis to a well-functioning crew. It's the place I've spent most of my life—it feels like home. I don't get overly excited anymore, but I love being there.

VIC: I thought you were very brave to do *Partition*. It was such a different culture, with complex nuances. You weren't stereotyped, and the essence of the film was powerful—about bridging divisions and simply being human.

KRISTIN: Thank you. I think we were all brave in that project. It was far outside my usual experience. I had a lot of help preparing for it—coaches, research, everything. At the time, it was a breath of fresh air. I was on *Smallville*, and they let me go to India to shoot it. I was thrilled. It was challenging—I never knew if I could pull off the scene, which was exhilarating. The story was beautiful. It was about love, about bridging divisions, about finding shared humanity underneath religion and politics. At its heart, it was about people. That message still matters. I felt like I was doing something important, something that mattered. And it challenged me. I think that's what we all want—purpose and challenge. When they come together, that's a gift.

VIC: What matters to you now?

KRISTIN: Oh—probably the same things that have always mattered. What matters is community. What matters is connection. Building deep relationships with people, having meaningful engagement across different cultures—all of that. In the end, that's what's come to matter the most to me.

VIC: Beyond acting, what else do you do?

KRISTIN: I read voraciously. I'm deeply curious. I love learning. Like I said, I went back to school and got my bachelor's degree. I'm even considering doing a master's. I love being in nature, exploring. And of course, I love storytelling—not just on set, but in other ways too. Whether it's sharing other people's stories or experimenting in different mediums, that brings me joy.

VIC: Do you feel good about your life?

KRISTIN: I do. I'm really happy. I feel lucky. I get to travel the world, read books, meet amazing people. I have free time. I sleep well. Let's be honest, that's a real blessing.

VIC: Thank you so much. If you're happy, I'm happy.

Chapter 16

MARTIN DUCKWORTH

Martin Duckworth is an acclaimed cinematographer and filmmaker whose work at the National Film Board of Canada spans over 50 films. With a distinctive eye for the human condition, his documentaries explore peace, activism, disability rights, and the nuances of everyday life. He has also taught generations of documentary filmmakers at Concordia University, combining artistic vision with social commitment. Duckworth's body of work is widely celebrated for its depth, empathy, and enduring relevance.

VIC: What was it like growing up in Nova Scotia? Where did you grow up?

MARTIN DUCKWORTH: I didn't grow up in Nova Scotia. I grew up in NDG, Notre-Dame-de-Grâce, when it was an anglophone ghetto in Montreal. I moved to Nova Scotia at the age of 17. I went to high school there and lived in Nova Scotia for four years. Northern Nova Scotia is a military town, but what was interesting about it was that my mother was a pacifist, an anti-imperialist pacifist. She ended up as a feminist anti-war activist in Halifax. She was always demonstrating in front of the naval yards in Halifax. So that's what I remember most about my high school years.

VIC: Was there any video at that time? There was no television yet, right?

MARTIN: Correct. No television at that time. What did I listen to on the radio? I listened to Paul Robeson singing. That was my main source of inspiration. We listened to Paul Robeson every Sunday afternoon, and Marian Anderson too. That's my strongest media memory from my teenage years — CBC radio.

VIC: CBC was around then?

MARTIN: It must have been, but my goodness, I don't think I paid much attention to it. I wasn't paying much attention to films either. I got turned off films by *The Wizard of Oz*, which I saw when I was 8 years old. It frightened me so much that I didn't want to see another film for the rest of my life. I didn't watch a film again until I was at university. I was teaching at Mount Allison, and they wanted me to help start a film club. That's when I saw *Jules and Jim*— the first film I saw since I was eight years old. That was when I was about 22 or 23—16 years after *Wizard of Oz* turned me off films!

I experienced a dramatic turn in my life in 1961. I was teaching at Mount Allison University in New Brunswick, organizing a summer institute on French Canadian culture. We brought Don Francks and Fernand Dansereau from the Film Board. Fernand brought the *cinéma vérité* film *Golden Gloves* by Gilles Groulx, about young boxers in Montreal trying to break into the sport. When I saw that film, I decided I wanted to make documentaries. I asked if he could introduce me to the right people at the Film Board. He introduced me to Tom Daly in Montreal, and Tom got me a job as an assistant cameraman. *Golden Gloves* changed my life.

VIC: So you started in cinematography, as an assistant cameraman?

MARTIN: Yes. They hired me based on still photographs I had been taking since I was a teenager. I'd done a lot of still photography.

VIC: Do you remember the first film you worked on?

MARTIN: At the Film Board? Gee, I think it might have been *60 Cycle* by Jean-Claude Labrecque. Also around that time, I worked with Michel Brault.

VIC: What was your experience like on that first film?

MARTIN: It was a very exciting time. Those were the golden years of the Film Board — when all the great filmmakers were being trained: Gilles Carle, Don Owen, Michel Brault. I was assistant cameraman on films by nearly all of them. The cafeteria was the creative hub. I was probably the only English speaker who sat at the French tables, and that got me hired on their films too.

VIC: When did you start shooting your own films?

MARTIN: I was hired in '63, and I think I shot my first film in '66 — a film about my children called *The Wish*. I was 33 years old.

VIC: Did you have trouble getting it off the ground?

MARTIN: Not with Tom Daly as producer! He backed that film and my next few projects: *Accident*, *Untouched and Pure*, and *Passing Through Sweden*. He was a great supporter.

VIC: Did you ever consider going to the States, to Hollywood?

MARTIN: Well, when I met Audrey, my wife, I was working on a film about the Hiroshima bombing. I promised her I'd look for work in Boston, her hometown, if she moved to Montreal with me. I tried, but couldn't find work there. She stayed anyway. We bought this house, raised three children here. That was 48 years ago.

VIC: Seems like you had two great passions — filmmaking and women.

MARTIN: That's probably true. A pretty good balance between the two.

VIC: Did you write your own films?

MARTIN: Yes. All of them were my ideas. I wrote the proposals. Back then, all you needed was one page to get a documentary budget. Now it takes 20. So I haven't done that in a few years.

VIC: Who do you credit most for your career?

MARTIN: Tom Daly, Colin Low, and Jacques Vallée, who produced four or five of my films.

VIC: What film are you most proud of?

MARTIN: *Dear Santa Claus*. It's about children writing letters to Santa. I made it for my daughter, who's handicapped and still believes in Santa. She's 48 now. It's a very pro-Santa film. It was shown at Christmas for years.

VIC: And politically?

MARTIN: *Peacekeeper at War*. It announced Canada's role in the first Gulf War. A big-budget film — lots of archival material. It's expensive to keep online because of rights, but it was widely used in high schools at the time.

VIC: You seem very socially conscious.

MARTIN: I come from a family that was. My father was a YMCA secretary. He believed Jesus was a socialist, and so he preached social Christianity as a way of raising money for the YMCA. My mother became very active under his influence in the peace movement during the Second World War. They resisted Canada's involvement in the war, which was very dangerous at the time. I come from a very socially active family.

VIC: What makes your life richer? What makes life worthwhile?

MARTIN: Grandchildren. And Rachmaninoff. I'm crazy about him right now. I listen to Rachmaninoff piano sonatas almost every night when I go to bed.

VIC: Looking back, do you ever regret getting into the film business?

MARTIN: No, my only regret is that I didn't get into it earlier. I think I could have been a better filmmaker if I had met Fernand Dansereau earlier. I didn't meet him until I was 28.

VIC: You and I have similar background. We both started out as cinematographers, then moved into directing. A lot of directors come from editing, but we came from the camera side. Do you think that was an asset?

MARTIN: Absolutely. If you're going to be a documentary filmmaker, that's the best background to come from. You don't need a script to make a good documentary. All you need is good characters and a good storyline. Once you've lined those up, you go out and find them with your camera.

VIC: You were very focused and driven to make films. Who do you thank for that? You needed funding to make those films.

MARTIN: Well, for the first seven years of my filmmaking career, I was at the Film Board. I got all my funding from them, thanks to Tom Daly, who always made sure I had a decent budget. Later on, Jacques Vallée supported me in French production. The Film Board gave me not only production funding, but also a salary. They hired me in 1963 as an untrained assistant, trained me to be a cameraman, and paid me while doing it. That just doesn't happen anymore. The 1960s were the last time for that kind of opportunity. I was hired at the same time as Robin Spry, Mike Rubbo, and Tanya Ballantyne. A lot of us got our start then, and they trained us because they expected us to produce films that would build the Film Board's reputation.

VIC: How long were you at the Film Board?

MARTIN: From 1963 to 1970. In 1970, I met a woman in Sweden while filming there. She told me that if I stayed on staff at the Film Board, I'd become corrupt—an established bureaucrat. So, she persuaded me to quit. I was 40 years old. I was crazy about her and wanted to stay in her good graces. We had two children together, so it paid off in the long run.

VIC: Do you regret leaving the Film Board?

MARTIN: No. I became very active in organizing freelance English filmmakers. I helped to establish DOC—Documentary Organization of Canada—which started here in Montreal in the 1970s.

VIC: You've done mostly social commentary films. But did you ever do anything light?

MARTIN: I made a film about Oliver Jones—about his jazz music, which I like very much.

VIC: What was the most difficult project you tackled?

MARTIN: The film about the First Gulf War, *Peacekeeper at War*. The director of English production at the time didn't approve of it—he said I was fired.

That was tough. I gathered the other filmmakers around, showed them the film, and they all spoke in favour of it. That persuaded the Board to let me finish it.

VIC: Did you ever reconcile with that producer?

MARTIN: Yes. A few years later, we ran into each other at a Film Board old-timers' lunch. He asked what I was working on, and I told him I was trying to make a film about Palestine, about a friend trying to reclaim a hotel in Haifa. He asked, "Do you have a producer?" I said, "No." He replied, "I'll produce it." So, we became friends again. It was very nice.

VIC: You seem to have been drawn very much to subjects elsewhere. What about this country itself? At the time, there was the FLQ crisis going on, and Indigenous Peoples didn't have a strong voice yet. Given that you were always drawn to social issues, did you ever think about taking on some of those topics?

MARTIN: Well, have you seen the film I made about the Sudbury miners' strike? It was in 1980, I think. That's the strongest film I've made about labour struggles in Canada. It's called *Wives' Tale*. I think there were about ten thousand nickel miners on strike. I wanted to be involved in some way, so I got to know one of the women who was organizing wives to support their husbands during the strike. I ended up spending maybe six or eight months living in Sudbury with some of the families. I found a brilliant young filmmaker to help with sound recording. So together we made the film about women organizing to support the strike against Inco.

VIC: So that was your most relevant film on Canadian labour?

MARTIN: Yes, definitely. I also tried to get a film going about the history of labour unions in Canada. Actually, I got fired over that one too. I had shown a first cut to the director of English production, and he didn't like it. That wasn't the Gulf War film I mentioned earlier—it was about Canadian trade unions. But the same producer later made up for it by producing the film I wanted to make about Palestine.

VIC: You also did a film about coal miners?

MARTIN: Yes, I made *12,000 Men*, a film about Cape Breton coal miners. That might be one of the films I'm most proud of. It was approved by the coal miners' union, and they used it in their union hall for years afterward—constantly showing it in Cape Breton.

VIC: When you were making films—shooting, directing, doing everything—what aspect did you enjoy the most?

MARTIN: Having one eye on the eyepiece and the other eye looking around. That's what I liked most—seeing, really seeing. And pushing the record button on the camera.

VIC: Not the interaction with your subjects?

MARTIN: Well, that's what leads to the moment when you push the button. The camera comes after you've established a good relationship with your characters. When they start to feel that what you're doing is important to them, they let you in. That's when it becomes possible to really film them.

VIC: You've made so many films. Can you share some of your most memorable moments—times where you felt deeply fulfilled in your work?

MARTIN: I think the most important, most memorable experience was making the film *No More Hiroshima*, with my wife, Audrey. That was a high point emotionally and politically. It was also the high point of our relationship—we were together for 48 years. The film followed Canadian survivors and peace activists, who were exploring both the personal and political aftermath of nuclear warfare. The film board supported us really well. Audrey was given a contract to ensure it was widely seen in the U.S., and she travelled with the main character.

We both attended screenings in Quebec and Ontario. That was probably the most meaningful project I've ever worked on. We filmed for about two months—partly in Hiroshima and partly in New York City. But Audrey and I spent a couple of years researching and preparing before we even started shooting. We had a Canada Council grant that allowed us to travel and meet people a year in advance. Audrey brought our one-year-old son, Nicholas, and he helped us build relationships. People would open their doors and invite us in when they saw the baby.

It was very difficult emotionally. We were speaking with people who had seen their children and loved ones walking around with their skin falling off. It was horrific. But the humanity of the survivors helped us stay sane. They still believed it was possible to eliminate nuclear weapons, if people around the world came together. That was their motivation for participating in our film—to spread that message.

VIC: How many films have you done?

MARTIN: Well, I was trying to count the other day. I've made 25 that I feel proud of. And maybe another half-dozen that were less relevant but I think they were all worth doing. I don't think I would have done them if I hadn't believed in their worth. I can't remember doing any camera work that I didn't feel strongly about—whatever the issue was. I need that motivation, or I just couldn't do it.

VIC: Did you ever do camera work on something that didn't involve you emotionally?

MARTIN: No. I've been very lucky. I don't do action films. I say no. But to be honest, I've never really been asked to do other kinds of films. I seem to be part of a kind of cult—progressive-thinking filmmakers. We all believe we're sailing in the same boat.

VIC: Where does your inspiration come from?

MARTIN: My father, the social gospel preacher. He raised money for the YMCA by convincing millionaires they should feel guilty about their wealth—and that they could deal with that guilt by donating to the YMCA. He was very successful at it.

VIC: And he passed on those values to you?

MARTIN: Absolutely. He showed me that you could be a socialist, a pacifist even, and still succeed in life. He kept his job at the YMCA even though he spoke out against Canada going to war during World War II. He stood alongside one of the leaders of the NDP at the time. Before Tommy Douglas. Anyway, my father was one of the few public voices against declaring war on Germany in 1938. He didn't hide his views, but he was such a powerful speaker, people listened—even those who disagreed.

VIC: So those seeds of social justice were planted early. Did you take on anything like that yourself?

MARTIN: The Hiroshima film, definitely—that was the best thing I did for the peace movement. I also made a film in 1986 about Dresden during the Cold War, *Return to Dresden* it was called. I travelled there with an old family friend—a McGill professor who'd been a pilot during the bombing of Dresden. It was a moving film, about his apology to the people of Dresden. That one meant a lot to me.

Then there was *Our Last Days* the film I made in Moscow, also during the Cold War. It followed two Montreal musicians who performed there at a peace event in 1986, right at the height of tensions. That was a hard one. Soviet inspectors were with us constantly, making it hard to get material. I didn't even know if there was a film in it until I got back to the Film Board and started editing. But eventually, I found the story. I'm proud of that.

VIC: You've taken on some very challenging political and social subjects. Did the Film Board ever interfere?

MARTIN: Only once—on a film about the history of the Canadian labour movement. They withdrew their support. But otherwise, they've been great. I don't think the Film Board would have survived if Donald Trump had been in charge back then. He would've seen it as a bastion of liberal thinking.

VIC: How important is independence for filmmakers?

MARTIN: It's everything. But now, the Film Board barely has a budget. You need a TV outlet lined up before you can get a film made there. You have to arrive with half your funding already secured from a broadcaster.

VIC: So it's about selling your idea?

MARTIN: Exactly. It comes down to writing a strong proposal. That's not something I was particularly good at. I started phasing out about ten years ago, partly because of that.

VIC: Were you ever offered work in the States?

MARTIN: Well, one film I shot for the Film Board was about an archaeologist from Bulgaria who had worked extensively with Indigenous people in northern Canada. He was also a photographer, and some of his images showed children breastfeeding. These photos were distributed in U.S. archaeological circles, but when a certain senator found out about them, he declared them immoral—said they violated American values. We brought the archaeologist over, followed him around and made a film called *Mother Tongue*. There's quite a strong sequence of him speaking to the senator—the one who made sure those breastfeeding photographs couldn't be seen in the U.S. That, and the big peace march in New York City in 1986 with the survivors from here, are my strongest memories of filming in the States.

VIC: But you never had any desire to move to the States?

MARTIN: Yeah, I thought about it when I met Audrey. I would've loved to move to Boston with her. Her father was a strong historian of the American empire. He's actually the one who encouraged us to make a film about Hiroshima. He was similar to my father in some ways—only he preached the communist line instead of the Christian one. He was in favour of war with Germany. I really loved him and would've loved to find work in Boston, but I couldn't make it happen.

Oh, I did do one progressive American film. I worked camera on a documentary about the history of the American Communist Party, *Seeing Red: Stories of American Communists*. It was a very good film and was even nominated for an Academy Award. It was directed by Jim Klein and Julia Reichert.

VIC: Is there anything you'd like to do now? Any film project?

MARTIN: Yes. I want to make a film about Elizabeth Pion, a young pianist. She's a great interpreter of Rachmaninoff—and she also plays Prokofiev beautifully, which is very difficult. She's brilliant with concertos.

VIC: You like Russian music?

MARTIN: Yes. Very much.

VIC: Now, when you work as a filmmaker—as a cinematographer—you're only as good as the team around you. One person can't do everything. Could you talk a bit about the support you received and how much that meant?

MARTIN: Absolutely. My favourite sound man is Glenn Hodgins. He lives in Amaranth, Ontario, and he's one of my best friends. He comes from a mining town. He's got a great story about his father, who was a miner. Glenn runs a honey and hay farm now, with hummingbirds flying around. Another important collaborator is Dorothy Todd Hénaut. She produced several of my films at the Film Board. She's a neighbour, and we often talk about politics and what films are worth watching. And I still stay in touch with Tom Daly's people. Tom's been gone for about ten years now, but I visit his family in the Eastern Townships every year.

VIC: Did you ever have any desire to move into fiction?

MARTIN: Only one skinny experience. I worked camera for Don Owen's first film. Anyway, I joined the Film Board in '83 as an assistant cameraman, and Don asked me to do the DP work for his first feature, *Nobody Waved Good-bye.* I didn't feel ready, so I suggested he hire Jean-Claude Labrecque for DP and keep me on as camera operator. That's what he did. I operated the camera using an O'Connor gear head. It was a great experience, but that's the only time I worked on a feature film.

VIC: I was thinking more of directing fiction.

MARTIN: I never had the urge. I've always been completely inspired by documentary. It's what turns me on. Fiction is too complicated for me. You have to write scripts, deal with lots of people, raise funding—it's not my world. With documentary, you just have to feel strongly about the person you're filming. That's your motivation. That's what gets you through all the challenges. You just have to care deeply.

VIC: For me, documentaries give me real-life experience—and that helps when I do fiction. It's the honesty of real life. If I feel strongly about an idea, I want to push it forward to the masses.

MARTIN: Yeah, but you've got to deal with producers—more trouble there.

VIC: I've been lucky. My producers have been supportive—financially, ethically, professionally. They've played a very positive role. But I know not everyone gets that. Still, I think producers can be creatively engaged too.

MARTIN: Well, I've had good producers too. It's not that. It's just, with drama, everything has to be just right. You feel strongly about the story, and you want to shape every element to have that emotional impact. I like to have that control on all those. I think one reason I have not been attracted to making fiction is that I would have less time for love of a woman and children. Yeah. I think that is one reason I didn't get into fiction. I wanted to spend as much time at home with them as I did on location.

Time is limited in life, yeah? And people do love you when you're with them. Another reason I didn't follow your path was that Audrey had work here in Montreal—two kinds. I mean, she went with me on location to Hiroshima, but... Oh, and she also came with me to Sudbury for a while. But she had two things to do here in Montreal. One was to look after our handicapped child, and the other was that she was a teacher of photography. She set up the photography department at the Saidye Bronfman Centre. She worked there about 17 or 18 years. She was heavily responsible for running a good program, and that kept her in Montreal.

VIC: What about your footprints—which I call the films you've made? Do you feel good about having left those footprints?

MARTIN: Each film opens a new door: a door I've never opened before. You know, what makes life rich for me is the experience of life. It's not the money, it's not the fame. It's the experience of life. I would never have met you if I wasn't doing this.

VIC: Can you share more about friendships you made through films?

MARTIN: Yeah. Well, I don't think you can make a good film unless you become friends with your subjects. Unless you're out to make a film against someone. I became good friends with a journalist who lived nearby. He was the press foreign affairs correspondent for many years before he retired. He came with me as my guide for the film I was making about the first Gulf War, *Peacekeeper at War*. He came with me to Kuwait and made sure I saw the right people there. I'm just saying—the relationships you make—they're just so close, you become best friends. You become intimate friends, because making a film together is a very intimate thing. You're exposing another person's life and activities.

MARTIN: The dancer, Margie Gillis—she's a good friend of mine. I didn't direct, but I worked on a film about her by Tanya Ballantyne Tree, *Margie Gillis: Inside Out*. We became good friends.

VIC: Have you done any other filming about dance?

MARTIN: Not quite. But my favourite film is *Strictly Ballroom*, and I've seen a lot of documentaries, especially Spanish flamenco dancing and all that.

VIC: What are your other favourite subjects?

MARTIN: I think music. I love music more than anything. I have to hear good music every day. I've got a good collection of CDs and LPs.

VIC: Did you do anything in that area as well?

MARTIN: I used to be a pipe organist. I put myself through high school with a part-time job playing pipe organ at a local Anglican church in Halifax. I loved playing the pipe organ. But I gave it up for football when I went to Yale. I wanted to make the freshman football team, so I gave up pipe organ to train for that.

VIC: And did you make the team?

MARTIN: I didn't make the team—and I never went back to the pipe organ. That was the greatest regret of my life. I loved playing Bach, and I used to be quite good. I won some prizes.

VIC: Do you ever regret not going in that direction?

MARTIN: I look upon my career as a filmmaker—as a cameraman—as making up for that bad decision.

VIC: What film are you most proud of right now? The number one in your mind?

MARTIN: That might be a film called *Peaceable Kingdom*. It's a 25-minute portrait of my ancestor, who was a Quaker. He immigrated from New Hampshire in 1783 to establish the first settlement in the Eastern Townships of Quebec. He settled on Lake Memphremagog. He set up a town, now called Austin. He tried to establish a committed, peaceful Quaker community here, but he didn't succeed. He couldn't find enough supporters. So he died an unhappy man. He's buried there. But I'm proud of that film—it's a nice portrait. That film was supported by Peter Raymond—you know Peter Raymond? It was for his series, *Multiculturalism*, or something like that. He did a series about immigrant filmmakers making films about their ancestors who were immigrants.

VIC: What role did the Film Board play in your life, do you think?

MARTIN: They started me in a new direction. I was on an academic path before I met Fernand Dansereau. And he switched me over to a film career at the Film Board. That became my employer for seven years.

VIC: Has the Film Board changed over the years?

MARTIN: It's never been the same as those golden years of the 1960s— the golden years, when all of Quebec's great filmmakers were formed there. I was very lucky to be one of the last generation of filmmakers trained at the Film Board. It's gone downhill. Pierre Elliott Trudeau started taking money away from the Film Board—what the hell was his reason for doing that? Private producers were after him, I think, for giving such unfair advantage to Film Board productions. We have to find half the budget for our films before we can even pitch an idea to the Film Board.

VIC: When we start doing a business, and even to the end, there's always someone who has been your mentor. Who was your mentor?

MARTIN: Tom Daly. He was an exceptional producer. He got you reading Plato to discuss how to edit your film. "Read the Dialogues," he'd say, "and we'll talk about editing." He produced my first three or four films.

VIC: Anyone else?

MARTIN: Peter Raymond. He produced a few of my films after he left the Film Board.

VIC: Anyone else you related strongly to or looked up to?

MARTIN: Audrey. I think she was the biggest influence in my life. She came from a communist background. Her parents were politically active in the civil rights movement in the U.S. They were active with Black communities and civil rights. Audrey had that amazing combination of political consciousness and saintliness. She loved everyone, made everyone feel at home, opened people up. She was a fantastic lady. I directed the film *Dear Audrey* about her in 1994. The film is a portrait of her life, her creative work as a photographer, and the way we navigated her multiple sclerosis.

VIC: Do you still watch that film, *Dear Audrey*?

MARTIN: I go to screenings with it quite frequently. We have another screening next week at the Jewish General. Now it's in the Antigua Library.

VIC: What's your favourite scene?

MARTIN: When she flies into heaven at the end. The film has many beautiful scenes, but that's the one that stays with me. It represents her flying into the cosmos—where we all belong. She's getting there first, paving the way.

VIC: Last thing. Tell me about Alanis Obomsawin.

MARTIN: I shot one of her films. She had to fight for her survival at the Film Board. One administration after another tried to keep her quiet. They thought she was too loud. She made sure films about Indigenous People got programmed.

She had a hard fight. She kept going by maintaining an active political and cultural presence outside the Film Board—as a singer and poet. She did public readings and musical performances. So, the country became aware of her struggles and efforts. Eventually, the Film Board stopped resisting and let her finance what she thought was needed. The last 20 years have been easier for her there. Now, the Film Board is proud of her. They can say, "We helped her become an important voice for her people."

VIC: What film did you do with her?

MARTIN: I don't quite remember the title—*Kattawapiskak* perhaps. It was about a water and housing crisis in a Cree community in Northern Ontario.

VIC: What was that experience like for you?

MARTIN: It was freeing. She lets her crews play central roles. I felt in command. She didn't tell me which angles to take, when to roll or cut. She gave me confidence. I think she does that for her subjects, too. She doesn't direct them in a traditional way—she empowers them. She lets them show her when it's time to film. She gives her crews and her subjects real roles to play. She's a very talented singer and songwriter. She sang at my mother's funeral which was very, very moving.

VIC: You're quite political yourself, whether you acknowledge it or not.

MARTIN: My father, the war, myself—we all tried to live with purpose.

VIC: Strange question. Do you dream, Martin?

MARTIN: Oh, I have vivid dreams every night. They're always inspired by the films I've made. The settings are from my films.

VIC: Any recurring dream?

MARTIN: Yes. Making love with Audrey. That comes back a lot. Probably the one that recurs the most. It's a very good feeling.

VIC: Very nice theme to end up on. Thank you Martin.

ENGLISH

Chapter 17

JOHN KENNEDY

John Kennedy served as Head of CBC Drama, guiding the network through a vibrant era of original Canadian storytelling. With a background in production and a sharp creative eye, Kennedy nurtured emerging talent and championed high-quality scripted programming. His leadership was instrumental in bringing bold, homegrown series to national and international audiences.

VIC: When you took on the role of Head of Drama, what was the environment like at CBC?

JOHN: When I arrived, I already knew a lot of the people in CBC Television Drama—I'd been working there off and on for about ten years. I knew just how incredibly talented they were. Now, I have my own talents, but I never claimed to be one of the creative visionaries. What I could do—and did well—was recognize talent and help shape conditions for it to flourish. I didn't come in thinking, "Now's my chance to impose a vision." Quite the opposite. My thought was: "How can I help these people—this pool of gifted writers, directors, producers—do their best work in a system that's under pressure from all sides?"

VIC: Pressure from above?

JOHN: Very much so. The CBC is a big organization, and a complex one. Here's a small example that speaks volumes: we were producing television drama on two-inch videotape back then. These reels were expensive, huge, and they got used up fast. There was a lot of pressure to reuse them, which meant wiping previous material. But we weren't talking about erasing rehearsal tapes—we were talking about erasing finished productions. Works of art. Archives of real value. I had to push back—sometimes quite forcefully—against the bureaucracy to preserve those recordings. It was a fight for cultural memory. You pay a lot of money for one of those reels—and we'd use, like, ten of them to do a show. We shot over here… and we shot over there… we would keep going and do a third take and a fourth take and a fifth take sometimes. Nevertheless, you still had to protect that stuff.

VIC: Were those kinds of resource pressures common?

JOHN: Constant. All the production departments—drama, news, current affairs, children's—had access to the same pool of designers, set painters, makeup artists, editors, and camera operators. There was always a fight for time and talent. And in television, it's not just about getting a designer or an editor—you want a specific person. You don't just ask for a camera operator; you ask for Vic Sarin. It's about chemistry. You build a team, and that team chemistry matters deeply.

VIC: But Drama didn't have full control over those people?

JOHN: No, not at all. We could express preferences, and most of the time, we got them. But those people didn't report to us. They were shared resources, and coordination was everything. The creative outcome always depended on those relationships—on getting the right mix of people together.

VIC: Your predecessor, John Hirsch, was a titan of theatre. Founder of the Manitoba Theatre Centre, a major figure at Stratford... and then they brought you in, someone with a very different background. Do you know why?

JOHN: As far as I know, it was Dennis Harvey who made that decision. Whether someone advised him, I can't say—I'd be speculating. But yes, it was a big shift. Hirsch was a pure artist. I came in with a broader perspective—someone who could see the organizational pieces and make the whole thing work.

VIC: Did you feel intimidated stepping into that role?

JOHN: Not at all. I knew the people, I knew the shows, and I had a pretty good sense of the strengths and weaknesses within the department. I also knew my limits, which is why one of the first things I did was reach outside the corporation. I asked Jean Roberts—then head of theatre at the National Arts Centre—to come work with us. She was terrific. She understood the theatre world, and she knew the people in it—actors, writers, all of them. That was a major strength. I also made a point of welcoming people from outside CBC Drama. Jeannine Locke is one example—she became a key contributor. There was great talent in the wider community, and we needed to bring it in.

VIC: What made Jeannine such a strong creative force?

JOHN: Jeannine knew how to make television, plain and simple. She wasn't the only one, but she stood out. She had very strong opinions about how things should be done, and a refined sense of taste—just fabulous instincts. On top of that, she had persuasive powers that worked on just about everyone. She could talk me into things, certainly, but also actors, directors, even cinematographers. She knew how to shape a vision and get people on board.

I spent seven years working with her, mostly on her documentaries. We travelled a lot. Looking back, I truly cherish that time. She wasn't easy—she had a firm point of view, quite conservative in some ways, but she knew this country inside out. And though I've never been a big reader myself, I learned a great deal from her, especially her passion for Canada and its history.

Coming into the drama department from the outside gave me a different perspective. I learned how to work with people by focusing on their strengths, not trying to reshape them. It was about drawing the best out of everyone and blending the disciplines.

VIC: That kind of freedom and collaboration sounds rare. Did you face resistance from the top?

JOHN: Actually, one of the great joys of that time was how little interference I had. My immediate supervisors were very supportive. I'd say I was generously backed by the executives in English Television, and even some on the French side. I built good relationships with colleagues across both language groups, and it helped tremendously. I never felt constrained by upper management.

The real challenge wasn't internal friction—it was making the whole operation work. Making it hum. Creating an environment where people could thrive doing the kinds of projects they believed in. Everything still had to go through approvals, but we tried to let good ideas grow.

If there was one major roadblock, it was budget cuts. That was the pressure point—politicized at times, and relentless. I remember having to call a departmental meeting after one of those rounds of cuts. I had to tell people that jobs would be lost. It was awful. And it wasn't the last time I had to do that—later in my career, when I moved to B.C., I faced the same thing. I took those moments very personally. I probably should've had a thicker skin, but I didn't.

One day in particular sticks with me. After delivering the news in a big meeting—lots of heavy silences, a few voices of hope trying to rally the team—I walked down to the waterfront and wept the whole way. By the time

I got back to 790 Bay, maybe an hour later, I'd steadied myself. But that was a hard day. I remember it vividly.

And then there were all the unpredictable things that just come with production life—a snowstorm shutting things down for days, or a work stoppage. It was never boring. I was Head of Drama for nearly ten years, and more than once I wondered how they kept letting me do it.

VIC: That period was special, no question. There was so much going—TV series, movies, sitcoms.

JOHN: We brought in new people—some who'd never done drama before. Phil Goff, for instance, came from Newfoundland and was doing current affairs. We brought him into *For the Record*,

VIC: The *You've Come a Long Way, Katie* series is some of the best work I've seen on Canadian television.

JOHN: We encouraged people to lead with their creativity. I tried to make space for that. Of course, it wasn't all free-flowing. We had passionate discussions about direction, about tone. And sitcoms, in particular, become machines—you have to write quickly, shoot quickly, and keep the whole thing on schedule. That pressure's real. But the people we had… they rose to it.

VIC: You were good with numbers. How did that translate into the day-to-day of running Drama?

JOHN: Well, television is still a business. No one was handing us a blank cheque, saying: "Here's a million dollars—go have fun." Every one of those dollars came with consequences. I had a solid understanding of the financial side—what the limits were and what those limits meant for production. I never panicked during a financial crunch, at least not one I can remember. I always felt there were ways to deal with it. And I think that helped some of the producers breathe easier. They knew I wasn't going to react with, "Off with your head!" every time we hit a financial snag. My job was to understand the constraints and try to do something about them, not add to the pressure.

That goes back to something I said earlier—I had some talent for working with people. I wasn't too bad at choosing the right person for a role or encouraging someone to stretch into something new. Sometimes that meant asking more of someone than they'd been asked before, and sometimes it meant simply agreeing with them that they could do more.

VIC: Like when Jeannine Locke said she wanted to direct?

JOHN: Exactly. She said she wanted to direct, and I agreed. It seemed like a good idea, and she proved it was. And that kind of thing went on for ten years. Not every day was glorious, of course, but they were productive days. People were doing strong work. Not all of it succeeded—some things didn't work, and I won't name names. But that's the nature of the business.

VIC: What about the public broadcasting model? These days, it feels like everything hinges on ratings and commercial success.

JOHN: We didn't have that luxury. Our operation was far more constrained. We had a fixed number of hours to deliver each year and a set pool of resources to make them happen. That was the reality. We weren't free agents—we had a palette, and we had to create within its bounds. A limited number of colours, and a strict frame. But that's what we did, day after day. And within those boundaries, people made great work. We had an especially strong group of women in the department. By the time I left, I'd say the number of women had doubled compared to what it had been 15 or 20 years earlier.

VIC: Was that a conscious decision on your part?

JOHN: It was a talent decision, first and foremost. But yes, part of it was conscious. It seemed right to move closer to actual representation. Different voices bring different perspectives. That includes perspectives from other cultures too—not just gender. There's value in hearing from people who didn't grow up in the same world I did, which some days feels like it was centuries ago.

VIC: You gave people freedom—the space to be creative. I miss that feeling in today's industry. Do you think it's still possible?

JOHN: I think it can still come from anywhere—public or private—but it has to be energy that's harnessed, not controlled. You can't go around saying, "I know how you should be shooting this." That kind of top-down control shuts creativity down. Now, I take your point that it's harder today. There are more layers, more noise. And yes, my tenure was from 1978 to 1988. That's a long time ago. I have friends who were born in 1988. The whole media landscape has changed.

I left in 1987, partly because I sensed that shift coming. The corporation was beginning to turn, to become more managerial. That shift, I think, was inevitable. But I came from a tradition—like you did—of the ABC in Australia, the CBC here, even the BBC model. Public service broadcasting, designed to serve a cross-section of society. That was the philosophy.

VIC: How much breathing room does a creative person really need?

JOHN: A lot. If you want excellence, they need that space. And to the CBC's credit, we gave a good amount of it—not just inside the building, but also with independent producers. Some of them had tremendous freedom. I won't name companies, but they did brilliant work, and they had to take risks, too—personal, financial risks. They had to borrow money, negotiate with funders, juggle expectations. They faced the same pressures we did, maybe more. But despite that, they made beautiful, meaningful work.

Even with all the constraints—concrete budgets, unpredictable crises—great things got made. I'm not sure how it works now. I've been out of the loop for a while. But back then, if a designer quit mid-production, yes, it was a headache. You had to replace them fast, and it could cost a fortune. But the production carried on. That's what professionals do.

And for my part, whether it was business or life, I tried to operate the same way: give people space, and benefit from their talent. I was always grateful for that.

VIC: You weren't an artist yourself, but you seemed to have a deep appreciation for it.

JOHN: Absolutely. I couldn't draw to save my life, but I loved going to art shows. I got something out of it—deeply. And I think that same feeling extended to the way I approached television. In many ways, it comes down to the talent of the overseer—the person running the show, the conductor if you want to use a musical analogy. Like orchestras, some are consistently inspired. Others, not so much. Why? They're often playing the same material, but the difference lies in the leadership. It might be creative leadership or simply the ability to manage creatives well. Whoever is at the helm has the power to enable—or to shut things down.

That principle applied just as much in television. I heard it from the actors and directors we worked with—they often said the best thing was the freedom they had once the budget was approved. Total freedom. And yes, I tried to provide that. You were there—on *You've Come a Long Way, Katie*. You came in as a cinematographer, not a director, but you ended up doing both on a three-hour film. And you handled it beautifully.

I remember us sitting in that little fifth-floor room, you talking with excitement about the opening scene—just a quiet, visual moment. She walks in, sits by a rocking chair. Nothing seems to happen, and yet everything happens. That's what I loved. I wasn't looking for spectacle—I was listening to what the creators saw. If it made sense, if it had power, I got behind it. That openness, that support, was what helped people flourish. People like you, Bill Shatner, and countless others who went through that system—many of them became iconic. That early freedom helped shape their paths.

VIC: Were you conscious of offering that freedom, or was it just your nature?

JOHN: It was both. Yes, I was conscious of it, but it was also just who I am. I think people saw me as a decent guy. If you're decent and you have a few principles—and you know what you can't do—you don't waste time pretending. If someone knows how to draw and you don't, you don't say, "I could do that better." You say, "How can we make this happen?" That was my approach. If someone brought me a compelling story or a character worth exploring, I'd ask, "How do we do it?" There were places within the CBC—and certainly in the private sector—where that approach didn't fly. And I know it doesn't apply in every industry, especially now with how the media landscape has changed. Some of the big names today, the hotshot producers and directors—they've earned their control. But I think public broadcasting allowed for a different kind of space.

VIC: Was that because CBC was funded by the taxpayer?

JOHN: Yes, I think so. When you're publicly funded—by the Canadian taxpayer—you carry responsibilities. You have to answer to a mandate, the *Broadcasting Act*. It doesn't say "make hits." It tells you to reflect the country, to serve a cross-section of society. And that expectation can be interpreted in a dozen ways, but it's still there. CBC still does a lot. But TV drama—well, that's changed a lot since my time. I had my run, my moment to help shape things. But now it's a different world. And I don't know what's right or wrong in the current climate. I really don't. I do know that in my 36 years at CBC, I saw a lot of governments come and go—each with something strong to say about the corporation. The relationship between politics and public broadcasting was never simple.

The CBC has always had to respond to the country's needs. Sometimes that meant action—pressure from Ottawa or the public to ensure the corporation was doing what Canadians expected of it. There were impassioned debates about programming choices. TV Drama didn't escape criticism. I remember the reaction to some of John Kastner's films—demanding, often difficult pieces. They stirred people up, just like current affairs always has.

But that tension comes with the territory. The CBC offered tremendous freedom, and once funding was secured for the year—or sometimes longer—that money was guaranteed. That's rare. But with that freedom came a serious responsibility: to meet the mandate and to reflect the incredible breadth and diversity of this country.

VIC: Looking back now, was there a moment or project that stands out as something you're especially proud of?

JOHN: I'm not sure I'd use the word "proud." There were events I loved—things I was privileged to help make happen. And there were others I didn't love, but I'm still glad they came to be. You always learn from the mistakes. But I've never been one for that "proud daddy" feeling. I'm a father, and even with my kids and grandkids, it's not pride I feel—it's respect.

I feel good about what we accomplished. I feel good that I was able to encourage and support a wide array of talented people over many years. They were all different—passionate, challenging, brilliant. I wouldn't want to be married to any of them, but I truly valued their company. I understood their crises—some personal, some professional—and I feel lucky that I was in a position to help create an environment where that kind of creativity could thrive.

VIC: And it sounds like you had genuine support from higher up. That kind of trust makes a big difference.

JOHN: It does. I was lucky to be trusted. I didn't do it alone—I could only work with what was given to me. I'm no magician. I think of something Tenzing Norgay once said—you know, the man who climbed Everest with Hillary. I met him once, and I remember telling him how great I thought he was. He looked at me and said, "I am only as good as the team I climb with." That stuck with me. I feel the same way.

So yes, I was able to spark a lot of interesting projects. But I also had help. Support came from all sides—some from the higher-ups, some from colleagues, some from friends, even family. And definitely from the other department heads. We used to meet regularly to talk about shared challenges—after all, we were all drawing from the same staff pool: editors, camera people, designers.

VIC: That freedom you spoke of earlier—it wasn't absolute, was it?

JOHN: No, it wasn't. It came with a huge sense of responsibility. Freedom meant I had to deliver. That meant getting programming to air that was compelling, entertaining, emotionally engaging—and all within budget and on time. And "on time" was no small thing. A big part of production planning was being able to say, ten months from now, we'll be ready to produce a three-part miniseries. It'll air in 15 months. That's a serious gamble. A lot has to align. You have to be confident—about people, about equipment, about story.

Take Studio Seven, for instance. That was our largest studio, equipped with the best video cameras. These things were like Volkswagens tipped on their sides—enormous, heavy machines that needed to be pushed around the floor. That's what we worked with. And yet, somehow, we made it work.

A lot of what we did came down to careful production planning. It sounds dull, but it's crucial. You're constantly thinking: how do we line up all the resources to produce a three-part series ten or fifteen months from now? How do we budget it, hire the right people, secure studio time? It's the granular stuff of a business built around imagination. Yet, that imagination is the reason we were all there. If you can't create space for creativity to flourish—what's the point? We weren't making fortunes. No one got rich at the CBC. But everyone deserved to be paid fairly, and when things worked, they worked pretty darn well. I still remember a lot of it vividly. I had the energy for it then. I'm glad I don't have to do it now.

VIC: Was there a particular show that still sticks with you?

JOHN: One that really stands out is "A Far Cry From Home," part of the *For the Record* series. It was produced by Anne Frank and directed by Gordon Pinsent. The film tackled family abuse and divorce—tough themes. But it was done so well. I remember how powerful it was, and how they included resources at the end for people seeking help across the country.

I mentioned it to Anne a few years ago when she was briefly in Vancouver. I told her how much I still admired the show. She said, "I wouldn't feel comfortable showing it today." The core issue hasn't changed—but how we talk about it has. The complexity has evolved. Still, I think it was an important piece. Not a happy show, but a good one.

This business, in the end, is about storytelling. Some stories are dark, some light, some both. Another one I'll never forget is *Chautauqua Girl*. There's a scene where Jackie Burroughs, playing an elderly woman, sits in silence as "Unto the Hills" plays. No dialogue—just music and performance. It goes on and on, and it grabs you by the heart. You can't not tear up. It was a deeply human moment in a very human film.

VIC: You really connected with the emotional side of the work.

JOHN: Yes. The closer a show got to my emotional core, the more engaged I became. I remember moments from *The Beachcombers*, too—small, meaningful scenes that hit home. Sure, I liked some more than others. That's natural. But there's not a single one I regret making. Not one. There were challenging days. There were mistakes. But there was also real beauty in what we did.

VIC: John, let's talk a little about regional pressure. You were based in Toronto, but there was often concern from places like Vancouver that they were being overlooked. How did you handle that side of CBC politics?

JOHN: That was always part of the job—balancing national representation. Across the CBC, in virtually every office, there were exceptionally talented people. You still hear that, especially in radio—voices from across the country reporting on what's happening in their region.

It was the same during my time in TV drama. There were two main pressures. One was to reflect the country's grandeur and complexity—to make sure our programming wasn't just Toronto-centric, but truly national. The other was to tap into the different stories, voices, and concerns across those regions.

We did a decent job, I'd say. And that's thanks in no small part to people like Phillip Keatley in Vancouver. He was a drama program producer at CBC Vancouver and had a profound understanding of the role of Indigenous people in Canadian storytelling. He recognized talent, and he encouraged it. He helped bring forward voices like Chief Dan George and created one-shot dramas that captured regional and cultural specificity with real care. Toronto produced those kinds of stories, too, but Vancouver was strong—very creative, very engaged.

VIC: And your later years—did you find some peace away from all that pressure?

Yes, absolutely. These days, I've stepped back. I'm not used to being in front of the camera. I've always been behind the lens, observing. But really, I'm at peace. I've lived in the same apartment now for 14 years. Before that, I had a lovely house, designed by my brother, an architect. It was right by the water. My children grew up there. It was beautiful. We had family, friends, a garden, and space to breathe. There's something about Vancouver—it's one of those rare places where you feel the balance of nature and art, silence, and story.

I still think about those I worked with. Dennis Hargraves comes to mind—he was in TV Children's when I first arrived, back in the fifties and sixties. And when he retired, he created a design space here on the coast.

I visited just recently—absolutely gorgeous. Time changes everything, but those memories stay vivid.

So yes, I've slowed down. But I still carry all those years at the CBC with me. The people, the stories, the lessons. I'm not a magician. I was only as good as the team I worked with—and they were damn good.

VIC: Thank you for your time and thoughtful responses, John.

Chapter 18

TREVOR EVANS

Trevor Evans is a Canadian director, writer, and producer whose work has shaped many hours of CBC programming. Over his career, he directed drama, documentary, and children's series, often finding the human stories behind the headlines. His projects reflect the breadth of Canadian experience, both within the public broadcaster and beyond. Evans has also shared his experience as a mentor to the next generation of filmmakers.

VIC: What was your relationship with CBC and what did you do there?

TREVOR: Most of my early stuff was actually at CTV. And then—how did I get to CBC? Through Ross McLean. He brought me in to do a show in Vancouver and then brought me to Toronto. Around that time, Lynn Starmer, who was an executive at CBC, got in touch. My first work at CBC was freelance. That's when they were looking for someone to direct *Wayne & Shuster* on film—they hadn't done much of that before. I should say, I was always a freelancer, never officially joined CBC staff. That would've been... 1970 or '71. Somewhere around then.

My earlier stuff was in the '60s, mostly with CTV out of Montreal. I did a show called *Magistrate Court*, and the guy who played the magistrate lived in Vancouver, though we shot in Montreal. It was a strip show—live to tape. He said to me one day, "You should get out to the coast. You're a creative kid with ideas. They're never going to let you run with them here at CTV." So my wife and I talked it over—we had two little kids—and we decided to take a flier. Moved from Montreal to Vancouver.

Now, he had some connections with the B.C. government, and I thought, "This is great. I'll get a kids' show going." The concept involved a "theatre in the trees" in Stanley Park, with TV monitors installed in the trees. Kids could go from tree to tree watching the story unfold. The forestry people loved the idea. The government was excited. And then they lost the election. Boom. Idea in the garbage can. So here we were, moved to Vancouver, no project. What now?

My wife said, "You did so much work for Ross McLean—his kids' show, his talk show. Give him a call." So I did. I said, "I'm available." He said, "When can you be here?" I said, "Tomorrow, if you've got something." He said, "Book the red-eye. I'll see you at the airport." So I flew back to Toronto that night, and the next morning, he took me downtown. He said, "I'm putting together a talk show like Johnny Carson. I want you to cut it." I got 13 weeks out of that. We moved everybody back east.

Then Ross called again. "You're going to get a call from a man named Len Starmer," he said. "He's the executive producer for *Wayne & Shuster*." So, I took the meeting. I misread it—they weren't just looking for a one-off. They needed someone to direct a whole filmed show. They had never worked in film.

VIC: Let's back up a little. Where were you born?

TREVOR: Calgary. 1936. I was an only child. My dad worked for the railroad, and my mom was a beautiful homemaker.

VIC: And how did you get into the arts?

TREVOR: Through a love of theatre. In grade school, I was always in plays—from Grade 2 through Grade 8. Then in junior high, more plays. In high school, same thing. They had a course—Drama 101—so I took that. I was also involved in the print shop at Western Canada High School in Calgary. They did all the printing for the theatre stuff, so I was on both sides of the stage, so to speak. I had little theatre obligations as well. One of the ladies in our little theatre group was a writer at the new TV section.

After one rehearsal, we were having a soda and she said, "You're a funny little fool. You should be on TV." I said, "Do you know anybody in the business?" She said, "Me. I'll get you something." At the time, I was working as an office boy for Mobil Oil. It paid well and they treated me like I'd invented the job, but I was eager to get out. The writer lady's name was Joanna Glass—she's now a playwright living in Florida. Her name is still Joanna McClelland Glass.

VIC: This woman got you an interview?

TREVOR: Yes! She got me an interview with the art director at a new TV station. I went down, and he had this very strong Hungarian accent—he was a talented artist, but not much of an interviewer, so what happened was the man hired me part-time—I thought it was full-time. I went back to the oil company and gave my notice. Then I showed up at the studio on Monday and he said, "What are you doing here? You're not supposed to start until Saturday." I said, "No—don't say that." And he said, "Sorry."

So I quickly found Joanna—the woman who got me the job—and she was in the studio. I said, "Joanna, I think I've blown it. I quit my job at Mobil Oil for a one-day-a-week gig." And she said, "Let's work on that."

She started calling people. Meanwhile, I went back to Mobil Oil, told them my sad little story. They fell on the floor laughing. You see, when I left, there were five office boys—they'd all moved up the ladder. Now, to take me back, they had to demote themselves again. They took a vote, decided they'd do it. So now there were six of us in the pool again. The woman who supervised us said, "There's a lesson in this, Trevor. Ask questions. Get everything in writing." I said, "Yes, ma'am. Lesson learned."

Anyway, I went back to the TV studio and said, "I'll do the Saturday gig for now, but please consider me for full-time." The next weekend came around, and I did what I was supposed to—setting up canned soups in display cases. Then they said, "Okay, now you can quit Mobil." So I did. And I started full-time at the Calgary TV station. I was there a year before they fired me.

VIC: Why?

TREVOR: The head of the department fired me because I was on air too much. Other writers kept casting me as a stooge in commercials, and he got jealous. So he let me go. But he did me the biggest favour in the world, because otherwise I might've stayed in my hometown. I went to Edmonton after that, and the rest is history.

You know, TV didn't even arrive in Canada until 1952. Life before that? It was all CBC Radio. I was passionate about it. There was always a time delay between the East and Alberta. An 8:00 p.m. show in Toronto would air at 6:00 in Calgary, which was a bit early, so they'd add a little disclaimer: "This programme originally aired at 8:00."

I loved CBC Radio. I had my favourite hosts—so funny—and I'd call into the shows sometimes. The next day at school, we'd talk about it. Radio was my connection to the creative world. There wasn't any showbiz in the family. But I was in Boy Scouts, sang in the church choir, joined any little club that would have me. I didn't like being home—my family was broken, and it was uncomfortable. So I found ways to justify being out of the house, in rehearsals, meetings, camps.

That was a formative time. I discovered I could make people laugh. I wasn't a jock—I wasn't playing hockey or football—but I could make the girls laugh. And the guys came along for the ride. That became my thing. I'd get cast in the school play in the funny part, and I'd milk it a bit. That gave me something—satisfaction, maybe even peace. There was freedom in saying words in an unreal world. And as I kept doing it, I got better. I took drama in high school. There was a woman who taught the class—bless her soul, I've forgotten her name—but she had a doctorate. She once said to me, "Trevor, there are only two places where overacting is useful, and you're very good at it. One is the circus, and the other is television." She said, "Get a job in either one and you'll be fine."

That was Grade 12. And I thought, "Well, circus clown—I love the circus. You get to dress up, be somebody else." That appealed to me. So one day, the circus came to Calgary and sent two clowns to our TV station—where I was working as a prop boy—to promote the show. They gave me passes and said, "Come backstage, we'll show you around." I went backstage to what they call "Clown Alley." There were all these old men putting on makeup. They weren't funny. The two main clowns were in their 50s—like uncles—and I was 18 or 20. I kept thinking, "When does it get funny?" It didn't. It was a business.

I asked, "If I joined, what would I be doing?" They said, "You'd be doing the 'come-in.'" That's where you walk around while the kids are finding their seats, blow up balloons, chat with them. I asked, "So do I ever get to do a routine?" They said, "No, the producing clowns do the routines." I said, "Okay, so how do I become a producing clown?" They said, "Practice—for years and years and years." That's when I realized maybe that wasn't the right path for me. So I stayed in little theatre. I kept at it until I got the opportunity to be a prop boy at a TV station in 1956.

VIC: I want to go back a bit—to your early life. When you were young, radio was the only thing around. What kinds of shows did you listen to? Do you remember any of them? And what was it like in your family—listening to radio together? Give me a sense of what life felt like at that time.

TREVOR: Sure. CBC was a lifeline for me—it connected me to the creative world. I loved the shows, especially when they were funny. CBC comedy was smart. It also gave me a window beyond Calgary. I grew up there, and the local stations mostly played music and read news scripts—pre-written stuff about what was happening elsewhere in the world.

As a kid, I didn't really care much about news or current affairs. I liked hockey—I listened to it on the radio. I think I liked some baseball too. But this was during the war years, and I don't remember spending much time listening to the radio because there were a lot of sad stories in the 1940s. Instead, I put myself into school productions—any play, any chance to wear a costume or be the centre of attention, especially if it involved making people laugh.

VIC: What about your family? Where I'm coming from is, I remember in the radio days, the whole family used to sit by the radio. It was the main source of information and entertainment. Can you talk a bit about what you saw—whether or not you were personally interested—about how your family or others engaged with radio back then?

TREVOR: Yes, radio did hold my attention. After supper, we'd often listen to drama shows. They were like soap operas. My mom loved those. I remember listening to *The Lone Ranger* on the radio—"Hi-yo Silver, away!" That one stands out.

Most of the shows were episodic serials. For me, radio time was usually from about 7 to 8 p.m. That was the family hour after dinner. I listened to whatever was on. I don't remember all the show names, but *Wayne & Shuster* was among them, and there were a few game shows too. I don't recall the names now, but they had funny hosts and I liked the laughter. I laughed along with the audience. I also remember wishing I could be there—sitting in the audience, laughing, seeing what it was like. I was always drawn to humour. That's what I liked. Johnny Wayne and Frank Shuster were always funny. Radio shows were strong because they used sound effects so well.

For me, radio was an escape. My family life wasn't happy. My mom and dad were always fighting. Dad had a drinking problem. He worked nights and slept during the day. Suppertime was when he'd wake up, and that's when my mom would start arguing with him. I'd turn up the radio to drown them out. I didn't want to hear them fight. I'm not sure if it was CBC because I didn't really pay attention to the station names back then. It was just whatever was on 690 or 580 on the dial.

VIC: So that seems to be the seed, right? The radio days planted something in you—an early love for comedy and performance. Later you directed *Wayne & Shuster* on television. Can you tell me how that relationship developed?

TREVOR: Sure. I came to *Wayne & Shuster* through another show that Ross McLean was producing in Toronto. He set up the meeting Len Starmer, and then I was invited to lunch with Johnny and Frank. They explained what they were looking for. They needed someone to direct a sketch called "City Golf." The idea was that city streets would be the golf course. They'd play it completely straight. That's why it needed to be shot on film. But they weren't used to working in film, and they didn't have a director familiar with it. So I told them how I'd set things up, and we began working together. They weren't comfortable with some of the technical aspects—how to frame shots or understand what a take might look like—so I gave them a few different versions of each shot. A little wider here, a little tighter there.

One bit had them getting on a streetcar with golf clubs, getting off at Yonge Street. We had the camera waiting for them. That was fun. They gave me room to invent, but I also kept in mind what they didn't like. For example, they didn't like wide shots. They said, "The comedy is in our faces." So I focused on that. I was hopeful I'd be signed to a contract, but it turned out I was hired just for that one sketch. The main sketch was about 12 minutes long, and it took all day to shoot. We were filming in the middle of downtown traffic, with a camera crew and a police officer managing traffic. It was scary, but it was fun.

At the end of the day, they said, "Thanks very much, the cheque's in the mail." That was it. I went home and told my wife. She asked, "How long is the contract?" I said, "That was it." She said, "Oh gosh, what are we going to do?" I made more phone calls. I thought I'd be going back to freelance work. But then—within a week—after the sketch was edited and added to their special, I got a call. I was invited to have lunch again with Johnny and Frank and they said, "We like what you did. Would you be interested in taking over for the director?" He was an American who was retiring and going back to New York. I said, "I'd be delighted. Thank you very much." We shook hands right there at the table, and that was that.

Then I went to my first pre-production meeting and started getting into the rhythm of it. The table read was great—25 or 30 people gathered at the Sumach Street building. I sat at one end of the table, Johnny and Frank sat at the other, with the actors in between. We could make eye contact. It felt as close to Hollywood as I'd ever been. I liked the energy, the team spirit—it was like sports. Everyone had a role to play. I had to figure out mine. I made suggestions, alternatives, just trying to find where I could make a mark.

Eventually, someone said, "Leonard wants to talk to you." Leonard Starmer was the executive producer. We had a sit-down, and he said, "Here's the deal. The boys, Johnny and Frank, are calling the shots. You're in the chair because we need a director in the chair." I asked, "So what does that mean? It's a non-job?" He said, "We don't see it that way. You've got great credentials. We're sure you'll find ways to bring your ideas in throughout the rehearsals." I said, "You can count on it."

I went home and talked it over with my wife, who was also a writer in the business. She said, "This will be hard for you. You're used to being the boss, but here you'll have the title without the control." Then she said, "Look at what's at stake. You've got two daughters in girls' school. University after that. You need cash flow." I said, "That's your version of creativity?" She said, "Take the money. Grin and bear it."

So I told myself, "I'll find a way to plant ideas." During rehearsal, I'd casually say, "Wouldn't it be funny if..." They'd shoot it down: "No, no, no. That won't work." Two days later, one of them would say, "Hey, wouldn't it be funny if..." and it'd be my idea—reinvented.

I talked to Leonard again. God bless him. He said, "It takes a strong person to submerge your identity in this kind of role. You're the director, like in film—but even a movie director has to answer to the person with the money. If the money guy wants a shot of a dog, that dog's in the movie, whether the director likes it or not." So I learned. To play in the big leagues, you have to define your role clearly.

And here's the truth: during rehearsal, if I did something that got a laugh, the guys would say, "Get out of here, you're fooling around." But later, that exact bit would show up in the final show. Later on, after Johnny passed away—God rest his soul—I had a talk with Frank. I asked him, "How did you last all those years? Johnny was a difficult man." He said, "Can you imagine being his partner since high school?" I said, "How did you manage?" Frank said, "I learned to throw my idea out early and let him reinvent it. That way, I still had the satisfaction of planting the seed. He'd grow the tree, and everyone else would help shape it. Then he'd cut it down and get the laugh."

That stuck with me. I've used that philosophy elsewhere in life too. When you realize what your real role is, it's not about credit. Even film directors are often just hoping the studio doesn't say, "This is crap—get us another director." So, unless you own the project and have lots of money in the bank, you're going to be accountable to someone—and that someone may not always be pleasant. Or you might not even like the project. But whoever has the money controls the demand. That's still true today.

VIC: So how long were you with *Wayne & Shuster?* How many shows?

TREVOR: Ten years. Four shows a year. Then I went to New York and spent five years with HBO, working with Jerry Stiller and Anne Meara on their show. It was a big promotional series for all the movies HBO was running. We did sketches in between the trailers. They were really funny—a husband-and-wife team. They lived just two blocks from the studio.

VIC: Let's go back—ten years, then away for five. So how long altogether?

TREVOR: I was there ten years total. The first stretch, then gone for five, and I came back for about a year and a half. Then Johnny died. After that, Frank did some retrospectives.

VIC: What was the reason behind the *Wayne & Shuster* show's success?

TREVOR: If I go by my mom and dad's reaction to their comedy, it was simple: setup and punchline. A guy walks into a doctor's office, that kind of thing. It was basic structure—funny voices, great timing. All their supporting players were strong comic performers.

They did 67 appearances on *The Ed Sullivan Show*. I might be off by one or two, but it was around that number. They did family comedy. Their sketches had a beginning, middle, and end. They'd often be placed in the final quarter of *Ed Sullivan*—around 25 to 35 minutes into the hour. Ed Sullivan would say, "You guys are running too long," and they'd reply, "We can't stop World War II in the middle just for a commercial."

Whatever the sketch was, they committed to it. They got a great response from Ed Sullivan's audience. And of course, that was the big show everyone in Canada watched on Sundays. The performers in their cast knew they might never get to deliver the punchline, but they could be in the scene—help set up the joke, get paid well, and be asked back again and again.

TREVOR: It was a legacy. When I look at it now, I see it in chunks—ten years with *Wayne & Shuster*, five years with HBO in New York, then back to Toronto for another five. After that, Johnny got sick and passed away. We did a few retrospective shows with Frank. So, in total, I'd say I was involved with them for 17 or 18 years.

VIC: There are two things I want to ask. One is about how the CBC hierarchy worked. Let's be honest—your show existed because of CBC. Did they ever interfere? Or were you left alone?

TREVOR: I wasn't aware of any interference from higher ups at CBC. Len Starmer was the executive producer—that's where my line of communication ended. If I had a concern—something Johnny and Frank didn't seem to grasp—I'd go to Len and say, "Can you explain this to them in your language?" That was the route. I was a freelancer. If I'd been staff, maybe I'd have been more involved. Most of the people working on the show were staff, except for the actors and people like me. We freelancers understood how the CBC hierarchy functioned, both at the network level and within broadcast operations. But here's the thing—this wasn't 20th Century Fox. It wasn't Metro-Goldwyn-Mayer. And CTV had long since exited that kind of entertainment. They'd co-finance something short or maybe run a Toronto-based series aimed at the U.S., but that was it.

In my view, CBC was the heart and soul of Canadian imagery. All the things we now associate with Canadian culture—like hockey, and *Wayne & Shuster*—came from CBC. Johnny and Frank were loyal Canadians. They believed in this country. They believed Canada deserved more than it was getting. But we were only 10 percent of the North American population.

VIC: Why didn't Johnny and Frank just stay in the U.S.?

TREVOR: They tried. They did a full season in the U.S. But they didn't like it. They weren't in control. They had to fight producers and executives just to do things their way. In the U.S., it was all about money. If the client didn't like the joke, the joke was gone. Johnny and Frank would argue, "But it's a good joke!" The response would be, "Yeah, but we don't think it's funny." That was the end of it. They liked living in Los Angeles for a while, but they missed the consistency of working in Canada. In Canada, you knew who would be in the chair. In the U.S., someone could lose their job the day after a show aired, and the next week the whole control room would be filled with new people. They didn't like that.

They were loyal to Canada. They lived in Toronto their whole lives. And don't forget—they were in the Army. They did the Army Show during World War II. Frank once told me a story about that. He said they were behind the lines, doing a show. One night, he was staring up at the sky from the trench and said, "Oh, look—a plane's flashing its lights." Johnny grabbed him, pulled him headfirst into the trench, and said, "Those are tracer bullets, you idiot!" Frank said, "That's how dumb we were. We were 20." He told me he never took off his uniform during those years—he was afraid he wouldn't be able to get back into it fast enough if needed.

VIC: You know, it's funny—so many great comedians in Hollywood were Canadian. John Candy, Dan Aykroyd—there are so many. But in real life, Canadians are quiet, gentle people. How do you explain that?

TREVOR: I've thought about that too. Canadians are observers. We're on the outside looking in. We see things—the details, the absurdities—and we reflect them back. We see the big American football stars on TV and then look at our little high school team and say, "I want to be like them." But we don't have that kind of budget or infrastructure. What do we do? We laugh. Maybe there's a sense of national inferiority in there—just a bit. I don't know exactly what makes Canadians so funny, but in real life, we don't say much. On stage, though, we come alive. Maybe it's because we're used to being the "also-rans." We have to try harder. We can't buy our way into being funny. You either are or you aren't. And Canadian audiences are generous. They'll give you time. But if you give them something they don't care about, they'll let you know.

We're caught between two major English-speaking cultures—British and American. In some ways, we feel very British. But we're also drawn to what's south of the border. We're somewhere in between. We think of ourselves as the middle ground. On one side, you've got the high-powered money-driven culture of the U.S. On the other, the more social-minded systems of the British. Somehow, we sit between the two. And in that space, we try not to hurt anyone's feelings.

VIC: What about British comedy? Tony Hancock? Eric Sykes?

TREVOR: Oh, absolutely. You could watch someone like Eric Sykes sit in front of the camera for half an hour and end up on the floor laughing. With American comedy, it's all being thrown at you—fast, loud, big gestures. I think as Canadians, we like slapstick too. It's cause and effect. Bam! Pie in the face. That's funny. But the build-up matters. Sometimes it's not the husband or wife who gets the pie—it's the poor person trying to mediate between them. That twist is what makes it comedy. To me, surprise is at the core of humour. If the audience already sees the punchline coming, it's no good. But if you build the moment, and then pop the surprise somewhere unexpected—they laugh. And if they miss it, they stop and say, "Wait—what happened?" Now they're paying attention..

That's the difference I saw. When I worked in New York with Jerry Stiller and Anne Meara, they had a show called *Sneak Preview*. We talked comedy, and they asked, "How do you know all this stuff?" I said, "Well, I worked with *Wayne & Shuster*." And they said, "Oh yeah!" and I said, "You're the same idea, except you're married." Johnny and Frank were "Married in Queens" — strictly business, of course. Frank was the 'wife' character, and Johnny was the dominant 'husband.' Anne said, "Yes, and we reversed it. I'm the dumb one, and my husband is the smart one." We laughed about that. They appreciated Johnny and Frank. Johnny and Frank did 67 appearances on *Ed Sullivan*. Jerry and Anne did the next batch.

VIC: Looking back, how did the CBC fit into your career?

TREVOR: They allowed me freedom. CBC gave me licence to do things others couldn't. Other departments would come to me: "We know you direct, could you do this for us?" The Children's Department came one day and said, "We're having difficulty entertaining the 9–12-year-old audience." I said, "I thought that was my audience!" They laughed and said, "No, we need something more literate."

So, I said, "Let me think." I didn't have a handle on it right then. I asked if they could connect me with someone who might help. The head of the department gave me a number for a child psychologist at McGill. A friend of hers. I called him: "How do I write for 9–12-year-olds?" He said, "You don't. You write a script that's funny, and they'll get it. He told me there are only two audiences: preschool, and everyone else.

The 9-year-old thinks like his 10- or 11-year-old brother. He's not thinking, "I'm nine," he's thinking, "I'm almost ten. I'm sophisticated." So I said, "If I write a gentle script in an adult way, it'll work?" He said, "Have you ever watched *Gilligan's Island*?" Of course I had. He said, "It's an adult setup. But the professor couldn't fix that stupid boat." Exactly. We laughed.

So, my wife and I created a show called *Coming Up Rosie*, and CBC let me do it. I appreciated Don Elder—bless his soul. He just passed. I told him: "It'll be a sitcom, but with a premise that appeals to 9–12-year-olds—problem solving." All the characters were adults. No kids. But the adults solved problems like kids do—trial and error. They'd mess up, then have to recover. Adults do that too. Our lead, Rosie, was a video consultant for school teachers. She was the straight person. The rest had funny traits. Dan Aykroyd, for instance—he played the building superintendent. Very right-wing. Rosie was very left-wing. Not political, but mental attitude.

There were other middle-ground characters. The show was a gentle sitcom, transitioning from afternoon shows to early evening at 4:30. I wanted to make it more sophisticated—aim it at the 7:00 p.m. crowd, after supper, before prime time. I had hoped to bring Catherine O'Hara to her own show—make it more sophisticated that way. But that didn't work out. We ran out of production dollars. We were in the middle of a pilot. It had to be scrapped.

VIC: That would have been great. She is so talented. Thank you so much for your time, Trevor.

Chapter 19

ROSEMARY RADCLIFFE

Rosemary Radcliffe is a Canadian actress, writer, and comedian whose career has spanned television, film, and stage. She is known for her roles on King of Kensington, Coming Up Rosie, *and as Mrs. Barry in* Anne of Green Gables. *Like many performers, she describes acting as bittersweet, a craft filled with creative rewards and the uncertainties of the profession. Through it all, Radcliffe remains a respected presence in Canadian entertainment.*

VIC: I'm talking to a very informative, creative person. Rosemary, where were you born?

ROSEMARY: I was born in Stratford, Ontario, but I spent my early life on a farm near St. Mary's, which is about, you know, a few miles from London—between London and Stratford. I was born in a field, basically. My father was strict and believed the only acceptable thing near show business was radio. I came to Toronto when I was 17 to go to Ryerson to study Radio and Television Arts, but I couldn't concentrate. I think I might have been ADHD. I don't know. Anyway, here I am.

VIC: What made you decide to study art?

ROSEMARY: Well, although I'm the daughter of a pig farmer, I had a stage mother, and she started sticking me on the stage when I was around five. That was also the time I began to study piano. One of my earliest memories is from then. I had a hula skirt on, and there were a couple of twins who lived down the concession. Our mothers put us together, and I remember me singing "All the Nice Girls Love a Sailor." These little boys had hats on, and I had the hula. I must've been around five.

In those days, being an actor was seen as a very bad prospect. You were probably a wanton woman. You probably slept with everyone. Actresses had such a bad reputation. And I come from a Calvinist background, so it didn't go over well. My father didn't like it, but my mother encouraged it.

Although I was on a farm, I was given singing lessons, figure skating lessons, tap dance, ballet, and piano. But piano went out. Once I came to Toronto and started at Ryerson, I made friends, but it was terribly hard. Once I graduated, I had no idea how to make a living. I lived in a room, and one day I was lucky to run into a guy from my class. He said, "Why don't you go over to this agency and see them?" And I did. In the next two or three days, I did a commercial. I had a big overbite at that point, and they thought I'd be good to eat candy. So my first commercial was for those horrible, red dye #5 cheeses—you had to gobble them and act like you were in ecstasy. Then you had to spit them into a big barrel. That was my very first foray on camera into show business.

VIC: That was your first commercial?

ROSEMARY: It was the first one that made me some money. I was always on edge trying to pay my rent. I had no idea how to do it. There were tough times and hot dog dinners.

VIC: Did you listen to radio a lot?

ROSEMARY: I did, lying in bed. There was a comedy show that came from Chicago—I can't remember the name. But I couldn't believe people were acting like that. I couldn't believe they were funny. At some point, I auditioned for a casting director—she's passed away now. She kept her dog in a drawer. I read a script and put my heart into it, and she said, "Oh, you just can't not be funny, can you?" I thought, oh my God, what's wrong with me? The CBC was very strict at the time. This was before anyone was funny, except maybe Wayne and Shuster—and certainly not women.

VIC: Do you remember your first foray into television?

ROSEMARY: It's kind of fuzzy because I didn't keep a journal. But let me just say, I've had the gorilla suit on. I don't know if you know, but the CBC had this huge, old, furry gorilla suit. I fit in there. At some point, I needed to pay the rent and I guess they wanted the gorilla to do something, so I got in there, and the did the gorilla—whatever.

VIC: Do you remember your first show?

ROSEMARY: Well, I played an extra, and I got paid eight dollars. This would have been in 1969. But then, through circumstances or whatever, I thought I could be a pianist—a cocktail pianist. And I was, at some point. One night I was at the Royal York and a woman got locked in the bathroom. There was a whole furor. She couldn't get out—she was too fat to go underneath and all this stuff. I told that story on camera for an audition, and I landed on a morning show done out of CBLT, produced and directed by a boy named David Acomba. At that point, I didn't know what to do with myself because I wasn't very sexy. Those were the days of *Hair*, so I dyed my hair red and turned it into this great Afro bubble. I was just bizarre. But you know, as a woman, it's really hard to be sexy and funny. At least it certainly was then.

VIC: What was the name of the show?

ROSEMARY: Yeah, it was called *Sunday Morning*— just a local show on CBLT. But there were people like Murray McLauchlan and others—they discovered some wonderful people. It was a kind of mishmash variety show. I think it was about 1969. That'll tell you how old I am.

VIC: First experience—were you hooked on it?

ROSEMARY: Well, no. It was always sort of... I had pressure driving me. At some point I just thought, this is what I should do, because I couldn't get a job. I learned how to type and everything, but they wouldn't have anything to do with me. The irony was, the woman who interviewed me later became a casting director. So we meet in curious circumstances, all the time.

VIC: So, you went into performing?

ROSEMARY: I did, yeah—for necessity, more than anything else. At one point I did some modelling. I lived in a basement and didn't understand that I was being kind of groomed to be a model. But I had a terrible sense of balance. The first fashion show I did, I nearly fell off the stage. It was at Casa Loma. So, modelling didn't go that well for me—I can barely walk!

VIC: So you tried a few places?

ROSEMARY: I don't know. I found that my career was sort of built when somebody got sick. They'd say, "Well, okay, why don't we use Rosemary Radcliffe?" It was a fill-in career, and then it sort of blossomed.

VIC: Talk a little bit about some of the people you worked with at that time.

ROSEMARY: It took me many years to get to Second City. But at one point, I auditioned for a show with Leonard Cohen. I've done so many shows I can't even remember which one it was. Anyway, we all ended up in New York with Leonard Cohen, and we were all frightened. I was out of my league. He would stand in the balcony—on his head. While we were rehearsing in this little theatre on Christopher Street, you'd just see these feet poised above us. He was a wonderful man, very shy, with such a presence and always there off-camera or watching a rehearsal—just an excellent human being.

VIC: In the '60s, '70s, '80s—so many Canadians started here and went on to do bigger, better things.

ROSEMARY: Hollywood was full of Canadians. You had to buy a green card or win one by lottery. For some reason, I just didn't have the courage to go to Los Angeles on my own. Of course I thought of it, but people said, "You'll never make it. You're not pretty enough." Every second girl in Hollywood is absolutely exquisite. That was enough to make me consider other options.

VIC: But you stayed in performing?

ROSEMARY: I did. I stayed as long as I could. I ultimately ended up at Second City. But before that, there was a wonderful man named Trevor Evans at the CBC. Most of my CBC career was in the children's department. Trevor put me in this show called *Dr. Zonk and the Zunkins*. There was an early Dr. Tongue version with John Candy—he was playing Dr. Tongue—and Gilda Radner was in it, too. I remember once we went to the Dare Cookie factory and re-enacted the famous *I Love Lucy* conveyor belt scene. The belt got faster and faster, and we were trying to bag cookies. I loved it. That day, working with Gilda, was so fun. Somewhere in the CBC archives, it's still there.

VIC: If you talk to Americans—or even the British—they say Canadians are quiet, gentle, lovely people. Kind of boring, right? That's the persona. Yet, when you look at Hollywood, some of the most known comedians—like John Candy —are Canadian. What is it about Canadian comedians?

ROSEMARY: Maybe it's because we're cold, and we're making jokes to keep warm. I don't know. I guess I was just born this way—with some facial expressions. I can't speak for others. This is the body and personality I wear in the world.

VIC: Is it the writing or the physicality that leads you?

ROSEMARY: It's the physical expressions. I don't really write. I write poetry, but I hate sitting down with a piece of paper. I hate it. If I have any gift, it just comes naturally.

VIC: Right. Now, could you talk about your very first major break in the business? Looking back now, what would that be?

ROSEMARY: Well, I think that was Trevor Evans' confidence. Honestly, I don't know when that happened—there was never a clear moment. It was just me staggering around the city trying to pay my rent. But Trevor mentored me. He gave me a job and said, "Look, you can do this." And he added,

"By the way, I'm going to do ten takes and I'm not going to let you go until I get what I want." He put me in a variety show and later transferred me to another one called *Coming Up Rosie*. Then, little by little, I ended up in *King of Kensington*. At that time, KTTV was doing these shows with Kenny Rogers and others, and I'd be part of an ensemble cast. But I never thought of myself as a big star. I just got by and paid the rent, and in Canada, that seemed like all you could ask for—until Second City came along.

Andrew Alexander was the motivator behind that. He pushed and created new opportunities. I remember at one point, we swapped with Chicago's Second City and ended up performing at Terre Haute Federal Penitentiary: Catherine O'Hara, myself, maybe Dan Aykroyd—it was a scary place. I remember Catherine just crossed her legs and the whole auditorium roared.

We had adventures with Second City, but I didn't feel I had enough good ideas to keep going. It was like the shows in New York—you only get to perform what you think up, and then you have to talk someone into performing it with you. So you're constantly on edge, always looking for comedic ideas. It was very stressful. After ten months, I decided it was time to leave, though I had some wonderful adventures. The worst part for me was this thing called "Make a Song," where you had to stand up and make up a song on the spot. John Candy had a kind of Barry White routine—he'd talk-sing these love songs, and the pianist would accompany him. I tried doing blues. Everyone had their go-to act, but then you'd get prompts like "Do a song about geese," and I'd be like, "I was down by the bar, and I met some geese..." And then you'd have to rhyme. I couldn't do that.

VIC: So they wanted you to improvise?

ROSEMARY: Oh, for sure. Yes.

VIC: All the feedback came from the so-called creative team behind the cameras. Would they say, "Here's the subject, see where you want to go with it?" Or was it different?

ROSEMARY: Well, I was only with them on stage during the live shows at the Firehall. Later on, they rewrote everything. You'd come in with your idea and it would be typed out on a piece of paper.

VIC: So how much of the writing came from the writers and how much from you?

ROSEMARY: During the time I was in the CBC Children's Department, everything was scripted—by Trevor Evans and his wife Barbara. We had to memorize our lines.

VIC: So that must have been easier in a sense?

ROSEMARY: Yes. But I hate learning lines. It's the loneliest business in the world.

VIC: Talk to me a little about your relationships with other players at that time—especially the people we've mentioned.

ROSEMARY: I loved Gilda Radner. She used to give me rides home. She lived in a little house and was just so warm-hearted. She had a dog or a cat—I think named Snuffy—that had three legs. She was lovely. John Candy was lovely. Eugene Levy too. Everyone was extremely wonderful. We didn't know at the time that we were making history. People like John Candy were developing characters like Doctor Tongue, which would just emerge during improvisations. You'd see him bring that out in the middle of a scene.

VIC: How much of that humour was accidental or spontaneous?

ROSEMARY: You can't get laughs by just telling a joke. Nobody laughs. The best comedy comes from human behaviour in real situations. You had to prepare a character and then go on stage with it.

VIC: Could you talk a little about John Candy?

ROSEMARY: He was a very fine man. I only knew him for those ten months at Second City. At one point we all drove to Chicago. He had an old snowmobile, I think. He used to drive with one hand and his other arm out the window. He had an extreme hunger to be famous. I believe he got up in the morning hungry for fame—it was like food for him.

I've seen people who are now very famous, and they weren't necessarily more talented, but they had this hunger. I don't have that. I wish I did. Maybe I'm just too lazy. But they wanted it—fame—so badly.

VIC: You see the fame—for what reason? For money?

ROSEMARY: Fame? I have no idea. To me, my biggest joy, take making films, for example, is when someone is touched. The lights go down, and if someone comes to you afterwards and says, "That particular character, that scene, it touched me so much. I learned something. I felt something." That, to me, is what it's all about.

I cannot know another soul's motives. But if you're asking about John Candy's character—no, I don't think it was about money for him. He lived with his mother and grandmother, and I believe there was an onus on him to take care of the family because his father had died. But he had this wonderful soul. At Second City, if you came up with an idea, he would always, always work with you. Never nasty, never dismissive. He was generous and giving, though of course he had his own struggles. Everyone does. But you know, a clown always plays against pain.

VIC: Is there some honesty in that? That those who are so funny on screen are actually carrying sadness?

ROSEMARY: Oh, definitely. I'd say comedians are all troubled in some way. They see the sadness of the world, so they make a joke—but they carry that sadness inside them. Then they layer behaviour over it, and somehow, it creates this simpatico with the audience. Some people were always "on," always entertaining. Others needed a break. There were those who lived normal lives offstage, and then they'd light up when they got on stage—it would just explode out of them.

VIC: In your mind, was there a character or colleague you worked with where the chemistry was especially strong?

ROSEMARY: I loved *Coming Up Rosie*. But I was the straight man in that show—everyone else got the jokes. The premise was that we were in a basement and I was making documentaries, while these eccentric people surrounded me. Fiona Reid, Catherine O'Hara, John Candy, Dan Aykroyd

Dan played a sort of Travis Bickle type who looked after the building and wore a police uniform all the time. Trevor gave us incredible freedom to make a character our own. Dan Aykroyd always carried a trucker's wallet, or he did at the time. I doubt he still does—now he just makes vodka! But yes, that freedom was layered on top of the script. I can't tell you where these ideas came from. Some people are just given more light than others.

VIC: I did a few shows with these guys, as you know, and I couldn't keep a straight face. Off-camera, it was chaos. I'd look through the viewfinder and just lose it. It was like, "This is the ice cube here"—and then someone would just take the moment and run with it.

ROSEMARY: That would be the improvisation they learned at Second City. They couldn't be still. There was a constant search for humour. That's the hunger—the drive—that made them extraordinary. But you probably worked with them more than I did.

VIC: I did quite a bit, yeah. But I was more in the film world then—before digital—so I had to worry about film stock, exposure, Christmas deadlines, the whole thing. But I had so much fun doing it. My next question is—how much creative freedom did you have? On stage? In television?

ROSEMARY: All I know is that I got worn out being in Canada. I got worn out because people would say, "Can you get me someone like Rosemary Radcliffe? But not her." Unless you went to the States, or were part of a protected circle like *SCTV*, it was cold. Lonely. You could burn out fast. Shows that became famous, like *Schitt's Creek*, had protected nests. But in so many other circumstances, you weren't protected.

VIC: So how do you sustain it? Your character, or even your own presence?

ROSEMARY: That's just it. I didn't have to show up day after day in the same way. But it's a lot of pressure. When people look at comedy, they think, "Oh, they're funny all the time." But how much of it is real? And how much is acting?

VIC: Which is play-acting? For example, do you remember Peter Sellers?

ROSEMARY: Well, I have to say, although I thought he was an incredibly talented man, I didn't find him very funny. I don't like pratfalls—I don't see the point in them. There's wit now and then, but that English brand of humour just doesn't suit me. I don't find it funny.

VIC: So what kind of humour are you drawn to? Are you more into slapstick? Speech? American style?

ROSEMARY: I don't even know. I think you just have to have it in you—your whole being. You're either funny or you're not. You're born with it, or maybe you develop it because you needed to get out of terrible situations. Then all of a sudden you do something funny, but it's lying there dormant. You don't display it every day. Humour is very strange. I don't even know I have it. I can do it, but I'm not trying to do it for you now. I'm just being myself.

VIC: Are you afraid that if you're truly yourself, you'll lose that humour in front of people?

ROSEMARY: No, this is me. But I'll tell you—I got worn out. I didn't want to be an actor anymore. So for many years now, I haven't done much. Now I just write poetry, do a little music composition. I study composition. I just... I find acting is hard work. It demands that you give your whole body. And then you have to tamp things down, bury all that emotion, even in your voice, so that the audience can receive it and sense it, and love it.

VIC: I'm exploring the world of people who are funny—because I grew up watching and listening to that. And there are always two sides to it: the dark side and the light side. They always seem to act against the dark. That's what drives them. But from you, it sounds like it's not quite the same. Like you mentioned... John Candy, for example, came from a poor family—so he had that drive.

ROSEMARY: Yes, yes, that's what I call the hunger. The hunger to be more, to spread, to be larger. I think if you're very fortunate in life, you know from the start what you're meant to do. You know you're going to be a cameraman, for example, and you work toward that. And eventually it filters into a living. But there are people like me who just wake up and don't know what they're doing. They flop around. I'd say I'm a flopper.

VIC: Can you tell me any stories—looking back—of times you had a wonderful experience on set, in a sketch, an episode?

ROSEMARY: *Coming Up Rosie*, those were all fun. Every single one. You'd just report to set, and the makeup people would take care of you, the costume people would take care of you, and they'd put you together as this character. Then the director would say, "Take ten"—and you'd think, "What am I doing wrong? Am I not good enough?" But who knows what he was looking for? You never know the mind of a director—why he wants ten or twenty takes.

VIC: That was Trevor, right?

ROSEMARY: Yes, but I loved him. He was great. Great, great.

VIC: Did he give strong direction?

ROSEMARY: Well, he would just shoot. He never gave line readings. But he would shoot until you got grumpy with him—and then the emotion would be there.

VIC: He pushed you?

ROSEMARY: Yes. Yes. He was a pusher.

VIC: What about the other people you worked with? Did you enjoy working with them on *Coming Up Rosie*? Do you still keep in touch with any of them?

ROSEMARY: No. I think a hundred million dollars changes people. It makes you different. So, no—I'm not in touch with any of them.

VIC: Do you have any regrets?

ROSEMARY: I have no regrets at all. I did get burned out, but I feel incredibly fortunate to have experienced those people. But ultimately, it's human behaviour. It's about who's hungry—and who's not.

I would think, "Oh, I thought I was prettier." This is a hard society if you're not very, very pretty. Show business is harsh. Everything is judged—how you walk, how you put on makeup. And it grinds you down. If you truly see beauty—I once saw someone on an elevator—you can't take your eyes off it. You're just sucked into it. And the rest of us? We're staggering around doing the best we can. I tried to do the best I could. I had no real acting lessons. I wasn't even allowed to audition for theatre school. I was like one of those dandelions that grows in the crack of the sidewalk. I just came up. And then, little by little, more projects came.

Acting isn't as interesting as travelling. To see the world, to peek into places... to stand in the Karnak temple—there's nothing on the stage that compares to that. Nothing.

VIC: You know, I find that fascinating about show business people—these two sides. They make you feel good, but many suffer. Take Michael Jackson—wonderful talent, great dancer, and yet so much pain. That duality drives so many talented people. It fascinates me.

ROSEMARY: Well, that's the sadness of seeing the world. Knowing that life is unfair. Some are given more than others. And there's nothing to be done. What can you do? Some are given psychosis. Some are given beauty. Some humour. It's just what we were handed. It was written what we would be. I love that line in *Lawrence of Arabia*: "It is written."

VIC: What's your all-time favourite film?

ROSEMARY: Oh, I don't know. There are just so many brilliant ones. I like *My Brilliant Career*, for example. But I can't say. I just watch everything with joy. I love streaming. I swear I've watched everything. I even started watching Joe Rogan. I'll watch anything. He's not even that attractive, poor man, but he has authority.

VIC: Anything else you want to say?

ROSEMARY: It's up to you. I think I've said enough. I'm not one of the great stars you've interviewed. I'm not Adrienne Clarkson. But I did fill a small piece. And that's all I could do—given my circumstances, how I was brought up, and how I was taught that acting was, you know, for wild women. So I just did what I could to bring out what I was born with.

VIC: Still, you played your role. Maybe not a huge one, but meaningful in its time.

ROSEMARY: Yes, yes. Well, we're the ones who were here. Yes, I guess so. I guess so. Don't undermine yourself. We all can only play the piece we're given in history. We can't play the whole of it. We come, we go—some stay longer, some shorter. But the footsteps are there. I see you. Only one part of my life was acting. I thought it was everything. But then I discovered, it's not really. And I didn't really enjoy even being a little bit famous. Like, I'd be waiting outside a nightclub and get spotted, rushed in ahead of others. I felt uncomfortable with that. Or when people would buzz when I walked into a restaurant. I don't know. It's... uncertain.

VIC: So how do you feel today, sitting here, looking back?

ROSEMARY: I've managed to stay off social media. I've managed to fade away, because I thought there were other, more important things to do.

VIC: There's a nice soundbite in that. You're saying we have a choice.

ROSEMARY: Yes. That freedom—most people don't have it. So I cherish myself. Think of this...what about what you have? Nobody thinks of that. We always think about the other side—what we're missing—but not what we have. I'm not saying that you would be guilty of that, just... it's something to think about.

VIC: You've given lots of beautiful little thoughts, thank you, Rosemary.

Chapter 20

CHRISTOPHER HINTON

Christopher Hinton built an international reputation as one of Canada's most innovative animators through his many years with the National Film Board. His films, such as Blackfly *and* cNote, *often play with narrative form and push the boundaries of animated storytelling. Nominated for Oscars and widely celebrated, Hinton's work reflects both artistic independence and the collaborative spirit of the NFB.*

VIC SARIN: Let's start with where it all began. Where were you born, and what was your early environment like?

CHRISTOPHER HINTON: I was born in Galt, Ontario—which no longer exists under that name. It's now Cambridge. I grew up in Clarkson, Ontario, and that's changed too—it's now part of Mississauga. Then I moved from Winnipeg to Montreal, spent most of my life there, raised a family in Montreal West, which I think they were going to change the name of too. So, most everywhere I go ends up being erased.

Growing up in Clarkson was actually really lucky. At the time, it was remote from Toronto—just a small highway connected it. It was a farming community, mainly fruits and vegetables. The walk to school was full of plums, apples, pears, grapes, berries—it was beautiful. We were close to Lake Ontario, and we had free run of a local forest—the last Carolinian forest in southern Ontario. We built forts in the forest. In the winter, we built our own hockey rinks—the town gave us a hose, and the cold did the rest. Always outside. Evenings were for homework. Sometimes TV, but that was strictly limited, maybe an hour before dinner and a little after.

VIC: As a kid, did you feel drawn to anything in particular?

CHRIS: Not when I was really young. I didn't have a clear sense of direction. But in my early teens, I started to feel a pull toward art. I started drawing and painting, and I just gravitated to it without really knowing why. My parents weren't pushing me in any direction, so I had the freedom to explore it. In school, I became known as the "art guy" in class. I really enjoyed it, but I don't know why. Even now, I find it a mystery. I just kept doing it. I remember buying a case of oil paints and going out to sit in a field and paint. Then I'd go home and throw the painting out. I did that for years—painting and throwing it all away. It was a bit ridiculous in hindsight, but I couldn't stop. I never kept anything.

VIC: Was anyone encouraging you? Teachers? Friends? And do you remember what kinds of things you were drawing?

CHRIS: No, no one encouraged me. Not teachers, not friends. My parents, especially my father, were businesslike people. My dad was practical, he never understood what I was doing. He was supportive in his own way—he never asked me to change—but he was constantly mystified by me.

As for what I drew… I was drawn to what I saw in art books. Van Gogh, Gauguin, that kind of thing. I wanted to emulate that. Looking back now, it's kind of absurd, but that's where I thought I was headed. I was also fascinated by anatomy. When I got into college, I started trying to draw the human figure. I bought a copy of *Gray's Anatomy* and studied the muscles. I wasn't good at it, but I kept at it. I was really driven by it.

We were pretty isolated in Clarkson, so I wasn't seeing other artists' work firsthand. A visit to an art gallery meant a drive downtown. I remember maybe once or twice going to the Art Gallery of Ontario. Later, my parents took me to the McMichael Collection when it first opened. But otherwise, it was just me, books, and whatever I could figure out on my own.

I really enjoyed seeing the work of the Group of Seven. It moved me. I'd spent a lot of time in the scouting movement up in Muskoka—Algoma, Sudbury, and north of Superior—so I knew the landscapes they painted. Seeing their work captivated me.

VIC: That's a powerful connection, seeing places you know reflected in art.

CHRIS: Yes. I remember Harold Town as well. I'm not sure why, but I gravitated to his work. It fascinated me, even though I can't explain exactly what grabbed me about it. It was bold—very different from the Impressionist work I usually looked at. I was focused on Impressionism back then. That was my "this is for me" moment. But Harold Town wasn't that at all.

VIC: What about Michael Snow? Or Christopher Pratt?

CHRIS: Yes, Michael Snow. I liked his work. And Christopher Pratt, too. He was a close friend for a time. I really liked the clarity and starkness in his images. I think I was being steered mostly by books. I remember reading one about the New York painters—modernist stuff—and that really pulled me in.

VIC: Were you drawn to things like *Starry Night*, or other kinds of compositions?

CHRIS: Honestly, I don't think I really knew what I was doing. I just wanted to understand where these feelings came from—why the work affected me. But I never figured it out. I remember subscribing to a Canadian art magazine once and finding the language absolutely impenetrable. I couldn't make heads or tails of it. So, I just looked at the pictures.

VIC: And you weren't schooled in art or art history at that point?

CHRIS: No, no formal education. Just something I paid attention to, that mattered to me.

VIC: Let's go back a bit—you mentioned colour. You seem to lean toward stark lines and space rather than fullness of colour.

CHRIS: Possibly, yes. I think that's true. Some of my work reflects that. I suppose I liked the starkness, the form. More than the lushness of colour.

VIC: More line and form over painterly depth?

CHRIS: Yes. That feels accurate. One New York artist I really liked was Claes Oldenburg. I liked the way he tackled form. I never really had the skill to draw that well, but I was drawn to his work.

VIC: Do you think you were still trying to find your way at that point?

CHRIS: Absolutely. I hadn't developed yet as an artist—not with still work. I was just exploring, seeing what hit me, and trying to work with that. But it wasn't until I got into animation that I really found something with bones, something I wanted to dig into.

VIC: What was that moment when you crossed over into animation?

CHRIS: It was in my late teens. Sheridan College, which happened to be close to home, had a new animation course. Three years. I applied and dove into it completely. I'd be there first thing in the morning and last to leave at night. I don't know what it was about it, but the idea of combining visual art with time—of controlling how an image moves, how you look at it, what it makes you feel—that really intrigued me.

VIC: So not just the image, but the rhythm, the emotional impact.

CHRIS: Exactly. You could give a line or a shape weight, nervousness, energy. You could make an abstract object feel like it had a story. That really struck me. I remember in second year, everyone was doing characters for their films—cartoons, figures. But my film was just a leaf falling from a tree to the ground. That's all. I wanted to change the world with a leaf.

VIC: That's beautiful. Did anything come of it?

CHRIS: Not really, it was a bust. I don't even know where the film is now. But thinking back, it's funny. I'm still doing that kind of thing. Right now, I'm working with a pianist in Toronto. Still blending photography with non-figurative drawings and paintings, trying to find some power in that mixture.

VIC: So, in a way, you haven't travelled that far from that leaf?

CHRIS: Exactly. It's kind of interesting when I think about it.

VIC: And at that time, animation wasn't a big field in Canada. Who brought you in?

CHRIS: In my third year at Sheridan, a white knight rode in—so to speak. Someone from Winnipeg was looking for directors to work in animation.

CHRIS: He looked at my reel of student films and offered me a job directing. I wasn't about to turn that down. I just said, "If you want me, I'll come." So, I moved to Winnipeg—and it turned out to be the best move I ever made. His name was Ken Perkins. He ran a company called Ken Perkins Animation.

VIC: And right from the beginning, you were directing?

CHRIS: Yes, from day one. I was directing commercials. It was a terrific experience. I learned a lot.

VIC: Do you remember one of the early works you felt proud of from that time?

CHRIS: Honestly, I don't feel good about any of them when I look back. Nothing was very polished. It was all a work in progress—I was a work in progress. But I was surrounded by this community of Winnipeg artists who were incredibly warm and encouraging. Many of them are still friends to this day.

VIC: What did you take away from that early experience?

CHRIS: I learned how to work efficiently and quickly. We were making commercials—Alberta, Saskatchewan, Manitoba—and making a living at it. Ken hired me full-time to animate, and it was wonderful.

VIC: Any projects stand out?

CHRIS: One unusual client was K-tel, the record company. Every Friday, we'd get a new assignment, and by Thursday it had to be ready for air. We had to come up with an idea, draw it, animate it, shoot it. And this wasn't digital.

If you wanted sparkles, you had to wind the film back and do a second pass. Some of those jobs took multiple passes. It taught me discipline. Speed and precision.

VIC: But eventually, you left Ken Perkins?

CHRIS: Yeah, for reasons I still don't understand. I quit and went freelance. Looking back, I think—what was I thinking? I had no real skills. I was green. But somehow I leapt.

VIC: What happened next?

CHRIS: There was a new company forming, Credo Group—Brad Caslor and Derek Mazur started it. They had animation work, so I freelanced with them. Around that time, *Sesame Street* was looking for Canadian content, so we did quite a bit of that.

VIC: That was a good foothold.

CHRIS: Definitely. Around then, the National Film Board brought on a producer in Winnipeg—Michael Scott. Instead of outsourcing, he pulled the local community together. He said, "We'll animate here, direct here, record here." That really built up the animation community in Winnipeg. It gave us all confidence—and a chance to learn everything hands-on.

VIC: Did you sign on as staff with the NFB?

CHRIS: No, it was all freelance. I signed contracts for individual projects. I don't remember the financial details, but I was working regularly for the Film Board through Michael.

VIC: Michael Scott? He's still around?

CHRIS: Yes, I saw him a couple of years ago. He's a lovely guy. I always respected his opinion. He was a terrific producer. Cynthia Scott—his sister, I think?—was involved as well.

I got along really well with the Film Board. They treated me well. As I recall, Credo Group was asked to create several projects for the government—around the time metric was being introduced. Insulating your house, *The Charter of Rights and Freedoms,* that kind of public content. The contracts came through Credo, but I had a lot of autonomy—developing storyboards, storylines, whatever direction I thought worked.

VIC: And the first NFB commission? Do you remember what it was?

CHRIS: I think it was "Lady Frances Simpson," part of a series of historical vignettes. I did the research myself, at the Hudson's Bay archives. Found the story about her journey west and turned it into a one-minute animated short.

VIC: That played on television, didn't it?

CHRIS: Yes, quite a bit. I think it won some awards. I never heard anything negative about it, although I, of course, didn't want to see it again. I never like anything I do. But it got attention. It was useful.

VIC: If you look at the history of the Film Board, they were real pioneers, particularly in animation.

CHRIS: Absolutely. Especially in the 1950s, they were the norm-setters. Norman McLaren really put Canada on the map in animation. He laid the foundation for everything that followed.

VIC: And Michael Scott picked up that thread in Winnipeg?

CHRIS: Yes, I think so. Michael helped build a real community there—a kind of broadcaster-hub model. You had animators like Cordell Barker, Richard Condie, and others. We all gelled. People started calling it the "Winnipeg look" or the "Winnipeg school." It was a very vibrant, collaborative space. You'd show your storyboards to anyone—animators, directors, producers—and get feedback without intimidation. It was warm and generous.

VIC: Why do you think the Film Board nurtured talent in that region?

CHRIS: I think it was an extension of the McLaren legacy. There was a community of people genuinely excited to explore animation. Canada had some international success at festivals, and the Film Board seemed keen to build on that momentum. I didn't get to Montreal until later, so I can really only speak for Winnipeg, but that community spirit was strong.

VIC: When did you make the move to Montreal?

CHRIS: After three years in Winnipeg, I moved to Nova Scotia. Didn't love it. Then I moved to Montreal and started freelancing out of the Film Board's office there.

VIC: What was the vibe like at the Montreal office?

CHRIS: In a word, encouraging. The Film Board was supportive at every stage. They gave me opportunities and trusted me. I was desperate to deliver on time and do a professional job. That sense of responsibility pushed me.

VIC: Do you remember a specific film where you really felt that support?

CHRIS: Yes. A film I made in 2004 called *Flux*. They gave me all the room I needed to explore. I had this idea that the screen would have no up or down, no left or right—no horizon line. The layout would follow a kind of intuitive logic, inspired by how my daughter used to draw. What mattered to her took up space. What didn't, shrank away.

VIC: That's a beautiful concept. Did that influence the technique?

CHRIS: Absolutely. I wanted the visuals to shift constantly, what's important comes forward, what's not gets pushed aside. But technically, it was tough. The Film Board set me up with a camera on Roxbury, paints, glycerin—tools to move elements around under the camera. Then they gave me a state-of-the-art computer at the time, but I couldn't get it to work the way I wanted. I was out of my depth.

VIC: So, what did you do?

CHRIS: I went back to basics. Took writing paper, cut it into quarters, built a simple registration device, and used a quill pen with ink. Drew every single frame by hand. If I wanted something on screen, I drew it in. If I didn't, I scribbled it out and moved on. It was always bubbling—always in flux.

VIC: And conceptually, it tied into memory?

CHRIS: Exactly. I realized my memories didn't match my wife's or my kids'. There was no overlap. We each remembered things differently. I wanted the film to reflect that fragmentation and impermanence—how time and space are unstable in our minds.

VIC: The Film Board supported not just the finished work but your whole process?

CHRIS: Yes, they gave me the freedom to explore. They offered other approaches—maybe faster ones—but they never imposed anything. I got to the final method through their support of that exploration. And that meant everything.

VIC: Looking back now, what would you say has been the most satisfying project for you?

CHRIS: *Flux*. Definitely *Flux*. It was the one that really stands out to me. It took a long time to even get to the animation stage. Normally, when I start a film, I just jump in—start animating, show some samples, and then ask if anyone wants to make the film. But with *Flux*, I couldn't do that. I had to figure out what it was first—what I wanted to say, how I was going to say it, how to manipulate the space. None of it was clear.

VIC: Was there was a long development phase?

CHRIS: Yeah, about two years of just wrestling with it in my head before I put pen to paper. That's a long time in film. But the Film Board stayed with me. There was no pressure. They just let me find my way, which is incredibly generous. When I finally made it, it felt like it came out of nowhere. But it was an original way to think about the screen, and time, and I'm proud of that.

VIC: And your first Oscar nomination came from *Blackfly*, right?

CHRIS: Yes. *Blackfly* happened because a producer at the Film Board suggested animating "The Blackfly Song." I knew the song but hadn't really listened closely to the lyrics. Still, I liked its pace. I like speed in my work, so I thought, yeah, I can do something with this. They gave me full freedom to choose the technique.

VIC: And you didn't use traditional cell animation?

CHRIS: No, I went with paper again, like in *Flux*. A small field. I didn't want sharp cuts. I wanted the transitions to be fluid—one scene flowing into the next—just like the song rolls along. So, I animated it all on paper, and they liked it. We made the film.

VIC: You went to Los Angeles for the nomination?

CHRIS: I did. It was terrifying. I don't like being the centre of attention. If I'd won, I don't think I would've made it to the stage, I'd have frozen. But the Film Board was thrilled. They're always happy for a nomination because it brings attention and helps put them on the map.

VIC: Your second nomination was for *Nibbles*?

CHRIS: Yes. *Nibbles* came out of a fishing trip with my two boys. I don't think we caught anything, but we drove up north, fished all day, and drove back. Looking back, it was ridiculous. All they really cared about were donuts. Every donut shop we passed, they wanted to stop. That was the premise: all this effort to catch a fish while the kids were endlessly snacking. It was quick and funny, and drawn straight from life.

VIC: It sounds like a very personal piece.

CHRIS: It was. But if I had to pick another film I feel really good about, it would be *cNote*. That one marked a new direction. I don't have a portfolio that follows a straight line—I like exploring new territory. Like with that old leaf-falling film, I've always wanted to bring non-figurative elements to life.

VIC: What inspired *cNote* specifically?

CHRIS: A friend of mine was head of music education in North York. I went to see him about a grant, something music-related. And he pulled me aside and said, "Chris, I want to show you what modern music looks like." He had these scores by contemporary composers—beautiful in their own right, like visual art. He gave me suggestions, what to look at, what to listen to.

VIC: You decided to explore that musically?

CHRIS: Yes. I wanted to find a young Canadian composer writing contemporary music. I didn't want to influence them, I didn't want them composing "for animation" or trying to match the visuals. I just wanted pure music, something abstract, and I'd build something around that. It was a wonderful project. I had to think about the arc of the film. I had to think,"It's got to keep people in their seats. I don't want repetition. I want it to be fresh and develop as the film moves forward." I look back on that as a very interesting project.

I did a small test before that called *X-Man*. A colleague in the music department at the university composed a piece, played on the piano, and I took that and made a little film to show the Film Board what my intentions were. By doing this little project, I had something to show.

VIC: But you seem to take real issues and do something interesting.

CHRIS: Yeah. I get very excited about things. Like when I get the idea of working with non-figurative elements. I just wanted to start working right away and deal with the Film Board later. And the Film Board's usually receptive. I really liked what happened. And then I took it to the Film Board, and they produced *cNote*.

VIC: So much innovation came out of Canada. Who do you credit for that? Is it our long winters here? Is it the larger canvas of the country? Talk a little bit about what encourages people here.

CHRIS: Yeah, good question. Personally, I was given so many opportunities by the National Film Board. So much support. Technical expertise. Back in the early days—the analog days—there was a frightening amount of technical equipment, and really knowledgeable, skilled people to run it. People who knew how to operate cameras, optical printers, labs—all that stuff.

Today it's a little different. But back then, starting a film was daunting. And the Film Board just encouraged us—put projects in front of us—and we had to figure out how to do them. I still don't know how it would've all started without them. I doubt it would have. Because back then, you needed funding. You needed equipment. Nobody had that kind of setup.

The Film Board was trying to create a national arts program—a film world—and they wanted Canadians to do it. That was instrumental in the genesis of animation in this country. And we're known for the animation we produce here. Even today. Every year, we'd go to festivals, and the films were well received around the world.

VIC: Let's talk about the films coming from the animation world—both here and elsewhere. Do you watch animation from the U.S., or Europe, or other places? How does our work compare?

CHRIS: Well, I'd say it's just all different. You know, it's different. Back in the analog days, if your film was accepted by a festival—usually in Europe or Japan—you were invited. You were given a hotel room, maybe a flight. And the Film Board gave us per diem to feed us. So, we got to see the films being made around the world. It was a very exciting time. Because again, it was all done under the camera. It wasn't digital.

The films were really beautiful. People used a myriad of techniques—pushing paint under a camera, sand, pin screens, you name it. People found ways to generate moving art. Canadian films were well received. I think we had an amazing record of acceptance on the international stage.

VIC: Do you think you have a certain niche? Something that your mind gravitates to more than anything else?

CHRIS: Well, I'm fascinated with motion, animation motion. I'm just driven to find a way to make it sparkle. I don't know why. I like the challenge of working with visuals that people can't latch onto. For instance, a rectangle on the screen—how do I make that interesting? How can I keep you in your seat? That's what draws me in. What can I do to that shape? What feeling, what life can I bring to that goofy thing on the screen to keep the audience engaged? That's what really motivates me.

And I still do it. I do even more of it now. Over the last few years, I've been working with Eve Egoyan, a pianist. We started out with a kind of call-and-response collaboration. I saw a concert of hers—contemporary piano—and I asked if she'd be interested in working together. She gave me the rights to use some of her recordings, and I made a few little films.

Then she suggested, "Why don't I send you a piece of music and you animate visuals to it, and then you send me back 20 seconds of animation and I'll compose a score?" So, we did that for a few years. Then we decided to apply for a Canada Council grant, and we put together a performance. Not a film: a performance. That was a different way of thinking, because her piano was set up with an optical sensor. When she played a key, it triggered an animated clip on the screen. If she played multiple notes, you'd get multiple layers of animation—various clips—on screen at once. It always stayed in sync, no matter how she performed it, even on tour. So that turned out to be a really interesting project.

Again, it's just an extension of my fascination with the non-figurative world. Trying to make that kind of imagery connect. To have people feel as excited watching it as I feel while making it. But you never really know until you're in front of an audience—and they either applaud or kick you out. We had a couple of performances in Toronto. They seemed to be well received.

VIC: Do you take anything away from international audiences—something that feels uniquely Canadian? Or is animation becoming more homogeneous?

CHRIS: These days, I think it's more homogeneous. But in the earlier days, it was different. We definitely had a look, especially in Winnipeg. There was something distinct about that work. Maybe it's the long winters or the scale of the country, but I think we developed a sensibility in our films.

VIC: Why animation and not fiction?

CHRIS: I think it was just the luck of the draw. Animation is truly creative. Impressionistic. Dream-like, maybe.

VIC: See, I'm the opposite of you—I'm rooted in reality.

CHRIS: Yeah, totally understood. My mind just works differently, I guess. I like challenges—especially visual ones. Solving timing problems, working with an idea or technique, figuring out how to make something work—that's what excites me. I don't know where it comes from.

VIC: Are you working on anything right now?

CHRIS: I just finished three performances with Eve Egoyan. I never seem to stop—as much as it drives me nuts. Last year I took a solo trip through the Yukon, Northwest Territories, and Alaska. I'm working on a travel film about that—but it's not really about the places. It's about my mind. I kept a diary for the first time in my life, writing every day.

Now I want to put something on screen that reflects my mental process during the journey. I drove very slowly. Any time I saw something—like a rock that caught my eye—I'd stop. I didn't have a fixed destination. I had a van I could sleep in, so I just took my time, all the way to the Yukon and beyond. I've animated three or four minutes of it already, but I'm not sure I'll keep any of it. That's how I work.

I start animating, thinking I've got it figured out, then get two minutes in and realize I don't, and throw it out. I just finished a film about technology. I started that one six times. I wasn't even going to finish it, but someone convinced me to put a soundtrack to it and send it out.

These days, I think—at this stage of life—I'm fascinated with the ideas of humanity, and with opera, symphony orchestra, and dance. I just feel like I want to do something with those elements, but I don't yet know what. There's a possibility that a dance project at the Film Board will happen. About 15 years ago, we shot a dancer on a green screen. My idea was to take that figure and place it into an animated space, with non-figurative elements, and build something from there. That possibility still exists.

I like collaborating across disciplines. And if that project doesn't grow wings, I might see if there's a local dance community interested in exploring dance combined with animation. I just love the excitement of possibility. I've been very lucky, supported, and encouraged. When I'm in that creative world, I forget everything else. I get immersed, blinkered—it's not until my stomach starts growling that I even get out of my chair.

VIC: You've spoken about possibility and support. What are your thoughts on the importance of national institutions like the Film Board and the CBC in Canada today?

CHRIS: Oh, I'm a solid believer in national media for this country. Canada is so spread out—we can have very little communication between, say, Nova Scotia and the Prairies, or between all the various regions that make up Canada. I grew up on the CBC, on Peter Gzowski, and it was fascinating. I learned so much from it. The Film Board has been a huge contributor to national identity. I think it's vitally important, especially these days, to keep the country together—to give us pride in our history and cultures, and to celebrate the variety of languages and immigrant stories that make up Canada. I don't think we could survive without it. It would be a tragedy to kill those institutions.

I have a lot of very warm feelings about the Film Board and the people I had the opportunity to work with. I like the direction things are going today. It's not the same as when I was younger, but I love that they're bringing in new voices—young people, people with different backgrounds and nationalities—to express their own ideas. Sure, anyone with a laptop can make a film now, but there's something special about having a producer, or a body of expertise, to keep you focused. Someone who asks, "Why are you doing this instead of that?" That kind of questioning improves the work.

Guidance is important. I think the best work often comes from having barriers—technical challenges, colour limitations, timing constraints. Those restrictions force you to be creative. And the Film Board gives you community too. It connects filmmakers across the country, or just in the same neighbourhood. That cross-pollination, that artist-to-artist conversation—it improves everything. It's hard when someone in Quebec has an idea, and someone else out West has a similar one, and there's no way to bring them together. But the Film Board makes that possible. Personally, I think the CBC and the Film Board are vital to the survival of this country.

As for me, I'm looking forward to working with the human figure again. That's my next challenge. I'm hoping the Film Board can find those old frames we shot and that we can find a way to work with them. If not, I'll go low-tech again, as I've done before. It won't have the polish, but it'll still have the impact I'm looking for. You start with a grand idea, but once you're into it, things change. Ideas shift. Things become more malleable. It's a process—an exciting process. A real exploration.

I think we're very lucky to have three cultures in Canada—Indigenous, French, and English—and to be working, however imperfectly, at keeping that connection alive. National institutions like the Film Board and CBC have played a huge role in holding us together and giving us a voice. Personally, I still feel the excitement of animation. The Film Board's legacy in that area—being a pioneer—still motivates me. I'll wake up at 2:00 a.m. with an idea and go right to work. It just happens—I don't know why. Like this morning, I was sitting with a handful of olive pits, and I ended up arranging them on a textured piece of paper, photographing them because the shadows and textures inspired me. You never know when the spark will hit.

VIC: You've clearly stayed deeply connected with the animation community. Are there voices today you think we should be paying attention to?

CHRIS: Yes, absolutely. There's a film I'd highly recommend: *Shameless Propaganda*, made by Bob Lower. He was an editor and freelancer for the Film Board for years, now he's writing. This film might have been his last, and it's an attempt to distill the essence of what the Film Board really meant to Canada. What did it say about us? What did it do for us? It's not all positive—but it's deeply insightful. He narrates it himself.

These films are how we stay connected—not just practically, but culturally, spiritually. They help us understand each other across these enormous distances. And without that shared voice, what do we become?

VIC: Thank you so much for your thoughtful responses, Chris.

Chapter 21

IAN WEIR

Ian Weir is an award-winning Canadian screenwriter, novelist, playwright, and showrunner. His television credits include creating and producing the acclaimed series Arctic Air, Dragon Boys, *and numerous dramas for CBC, CTV, and international networks. As a novelist, his books such as* Daniel O'Thunder *and* Will Starling *have earned critical praise for their vivid historical storytelling. Weir has also been a longtime instructor and mentor in screenwriting and creative writing.*

VIC: I want to know you as a person. What was it like growing up?

IAN: I grew up in Kamloops. I was actually born in the States, but by sheer accident. My dad was doing a surgical internship at Duke University Hospital when I happened to come along. My parents were only down there for two years, and I was born right in the middle of it, in Durham, North Carolina. But I grew up in Kamloops, B.C. We only had one TV channel until I was in junior high school, and it was the CBC. So, I grew up watching the CBC, which of course included watching *Tommy Hunter* on Friday nights. Wasn't a big hit with the 8- and 9-year-old crowd, but that was the channel we had. I fell in love with theatre in high school. We had a very active drama program. For a time, I dreamed of being an actor until I discovered I had no talent. Which doesn't stop everybody, but it certainly stopped me. So, I moved into writing plays instead.

VIC: What did you and your friends do for fun?

IAN: Sports were very big. Organized sports, but also just pickup games after school on the playground. By the time I was in high school, we figured out we could get into some of the bars, so that became one of the regular entertainments, going to the pub on Friday and Saturday nights. It was still, in a way, quite an innocent time. You know, when parents could sort of send kids off to spend the day playing by themselves—"Here's your bike, away you go."

VIC: What about family time in the evenings?

IAN: We were, on the one hand, a very close family. On the other hand, my dad, as a surgeon in a small town, worked extraordinarily long hours. He was a wonderful man—I always felt supported by him and close to him—but if I think of enduring memories from childhood, it's hearing the phone ring at 2 a.m., then his footsteps going down the stairs, being called to the hospital, and not seeing him again until the following evening.

My mom was a writer, so she was at home a lot. And for someone who wanted to be a writer, that's such a gift—to have someone modelling writing as something real, something you can do seriously. Other friends I had growing up in Kamloops who had artistic talent, they didn't come from families that did "that sort of thing." So having a mother who wrote legitimized the whole process.

VIC: But you've written so much. Where does it come from?

IAN: That's a great question. I always loved writing. Always wanted to write. The first job I had as a writer was the four years after high school I worked as a newspaper reporter. What you learn in newspaper work is that there's no such thing as waiting for inspiration. You simply write. You put your bum in the chair and type. And having learned that, I've always been good at it. I can generate a lot of pages in a day. So basically anything that catches my fancy—new characters, interactions with people—that becomes fodder for the writing.

VIC: Anyone who inspired you? Looking back—someone you thought, "I want to be like you," or someone you read?

IAN: Yeah, yeah. So, a couple of huge figures for me—one, of course, was my mom. The fact that she was writing was a huge inspiration. In Kamloops back in the day, there was a tremendously strong high school drama program. Tom Kerr was the fellow who was running it, and at the same time as I was in high school, he was also starting up a semi-professional theatre company on the side. So, there was a chance to work with professionals, to play small parts in plays.

When I was going into Grade 12, I had a chance to be part of a trip to Edinburgh for the Edinburgh Festival. I didn't have much acting talent, so I was kept in very small parts in the productions, but I was part of the supporting cast. Being involved in productions at the Edinburgh Festival—at that age—was extraordinary. Tom's program had a huge influence on me, not just in terms of writing, but in terms of understanding art and what it means to work with professional actors. As a high school student, you start to understand what it takes—the kind of dedication and focus that professional work requires.

VIC: You've written so much in your life, but you also bring lived experience. Where does your inspiration come from?

IAN: I suppose anything I read becomes grist for the mill. I'm a huge, huge fan of Dickens. The three novels I've written were all strongly influenced by him. I haven't travelled extensively, not compared to you. I've been very provincial. But I try to observe deeply. Understanding characters and their situations is the foundation. And I love working. I love the process.

In terms of approach to character, I learned a lot working as a stage playwright. In theatre, when you're developing a new play, you're in the rehearsal hall with the actors. They pin you down on what you're doing with each character throughout the rehearsal process. That's something you rarely get in television or film. As a writer, you tend to be quite separate from the actors. When you're a producer on a TV series, yes, you interact more, but the chance to sit and really discuss what makes a character compelling—to watch gifted actors dig through the psychological layers of a character has had a huge effect on me.

VIC: For me, it's always been about life experience. Through the lens, I can go into any place and open a door. My entire journey has been about experiencing this one life fully. One life is enough. There's so much to learn, so much to see. And I see it through the lens, how people react, how they behave. It's all learning. That's why your mind, Ian, full of characters and stories—it's such a gift. I understand what you explore. Even if you don't write every character, they live in you.

IAN: Yeah, yeah. As for motivation, I confess—part of it is like you. I was never motivated by money. That wasn't the point. And fame wasn't really the point either. I think all of us want to do something we're good at. When I was a kid, I dreamed of being a professional hockey player, until I realized I didn't have that kind of ability. The only thing I was truly good at was writing and storytelling. So, I wanted to spend as much of my life and getting better at it.

That might not speak to inspiration, exactly, but it does speak to the love of the craft. The love of telling stories. And, as you know, as a filmmaker—if you don't love what you're doing, you can't do a particularly good job of it. You might manage the craft, but without that joy of getting up in the morning to work on your project—it falls flat.

VIC: You and I are blessed. I can work 18 hours a day. It doesn't feel like work anymore. One thing I wanted to ask: let's say you have an idea—you pitch it to a network, and they like it. Now comes the process: producers, actors, feedback from the network. It must be disheartening at times?

IAN: It can be challenging at times. But when you're working with good people, it's never really disheartening, because you're always getting feedback you respect and can learn from.

That said, I did hit a point in my career when I needed to step back from television entirely. It was around 2013, 2014, after we wrapped *Arctic Air*. I was just feeling burned out—not by the pace of the writing, but I'd taken so many millions of notes. And you must have felt this in your career too: I really couldn't take another note. I couldn't smile and find a way to incorporate it and make it part of what I was doing.

So, I went away and spent several years writing novels. Because writing novels is a private, individual, isolated activity. And I loved doing that. Then, after a few years, I realized I was getting really lonely. That, more than anything, is what drew me back to writing for television. Because as you know, television is the ultimate team sport.

VIC: But doesn't it sometimes bother you? You have this idea—a baby, a script—and then the end result is nothing like what you imagined?

IAN: Sometimes, yes. Though sometimes, it's gone ten times better than what I thought. Other times, not the same at all. I've been extraordinarily lucky with the people I've worked with. Not exclusively, but overwhelmingly, the end result has been better than I imagined—or at least exploring different elements than I would have imagined. Working as a dramatist in any form of drama, I think one of the essential things is remembering: drama isn't about the words. It's not about the writer. It's about the interplay between the actor and the audience. The characters and the audience.

Keeping that in mind, on every project I've ever done, I've always found great delight in actors making decisions and discovering things I didn't see. And when an actor finds gold, that moment of epiphany and joy, it's like, my God, they've taken this tool to a level I wouldn't have necessarily imagined.

VIC: Let's talk a little about your first foray into writing. What was the first thing you ever did? The beat-up story in school?

IAN: The first thing I tried to write semi-seriously was stage plays. And it took me a number of them before I wrote anything worth reading. I think that's a typical discovery: there's a lot of craft involved, and it's not nearly as straightforward as it might seem. So, I started wanting to write stage plays, and then—through a really happy accident—I found myself writing radio drama. It's not something I'd thought much about, but as soon as I started writing and listening to radio drama, I completely fell in love with the form.

Someone's made the argument that radio is the most visual of all forms, and I agree. It takes place inside your head. Writing for that, exploring that—it was wonderful. And you get to work with the most amazing actors in radio, because production happens quickly. When I was working on drama for the BBC, I remember being blown away—my first radio play with the BBC had one of the leads played by Michael Bryant.

VIC: Good heavens.

IAN: Yeah. And the next time I was in London—I went to university in London—I found that Michael Bryant was playing in *Uncle Vanya* at the National Theatre. I thought, "Oh my God." I waited outside the stage door, wanted to introduce myself. Michael Bryant came out—a very small man—and got on a very large motorcycle. He was heading off to meet friends. But we had a quick chat, and he remembered recording the play. He was just lovely about it. To have the chance to work with artists of that stature—it's such an inspiration.

VIC: What was your first foray into CBC?

IAN: My first foray into CBC television was a series called *Lies from Lotusland* in 1987. It was an anthology series produced by CBC Vancouver. Phil Keatley was the head of Western television at the time. It began when Phil approached the New Play Centre in Vancouver, asking them to recommend three stage playwrights who hadn't written for television but might be a good fit. So, I had a chance to write a play for *Lies from Lotusland*. I don't know that it revolutionized drama as a form—but it was produced. And I was so delighted with the process.

Lies from Lotusland opened some doors. On the basis of that show, I got to write several *Beachcombers* episodes—part of that whole generation of West Coast writers who learned some of their craft writing for *The Beachcombers*. And it kind of went from there. Around 1990, Nick Orchard was creating *Northwood* with the CBC, and I had a chance to write a bunch of scripts for that. Again, a CBC project. So much of my work over the years has been done for CBC. The first series I created as showrunner was *Edgemont*, which began in 2000—also a CBC production. That was Kristin Kreuk's first professional acting role, on *Edgemont*.And she was a revelation.

She was amazing. As you know. You worked with Kristin on *Partition*, which was a wonderful film.

VIC: Yeah. What was it like working in a corporation? You've also worked with commercial networks, not just government-funded ones.

IAN: Yeah, that's a really good question. CBC—I haven't done a show for them in a few years. But the earlier shows, there was always a sense of responsibility to the audience—that you were telling Canadian stories to Canadians. That was always taken very seriously. Some of the shows worked better than others, of course. There are so many ways for an artistic project to go wrong, and only a few ways for it to come together beautifully. But the desire was always there—to tell meaningful stories. To tell stories that matter.

That's not to say private broadcasters don't feel that too—but at CBC, it was an article of faith. Very strongly held. The executives I worked with took seriously the need to develop new talent—writers, actors, directors—anybody working in the form. They were committed to nurturing a new generation.

VIC: I think I know what you mean. I used to work in national news when I first started. Carol Off was there, and Bill Cunningham was the head of *CBC National* at the time. My nurturing came from that. Did you have a moment like that? As a writer?

IAN: The show *Edgemont* was that moment for me—the first show I did as a creator and showrunner. I'd written for television, worked on other people's shows, but never created or run my own. I thought: if I'm going to sell myself as someone able to run a show, I need to create something limited in production scope. Otherwise, I won't be taken seriously.

I worked out ten episodes before I pitched the idea. Creatively, I knew exactly what I wanted to do. I wanted to create a show that could be realized on a very tight budget. And of course, I went to CBC with it. That was in partnership with Michael Chechik, head of Omni Films.

I said, "I want to be the writer-producer on this show. But don't worry—it's not going to cost you $1 million an episode. So you can take the chance." CBC was wonderfully open to it. Getting *Edgemont* off the ground in that first season—we didn't have any Telefilm or CMF (or, back then, CCDF) money. We were kind of the last show CBC picked up that year. It was very much a "let's give them a chance and see what they can do" decision.

With the CBC licence fee, a distribution advance, money from the Shaw Fund, and tax credits—we were getting close to halfway to the budget. CBC

Vancouver also kicked in facilities. It was a good deal for them because their studio space in Vancouver wasn't being used much anymore. CBC was doing less and less in-house. We cobbled together a budget creatively. Michael and I kicked back our fees that season—reinvested them as producer equity. That got us to the finish line.

I think the entire first season cost $2.9 million—13 episodes at around $200,000 each. And the show actually worked. We were so blessed. It was CBC that made it possible. They were open, nurturing, and willing to create the conditions to make it work. God bless them.

VIC: How important was it to have that kind of freedom—as a writer, or filmmaker?

IAN: Very important. Of course, I've worked on other people's shows, and I enjoy that too. But getting the chance to do something that really matters to you—bringing other people into that vision—it's so important for the soul. And it's important for developing your craft. It lets you spread your wings and figure out how to do better at what you set out to do.

VIC: You've worked with various networks. Anything it takes to make the show, right?

IAN: CBC—certainly in the past—has tended to be more open to taking chances. And more open to allowing second chances if they see the seed of something they believe in. With private networks, there's less latitude for that. It's not that they don't want to—but they don't always have the luxury. They can't nurture and support development to the same extent that CBC traditionally has been able to do.

VIC: Could you talk a bit about development time? When working with producers and writers—how much freedom did you have in shaping the stories?

IAN: I had a lot of freedom in terms of the kinds of stories I wanted to tell. Of course, we were very much constrained in terms of sets. It was all a studio shoot, all interior locations. But I'd done a show like that before, which is why I was confident pitching the idea in the first place. It was a show called *Fifteen* for Nickelodeon. I was head writer on that for five seasons. A teen show, done at very high speed, all in-studio.

There are ways of creating something where you can tell the stories you want to tell within a very confined production model. As for the stories themselves, I had a lot of scope to tell the kinds of stories I wanted to tell. It's been a few years since I've done teen programming, but I always really enjoyed writing for that audience. It's a process of going back to being 15 years old and writing directly about the things that made me laugh, made me cry, that terrified or exhilarated me at that age.

VIC: When you write, what do you think is the most important thing—emotional connection or drama?

IAN: The emotional connection. And the truth of the characters. If you can get the characters in the script to ring true as three-dimensional human beings, then a gifted director and gifted actors will do wonderful things with those characters. If the characters don't ring true, there's no way to redeem the story.

So I always start with character and with the emotional connection. I don't begin with what makes "exciting drama." I start with: "Who are these people? What do they really want? How are they trying to get it?" That's always the process.

VIC: You've worked in the U.S. too. Is it different?

IAN: You can always tell a Canadian show. Not for the cynical reasons—like lower budgets, but because there tends to be a gentleness in Canadian storytelling. A warmth. Maybe not as much now, as the international marketplace defines so much. But there really is something distinct in great Canadian stories. And I respond to that deeply.

VIC: I've found Canadians are very gentle people. Not just in film but in real life. Peacekeeping came from Canada. We didn't get involved in Vietnam—even the Australians did. That's why we've held that position as peacemakers. But audiences still mostly watch American shows.

IAN: Yeah, exactly. It can be hard to sell a Canadian sensibility in your storytelling, because the audience is used to the American model of "drama." You do have to entertain. But I'd argue that if you create characters who resonate, who really live, then crafting an exciting story around them is a matter of craft. You can build story structure. That's a learnable skill. But creating those characters—that's where the art is. That's where the heart is.

As a viewer, the shows I love most have those resonant characters. I'm not drawn to stories that don't focus on that. And yes, there are international expectations versus Canadian ones. But I'll say this—the show I'm currently blessed to be working on, *Murder in a Small Town*, is with FOX Broadcasting. And they've been incredibly supportive of the kind of Canadian sensibility—humanity, gentleness—that we're bringing to it. They're creative partners in encouraging more of that.

VIC: Besides *Edgemont*, did you do anything else for CBC?

IAN: *Edgemont* was my first series as creator-writer. I've written for many CBC shows, but that was my first as showrunner. The second project I did was *Dragon Boys*, a CBC miniseries from 2006. That's a project I couldn't imagine doing today, given our evolved awareness of cultural authorship. All the primary characters in *Dragon Boys* were Chinese Canadian, and I'm not noticeably Chinese Canadian. But I'm grateful I got to do it. What made it possible was that, as the casting process unfolded, we attracted wonderful actors. They took the characters in hand and shaped them. Tzi Ma and Byron Mann had so much to do with the development of those roles and stories.

As a novelist, you don't get that collaboration. But in drama, you can sit down with the actor and ask: "Who was your character at 12 years old? How does he see this situation?" And the actors take that over. It becomes deeply collaborative. So yeah, *Dragon Boys* was my second project. That was in the days of CBC's four-hour miniseries. Then a few years later, Michael Chechik and I did *Arctic Air*. Adam Beach played the lead, and yeah, it was loads of fun. *Arctic Air* was set in Yellowknife, inspired slightly by Buffalo Airways, the real-life airline up there.

I'd never been to Yellowknife before we started doing the show. My first visit was eye-opening. Yellowknife was nothing like what I'd expected. To begin with, it's very cosmopolitan. I expected the population to be either predominantly First Nations or European, but it wasn't like that at all. Walking down the main streets, you'd hear voices from all over the world. It was quite wonderful. And like any smaller centre, any place off the beaten path, you find people who are absolutely brilliant in their own way, but who don't fit into someone else's box. They thrive there. They live life on their own terms.

VIC: How important is it to have a distinct voice in this country? I mean, we're a culture of multiple languages—French, English, Indigenous—spread across five time zones, with a small population, and massive winters. Isn't there enough here to do something really compelling? Why aren't we doing more to make that entertaining? And who's best suited to do it?

IAN: Great question. Traditionally, the broadcaster that's tried most earnestly to do that has been the CBC—more than anyone. Now, there's been criticism of Canadian shows, and fair enough—some have been more earnest than entertaining. Sometimes, in feeling the need to tell stories that matter, we've over-laboured the message. But I think that's part of the maturation of a culture. We're starting to relax a little—telling stories more freely, without needing to announce their significance.

That said, there's been glorious Canadian television too. And realistically, in any artistic field, what percentage of work is truly great? Five percent? Maybe ten? There's a big mushy middle, and some stuff that really doesn't work. That's just human creativity.

VIC: It's incredible when you think about the depth of human creativity. Dancing, singing, every day. I feel like, give me just one more lifetime! I'm in awe. Writing is where it all starts. Theatre especially—those desperate little productions—that's the foundation. So my question: what can we do to nurture that in this country?

IAN: The best and only way to nurture emerging writers is to create opportunities for them to write. It's not always viable, given budget constraints. But CBC accomplished so much in the days when they commissioned scripts knowing they wouldn't produce all of them. That was a way for writers to explore. In my own case, I had to get several thousand pages of sludge out of my system before I could write something halfway acceptable. You need to write and write and write and write and write.

I vividly remember one night—about 2 a.m., I was working on a stage play, I guess I was in my late twenties. And I had this moment of great excitement: "I know how to craft this scene!" Not a whole play, that's another story, but I knew how to build a scene. And that was thrilling. To reach that point, you need people to give you a chance to make mistakes—and learn from them. To point out those mistakes. And to give you more chances to keep writing.

VIC: What role do you think CBC—or the Film Board—can play? I mean, think of the work that came out of those institutions, even in the '50s. Oscars came to Canada through the Film Board. It was incredible. What could these organizations do now, in terms of nurturing writing?

IAN: I would love to see a world where the CBC—and the NFB as well—had the kind of public and political support to invest in what they do. The only way to support it effectively is to say: "Yes, it's going to cost some money." And it's worth it. Many of these projects aren't going to go anywhere—the same way that so much primary research in the sciences doesn't lead to a specific end, but it's essential. The exploration is what matters.

If it were possible to resurrect radio drama as a form, it would be tremendous. Radio drama is so inexpensive. You can produce an hour-long radio play for a couple thousand dollars. Podcasts fill that gap to some extent, but I still think broadcasters should be looking at those kinds of low-budget opportunities. You can get writers writing. You can get them learning how to tell stories. If you can separate the money from it and focus on lower-cost formats, it becomes much easier to let people fail. And if it only costs a few thousand dollars, there's less pressure to generate a financial return on every piece. I probably sound very idealistic here, but if CBC could get back to that impulse, it would be a huge benefit for Canadian writers.

VIC: What would you do if you had the mandate? For me, public broadcasting is essential. Public broadcasting serves the full cross-section of society. Commercial broadcasting chases ratings. But someone sitting in Churchill or in Saskatchewan—they're as Canadian as anyone in Toronto or Vancouver. They deserve stories too. Maybe I sound too socialistic?

IAN: No, no, I'm with you. I come from the same old-school thinking: honesty, inclusiveness, and catering to a full spectrum of people. These days, platforms like Netflix and Amazon are targeting young demographics. It's a selective audience now.

Let me tell you one of my favourite moments. It was during the casting process for *Edgemont*, the first season. Some roles had been filled, but we still hadn't found the right actor for one of the leads. And CBC wouldn't approve the rest of the cast until that role was nailed. We'd looked at every young actor in Vancouver, every agent submission. Finally, in desperation, our casting director, Carol Turlington, went around to the high schools. She called ahead, asked to see their acting students.

One afternoon, Carol phoned me—her voice was literally shaking. She said, "Ian, you've got to come down here. You've got to see this tape. I think I've found the real thing." It was Kristin Kreuk. I remember watching her audition at the Omni Films space on Water Street. Michael Chechik was there. The editing suite door was open. As Kristin's tape played, people walking by stopped. They leaned in. They watched. It was electric. She hadn't aspired to be a professional actor at that point—just a high school student in drama class. But the camera loved her. Her energy was astonishing. It's one of my absolute favourite memories.

As for challenges on *Edgemont*, it was my first time as writer-producer, as showrunner. Creatively, I felt confident in my storytelling. But I lacked confidence on the production side. And you can't fake it. You can't lie. I was lucky. One of our first ADs was Patricia Dyer Walden. She spotted right away that I often didn't know the answers—and sometimes didn't even know what questions I should be asking. But she was amazing. Quietly, at my elbow, she'd say things like, "Ian, have you thought about considering this...?" And I'd say, "Yes, let's do that." Without ever exposing me or making me feel unqualified, she walked me through a crash course in producing. I'll be forever grateful to her.

Here is another story. We had a slapping moment on *Dragon Boys*. Within our Chinese-Canadian cast, there was a moment involving Eric Tsang, one of the leads. Eric was from Hong Kong, with this incredible track record, just the most amazing stuff coming out of the Hong Kong film tradition. He was used to improvising. In the triad films, they didn't really work from scripts—just outlines. They created as they went. And Eric was a brilliant improviser.

It's always a challenge to make sure you've got other actors in the scene who can improvise at the same level, and we were so lucky. His character's wife was played by Jean Yoon, the mother from *Kim's Convenience*. Jean was also wonderful at improvising.

VIC: Oh, I didn't realize she had worked with you before *Kim's*.

IAN: Yes, and she brought such depth. At one point she had worked as a nanny in China, and though she's Korean, not Chinese, her Mandarin was quite good, her Cantonese, so-so. She and Eric decided that their characters would speak Mandarin at home. And when they improvised, Jean could dance right with him—improvising in Mandarin.

There was a scene, originally written as a confrontation. Eric's character was supposed to dump his plate and walk out. But in the moment, he dumped the plate, Jean looked at him, and slapped him. Eric slapped her back. And from there, it exploded into this amazing improvised scene in Mandarin.

After the first take, the on-set translator came over looking a bit anxious. She reminded us that CBC allowed "saltier" language after 9 p.m., but we had to be more careful between 8 and 9. Since the miniseries aired from 8 to 10, the time mattered. She asked nervously, "Is that scene airing after 9?" I said, "I can't remember—why?" She said, "Because Jean just told him to go sleep with his mother." And I thought, no, we can't say that at any time on the clock!

VIC: (Laughing) I think that settles the time slot issue. Here's a question for you. I've seen so many brilliant people come through this industry. But most of them end up going to the States. Bigger markets, more money. Why haven't we resonated more here at home?

IAN: Canadian films tend to have much smaller budgets. The audience is smaller. So, most of the great Canadian films tend to be arthouse, not commercial blockbusters. But the audience—the broad audience—is used to big commercial storytelling. They know the Marvel Cinematic Universe. I live in Langley, B.C. and the local multiplex almost never shows Canadian films. It's wall-to-wall American blockbusters. And honestly, most of them don't interest me.

VIC: So how do we change that? How do we get audiences into arthouse cinemas to see great Canadian work?

IAN: It's a challenge. Maybe it begins with telling better stories—but also with being honest about where we're starting from.

VIC: Here's my two cents: we stop making excuses. Stop saying we don't have the money. If we want to compete, we go all the way. Countries like Iran or Korea—they make their own films, in their own language, and they make it work.

IAN: Absolutely.

VIC: Well, anything else you'd like to share with me?

IAN: No, this has been great. I've really enjoyed it. We could go on for hours.

VIC: Perfect. Thank you so much for being part of this project.

Afterword

VIC SARIN

This Afterword offers twexcerpts from Vic Sarin's memoir, Eyepiece: Adventures in Canadian Film and Television *(Durvile, 2017). To Vic, film is a window to magic. Touching people with his art and celebrating the human side comes through in every chapter of the book, just as is comes through in his films.*

From Chapter 4, The Film Department

Riel (1979). The biggest thing that happened in the late 70s was when John Trent, a freelance producer that CBC used to worship, was asked to do a film about Louis Riel. *Riel* was a co-production between CBC and John Trent's own production company. *Riel* was a three-hour period story and they brought in celebrated Canadian actors from all over the world like Christopher Plummer, William Shatner, Neville Shute, and Barry Morse.

John Trent asked me if I would like to be Director of Photography on *Riel*. I had never done anything of this scale but he and I had done a TV movie previously titled *Crossbar* and he liked what we were able to do together, with an easy approach and a kind of natural look. Though some of my colleagues spoke disparagingly of John and his methods, I did not see that and got along with him very well. John was always trying to find the way to make things work. I enjoyed his passion and positive energy.

Riel was 60 days of shooting—a long shoot in those days when we used to shoot an hour show in fifteen days. We were supposed to shoot it in Saskatchewan but the budget wouldn't allow it so we ended up building sets at Kleinburg Studios, just outside Toronto. Bill Beeton, the production designer, designed some wonderful sets and gregarious George Bloomfield, who by then had finished several seasons of *SCTV*, was brought in to direct. Raymond Cloutier and Roger Blay came in from Montreal to play Louis Riel and Gabriel Dumont. Leslie Neilsen played Major Crozier, and Christopher Plummer got into his role as Prime Minister John A. Macdonald. The movie generated a lot of publicity because it was one of the biggest film productions CBC had attempted to do. So we were at the forefront, and the media paid attention.

As we got into production there was a scene where Plummer, as John A. Macdonald, had a model train. It was Macdonald's vision to build a railroad to unify Canada and connect us all. So the engine of the model train was set up right in front of the lens with Plummer in the background having his brandy. The script had him get up and walk over to the little model of the engine and the scene builds up to when he says, "This is my dream. We will build a railroad to bring Canada together." It was a pivotal and dramatic scene for the film, where Macdonald expresses his dream of uniting the country through a railroad. As the scene played out, Plummer put the brandy down, and moved toward the model of the engine, which was placed on a table in the foreground. He did his lines and we cut. George would usually turn to me at the end of the take to ask me if we needed another take. This time, I said to him, "I think we should do one more." He asked me if it was something technical. I replied, "Not really." Well, Plummer heard that and he just hit the roof, swearing, insisting that he knew exactly what the scene was about. I replied, "Mr. Plummer, I am just the camera man..." but he carried on into his rampage directed towards me. Plummer was an idolized actor at the time, and had just come off *The Sound of Music* so George, being the peacemaker, suggested we move on to the next scene.

In the evenings, John used to take Plummer to the Sutton Place Hotel in downtown Toronto and bring him to the set in the morning. Plummer got the star treatment, of course, and John and Christopher loved talking, both men being very gregarious. The next morning, John came running up to me and said, "I want to talk to you, I have a bone to pick with you." When I asked him what he meant he said, "What did you do to Plummer, he was so upset last night when I took him home." I stumbled through some kind of explanation and apology but later that morning back on set, George said, "Remember the scene we finished yesterday? I think we need another angle to finish it, so let's do another set-up from a different angle." What happened this time around on a fresh take was that Plummer, who was drinking brandy in the scene, played less drunk. As a result, his performance had much more impact as a powerful, and sober scene, telling the story of the foundation of this country. I think what happened was that Christopher was wondering why the camera guy would say 'one more take' when it wasn't a technical issue. After leaving the set, and I am speculating here, Plummer thought about my reaction and maybe decided that he was playing too drunk when he was giving his vision of uniting the country. At any rate, his performance was more calm and collected when give his empowering speech.

From Chapter 10, Documentaries

Hue: A Matter of Colour (2013). The National Film Board was good enough to ask me if i would like to do a film for them so I proposed a couple of ideas including *Hue*, which they went for. I put the principle of *let's see what we find out along the way* in place years later with *Hue: A Matter of Colour*, much as I had with *Solitary Journey.*

I don't like hypocrisy, which there is a lot of among the human race as a whole. The ethnicity I come from, the brown race, can be very hypocritical when it comes down to the shade of their skin. The Indian people are more conscious of colour than any other people on this planet. Throughout the history of mankind, lightness has always been in demand and globally, multi-billions of dollars of skin-lightening products are sold every year, notably in India, Philippines, Thailand, and Africa. In India, for example, in the same family, the child with the lighter skin is often favoured over those with darker skin and for that reason, might have a brighter future. That principle has been reflected for hundreds of years in the well-established caste system in India. I wanted to explore this problem and that is what *Hue* is about.

Before doing *Hue*, I knew colourism existed but to what extent, I did not know. When I met a woman in the Philippines who made a huge business out of skin whitening, and when I met a lady in South Africa who married an Indian man and how much pain and hurt it created with her siblings, I began to understand the extent of colourism and its hypocrisy.

In all the documentaries I make, I like to hit the topic head-on with honesty, and I also like to give some hope and anchor some meaning at the end. In *Hue*, a Brazilian street sweeper was able to make something of his life. He's a big star in Brazil now; he opened the 2014 Olympics with his dancing, in spite of his dark skin colour. It's inspiring to know that we all can do that. *Hue* is a serious film in one sense, an honest film, but is inspiring at the end, as in don't let this stop you. It didn't stop him. It hasn't stopped me!

As a side story, The National Film Board liked the subject I was working with, but they insisted that I be in it so it could become my personal story. I didn't feel it was necessary, but political correctness is very strong in the world now, so I went along with it. I felt that by placing my family and myself into the film, the Film Board would probably have less to worry about if there were any controversies resulting from taking on this highly charged subject material. If there was to be any heat, the answer could be, *Well it is a personal story of one filmmaker ... this is what Vic wanted to do.*

The Boy From Geita (2013). When I did *Hue*, a storyline came through about albino people in Tanzania who are persecuted because they have white skin. Albinos are known there as 'zero-zero people' as if they are not even human. It threw me off because my story theme from *Hue* was completely opposite. When I got into the subject, the more horrible I realized was this practice of oppression against albinos. In the year 2010 when I was doing this film, I could not believe as humans we were able to go the moon and here we were in East Africa killing people for body parts.

Peter Ash, founder of an organization called 'Under The Same Sun', facilitated the whole film and he himself has albinism. He was featured extensively in the film and it was very satisfying to hear him say that we had done a good job helping people out. He said, "Vic, this film has done so much good for us. The killing of albinos hasn't completely stopped, but it has slowed down and there is a lot more pressure to do something about it. But more than that, the local people are becoming more focused and educated."

There seems to be a tide turning where people in East Africa are saying, "These atrocities against albino people are horrible and intolerable." Meanwhile, through the efforts of people like Peter Ash, albino people in Africa are starting to enter more into the mainstream. In fact, in *The Boy from Geita*, we show how a Tanzanian albino Salum Khalfan Barwany, was elected as a Member of Parliament. When you educate people, the stigma diminishes, and we can see that *Geita* has made a huge dent toward giving the albino population equal rights.

Audiobook

Eyepiece:
Adventures in Canadian
Film and Television
ISBN: 9781988824024
Paperback and E-book

Gung Ho Filmmaking
ISBN: 9781988824093
Audiobook

Paperback/Ebook

The Voice Behind the Conversations

VIC SARIN

Vic Sarin, born in Kashmir, India, is a renowned Canadian filmmaker celebrated as a director, cinematographer, and screenwriter. After moving to Canada in 1963, he began a long career with CBC Television before founding his own company, Sepia Films. His cinematography credits include *Margaret's Museum, Whale Music, Nowhere to Hide, Heartaches, Dancing in the Dark*, and *Riel*. As a director, his fiction films include *Cold Comfort, Partition, Left Behind, Solitary Journey*, *A Shine of Rainbows*, and *The Lightkeeper*. His award-winning documentaries include *The David Milgaard Story, Hue, Keepers of the Magic*, and *The Boy from Geita*, which had a special screening at the United Nations. Among his honours are an Emmy Award, the Directors Guild of Canada Lifetime Achievement Award, the Canadian Society of Cinematographers' Kodak New Century Award, and appointment to the Order of Canada. He is the author of *Eyepiece: Adventures in Canadian Film and Television* and the audiobook *Gung Ho Filmmaking*.